"Bare Knees" Flapper

"Bare Knees" Flapper

The Life and Films
of Virginia Lee Corbin

TIM LUSSIER

McFarland & Company, Inc., Publishers

Jefferson, North Carolina

LIBRARY OF CONGRESS CATALOGUING-IN-PUBLICATION DATA

Names: Lussier, Tim, 1952– author.
Title: "Bare knees" flapper : the life and films of Virginia Lee Corbin /
Tim Lussier.
Description: Jefferson, North Carolina : McFarland & Company, Inc., 2018 |
Includes bibliographical references, filmography, and index.
Identifiers: LCCN 2018040238 | ISBN 9781476675688
(softcover : acid free paper) ∞
Subjects: LCSH: Corbin, Virginia Lee, 1910–1942. | Motion picture
actors and actresses—United States—Biography. |
Child actors—United States—Biography.
Classification: LCC PN1998.3.C674 L87 2018 | DDC 791.4302/8092 [B] —dc23
LC record available at https://lccn.loc.gov/2018040238

BRITISH LIBRARY CATALOGUING DATA ARE AVAILABLE

ISBN (print) 978-1-4766-7568-8
ISBN (ebook) 978-1-4766-3425-8

Front cover image of Virginia Lee Corbin,
publicity photograph from 1928 (author collection)

Printed in the United States of America

*McFarland & Company, Inc., Publishers
Box 611, Jefferson, North Carolina 28640
www.mcfarlandpub.com*

Table of Contents

Foreword by Kevin Brownlow

My reaction when I saw this book was "How did he do it?" I can appreciate why it took so long and how difficult it must have been; I had to research Virginia Lee Corbin's early career for a biography of one of her directors—Sidney Franklin—and I came up with hardly enough for one chapter, let alone 26!

Virginia Lee Corbin, at age six, was a leading player in the elaborate fairy tales acted largely by children, made by the Franklin brothers, Sidney and Chester, for the William Fox company in Hollywood in 1917–1918. She became one of the most popular child stars of her era.

When she grew up, she made an elegant heroine in pictures like *Play Safe* (1927) opposite Monty Banks. It was a comedy set aboard a railroad train, and one hopes she shared something of his sense of adventure for it was full of dangerous stunts. In the witty Civil War comedy *Hands Up* (1926) with the silk-hatted comedian Raymond Griffith as a Confederate spy, she plays, most charmingly, one of a pair of sisters who save him from the hangman's rope. When the Mormon leader Brigham Young makes a well-timed appearance at the last minute, Griffith rewards the girls: he marries them both.

I see from Virginia's filmography that her career included a surprising number of low-budget films—*program pictures*, as they were termed—made by such companies as Gotham, Chadwick, Tiffany and Perfection (!), and I wondered why. These studios, disparaged in the business as "Poverty Row," did rotten work. Their pictures were made cynically—six reels had to be shot in six days, whereas making a serious film on a big budget could take from six weeks to ten months. They advertised big names, but popular stars were hired for a day and close-ups were filmed *en masse* and sprinkled throughout the narrative.

By appearing in such pictures, an established actress would send a signal suggesting she had lowered her standards, but Virginia was different; she was growing up onscreen and, when she became a teenager, she had to make her mark all over again.

Not to be unfair, she also worked with several first-rate directors, and the results must have made her proud. Apart from the Franklins, Henry King, who would direct such classics as *Tol'able David* (1921) and *Stella Dallas* (1925), cast Virginia in *Vengeance of the Dead* (1917). King Vidor, who directed her in *Wine of Youth* (1924), would be responsible for *The Big Parade* (1925) and *The Crowd* (1928), two of the greatest films made in America. James Cruze, who had made an epic of *The Covered Wagon* in 1923, might have done the same for *The City That Never Sleeps* the following year, but we'll never know because Paramount allowed it to be destroyed. In a review of October 1, 1924, a critic for *Variety* wrote, "The story is admirably cast. Right at this time it must be said that Virginia Lee Corbin as the flapper makes a spot for herself in the picture world."

Her publicity, alas, seemed buried in the Victorian age: "Soon all the world saw what a wonderful child God had made," wrote Hector Ames in the June 1918 issue of *Motion Picture Magazine*. "So patient and natural was she when posing that many offers came from other artists, and she could have been a model to this day had not her mother wisely seen far greater glory ahead."

But once she started slipping, the fan magazines could be less than kind: "At present she is in the East in quest of a stage engagement," wrote Richard Mook in the December 1929 issue of *Picture Play*. "Her mother vouchsafes the opinion that Virginia has always been difficult to handle, possibly because she feels the deep, emotional power within herself and is, therefore, not content to portray the silly, flapper roles that are given her. Whatever the cause, Virginia's name appears less and less frequently on the billboards, and she has never done anything to justify the breaks she undoubtedly has had. My own opinion is that she grew up about ten years too late. Ten years ago, her blue-eyed, blonde prettiness would have made her an instant favorite. Today her type is passé."

Another child star, Diana Serra Cary, the indomitable Baby Peggy (known recently as the Last Silent Star Standing), wrote a sympathetic but sobering book about the tribulations child stars went through in early Hollywood. Tim Lussier has followed her example, telling us what *really* happened, rather than what we might prefer to hear. His excellent research reveals that this example of the "movie mother" was something of an affliction for poor Virginia, who suffered the usual miseries of child actors.

Sustaining role after role, even in minor pictures, took hard work and discipline. The competition was fierce—girls were migrating to Hollywood in such alarming numbers that producers were encouraged to make films warning them of the perils awaiting them.

Virginia Lee Corbin's career may have been minor compared to those of the big names of the silent era, but she did some good work against the odds. Just imagine how frustrating it must have been to hear yourself described enthusiastically as if you'd done your best work at four!

Kevin Brownlow is a filmmaker and film historian. He began collecting silent films at the age of 11 and started making films as an amateur in the 1950s. He joined the film industry in 1955 and eventually edited such films as *Charge of the Light Brigade* (1968). He is the author of *The Parade's Gone By...* (1968).

Preface

My youngest daughter answered the telephone one evening in 1998. The caller, she said, was Virginia Lee Corbin's son, and he'd like to talk to me. At that time, all I knew of Virginia was her appearance in *Bare Knees*, a delightful 1928 comedy she made for the Poverty Row studio Gotham Productions. I had purchased it from Grapevine Video not too long before this fateful evening, and I had found it a supremely enjoyable tale of a good-hearted flapper. As a matter of fact, I liked it so much, I wrote a review of it for the now-defunct website *The Silents Majority*.

The gentleman on the phone was Bob Krol, Virginia's second son, and someone I soon came to know very well and regard as a dear friend. He had seen the review on *The Silents Majority* and somehow obtained my phone number. Bob said that he was now in his sixties and finally felt the need to know a mother that he had never known and was seeking information about her from anyone who could help.

He explained that he and his older brother, Phil, had been raised by their father, Theodore Krol, from when Bob was 18 months old and Phil was four. His mother and father had gone through a bitter divorce in 1937, and his mother relinquished custody of them to their father. They never saw their mother again. She lived only five more years. Right before Virginia passed away, their stepmother tried to arrange for the boys to see their dying mother who was in a sanitarium outside Chicago, but, sadly, the meeting never materialized.

Bob said he and his brother had been raised with everyone in his father's family telling them they did not want to try and contact anyone in their mother's family—"no good will come of it," he remembered them saying. He had always regretted a missed opportunity to connect with his grandmother in the 1950s, right around when he and his wife, Connie, were married. An article appeared in a Chicago paper. The mother of Virginia Lee Corbin was seeking the whereabouts of her two grandsons. Bob said that as he was young and newly married with his whole future ahead of him, he took the advice of his father's family and did not follow up—a decision that, in his sixties, he looked back on with great remorse.

Now, as he began his quest to get to know his mother, he learned that she had a sister, Ruth, a fact he had discovered only recently, but she had passed away 12 years earlier in San Mateo, California. Of course, his grandmother had passed away years before. There seemed to be no other family members who would remember or could tell him anything about his mother. He had gotten some tidbits of information from a couple of members of his father's family, but since the two families did not interact, they were able to offer very little help.

Bob only had a few items in his possession that had belonged to his mother. There were six or eight 8" × 10" photographs—his favorite a beautiful shot of his mother holding him as a baby while his older brother looked on. He had seen *Bare Knees*, of course, but the only other movie he had of his mother's was a VHS tape of *The Three Keys*, one of Virginia's 1925 movies that a family member had secured from the Library of Congress. Other than those, he had never seen his mother in anything else.

The final possession was something he also cherished very much—a scrapbook that his grandmother kept on Virginia's career from its beginning in 1916 up until about 1919. Mostly newspaper clippings, it was, at least, a window into his mother's life during those heady years as a child star.

Over the next four years, I visited Bob and Connie several times—they lived only three hours away—and I spent the weekend with them on a couple of occasions. I was able to secure copies of seven or eight more of Virginia's movies. The first sound film of hers that I obtained was a Poverty Row picture entitled *X Marks the Spot*. In this 1931 film, Virginia is on screen for only about three minutes. We watched it at Bob and Connie's condo. After the end credits, Bob turned to me—he looked a little teary-eyed—and said, "You know, that's the first time I've ever heard my mother's voice," indicating the obvious, that he remembered nothing of his mother's voice from when he was two years old.

During those years I was able to locate and purchase a significant number of photos and magazine articles on Virginia, and I shared them with both Bob and Phil. Bob and I also worked together to create the *Virginia Lee Corbin Scrapbook* website, posted as a sub-site of my *Silents Are Golden* website. Bob wrote a letter about his quest for information that we included on the website along with a short bio of Virginia and a filmography—as best we could piece together then. The hope was that someone would see the website and come forward with more information on Virginia Lee Corbin. Alas, the effort did not generate any viable information, and, sadly, Bob passed away unexpectedly in November 2002. Bob was never short on gratitude for those things that I had been able to find for him, and, on more than one occasion, he said he felt as if he finally "really" knew his mother for the first time in his life.

I didn't stop my quest for information on Virginia Lee Corbin—a quest that has lasted for approximately 20 years. I stayed in contact with Bob's wife, Connie, until her passing, and have continued to stay in contact with Phil over the years, sharing with him each new "find" regarding his mother.

This book is something Bob and I talked about nearly 20 years ago, and it has finally come to fruition. It's all been for Bob and Phil even though Bob is not here to read it. I've also learned through my research that Bob and Phil's mother deserves to be remembered. She wasn't a major star, but she was well known and admired during the silent era. She made a lot of very good movies that are worthy of being preserved and seen by new fans. She was a good actress. She was most adept at comedy—and preferred doing comedies—but she could also do drama. During her tenure with Fox Film Corporation in the late 'teens, she was the most popular child star on the screen, and she did something very few child stars could do: she continued to have a busy and successful career as she grew and matured through the 1920s, and had it not been for some misfortunes and bad decisions, her career could have lasted many years longer than it did.

So this book is first and foremost for Bob and Phil, but it's also for silent movie fans who may not know this lovely and talented actress or those who want to know more about her. This biography attempts to give a fine balance between Virginia Lee Corbin's career and her personal life—which did have its trials and tribulations—but with her career at the forefront and not overshadowed by the personal problems she dealt with. There is no sensationalism here, just every attempt to give a straightforward and factual accounting of her life.

As with any biography of a star who has been gone for more than 75 years, so much must be culled from period publications as well as documents such as marriage records, obituaries, census data, court records, archive resources and other public information. Unfortunately, with the passing of so many years, personal reminisces are difficult to obtain and virtually non-existent after all these years. And, as noted, although children of stars are generally a significant source of information, Bob and Phil unfortunately have no memories of their mother.

Research for this book has uncovered several errors in online sources, so greater dependence has been placed on trade publications such as *Film Daily*, *Moving Picture World*, *Variety*, *Harrison's Reports* and other period publications designed for exhibitors, and even those occasionally have their faults. Fan magazines, which were fast and loose with the facts, were obviously used but with added caution. Newspapers tended to be mostly reliable and were particularly helpful in confirming when a film was in the theaters and where Virginia made personal appearances. In each chapter, sources are for the reader who may wish to delve further into a particular source of information.

Biographers invariably must depend heavily on assistance from others. This book would not have been completed or be as complete as it is if not for the following (most certainly and apologetically an incomplete) list of people (some who have passed on), all to whom I am very grateful: Bob Krol, Connie Krol, Phil Krol, Kevin Brownlow, Anthony Slide, Diana Serra Cary, Douglas Fairbanks, Jr., Lon Davis, Susan Hatch, Barbara Benes, Kathy Soto, Catherine Farrell (Virginia's great niece), Patsy Karp (Virginia's niece), Esther Linn, Sally Dumaux, Annette D'Agostino Lloyd, Barbara Hall, Dave Drazin, Carol Seymour, Dean Thompson, Mary Cade, Tony Luke Scott, Dave Hanauer, Jay Rubin, Bonnie Portnoy, Carl A. Hällström, Ate van Delden, Ken Steiner, Catherine Cormon of the EYE Institute, Mike Mashon of the Library of Congress, Marc Wanamaker of Bison Archives, Dino Everett of the USC School of Cinematic Arts, my wife Debbie, and all of our children and grandchildren whose love and support mean so much.

1. Looking Back

June 1942 had just turned the corner, and Virginia knew that she would never leave the sanitarium. Her husband, Charles, was good and faithful, and she was grateful for his devotion, but as she stared at the photo of her two sons, Phil and Bob, on the nightstand beside her bed, she had one last hope that she would see them—just once more—before her life ended.

Looking back over the years, she wondered how things could have been different. The only good to come out of her first marriage was the two boys, and she couldn't even hold on to them. Teddy Krol had beaten her in two years of court battles and gotten custody of the boys. They were so young when the divorce took place. Phil was almost ten now, and Bob was seven and a half. It had been nearly five years since she had seen them. How much the boys must have grown! Jean, Teddy's present wife, said she was going to bring them to the sanitarium. Virginia felt sure Teddy wouldn't approve, but maybe Jean could make it happen.

She had thought many times what life would have been like if she hadn't married Teddy. When he came along in 1929, she wasn't quite 18, but he seemed to be her knight in shining armor—her rescuer from the hell she felt she was living in with her mother. Her last years at home had just been a series of court cases, negative publicity, lost roles and the realization that after working in the movies since she was four years old, she had nothing to show for it. The fame had come, especially as a child star—she was the most popular child star in the world when she was making those Fox Kiddie Pictures. What fun that was acting in all of her favorite fairy tales! She was so happy then. She was even a success in vaudeville. The reviews were good—people came out to see her. Then she did what so few child stars have been able to do—she came back, and she made movies. Sure, she was playing roles that were older than she actually was, but she pulled it off. Being cast as a flapper was just fine with her—after all, she was a bit of a flapper herself! It wasn't the career that was bad—actually, it was her refuge. It was home. Her father and mother had separated at the beginning of her career—he was not around to help, and things could have been much better if he had been—but he didn't agree with her going into movies and couldn't live with her mother any longer. Yes, she got her dream—and her mother's dream—of fame and a lot of money, but then, by the time she was old enough to question it, she found out her mother had wasted it all away. There was nothing. They argued constantly. Her mother just couldn't let her grow up and enjoy life. She wanted parties, friends—nothing bad, but just to get out and have fun. Then there was her mother's suicide attempt, and that was the final straw. Since she wasn't old enough to go out on her own, she asked the court for a guardian, and that didn't work out either. The bad publicity cost her roles. Her career was negatively affected, and she felt her life was out of control.

In the midst of all of this, Teddy had arrived—at just the right moment, or so it appeared—and the year they honeymooned in England was just what she needed. It was glorious—she was deeply in love, seeing a foreign country for the first time, had no worries about money, and was far away from the turmoil back home. Also, although she had made one sound film, the transitions in the movie industry, sound films killing silent movies, and stars' futures depending on silly voice tests—all of this seemed to help justify a long stay in England. Study elocution, she thought, and then come back to Hollywood and be a success again.

Unfortunately, things didn't turn out the way she had planned after they returned. It was as if the movies had forgotten her. She had been a star—no, not of the caliber of a Mary Pickford, Clara Bow or one of the Talmadge sisters—but she was in demand and got darned good roles. Now, after returning, the only thing she could get was bit roles, or, at best, a second lead in a "B" western, the true sign that a career had taken a nose-dive, but this wasn't the worst of it. Before long, she began to realize the idyllic marriage she had envisioned was turning into its own hell. Teddy certainly wasn't the devoted husband she thought he would be. The fights were terrible. She had begun to drink, and, yes, when Teddy was away from home for as much as a year at a stretch, she did meet someone else. What could he expect of her?

So what if she hadn't married Teddy? Would she have maintained her popularity in sound films? Did her year overseas have a negative effect on her future film career? She was willing to do the bit parts and Poverty Row films if it could lead to better roles, but the time she spent away from the screen having children and going through that terrible divorce with Teddy were most likely the final death knell. After the divorce and in the last few years her hopes had risen again. She had gotten some work at the studios. Sure, they were uncredited parts or stand-ins, but it was a way to get her foot in the door. She just knew a real part was going to come along, but then the tuberculosis took her down.

Prescott, Arizona, and her dreams of becoming a movie star were so long ago. It's nice to have dreams—especially when they come true—but sometimes life just gets in the way, and fate has a way of stomping on those dreams and creating nightmares in their place.

2. From Prescott to Hollywood

*P*rescott, Arizona, is the county seat for Yavapai County, the largest county in the state. In 1910, the census reported that Yavapai County had less than 17,000 residents—or about two people per square mile. Approximately 6,000 of the county's residents lived in Prescott. At 5,347 feet above sea level, it was considered one of the country's prettiest mountain resorts with "an abundant supply of mountain spring water, equal in purity to that of any incorporated city in the country, broad and well-graded streets, fine and artistic business and fraternal buildings, well-equipped hotels, churches of nearly every denomination, adequate gas and electric light service; in short, all comforts and conveniences necessary to induce and care for all seeking advantages whether for health, pleasure or business."[1]

This beautiful city was where Leon Ernest Corbin and his wife, Mary Etta, came to live shortly after the turn of the century. He and Mary Etta had married in late 1890 or early 1891 in the town where he lived with his family and where he had started out working as a pharmacist—Huron, South Dakota. His father had been one of the original settlers of Huron when he moved there from Illinois. By 1900, the census indicates that he and Mary Etta were living in San Diego where his occupation was once again listed as "pharmacist." In Prescott, he was in partnership with Alfred William Bork in the Brisley Drug Company located in the Burke Hotel at the corner of Montezuma and Gurley Streets. The hotel still stands today as the Hotel St. Michael, one of Prescott's finest. The first newspaper advertisements for Corbin & Bork appear in February 1903, so it appears this is approximately when Leon and Mary Etta moved to the city. In later years, according to the 1913 Yavapai County Directory, the team of Corbin and Bork had joined Ed Shumate in the Owl Drug & Candy Company located across the street from the Burke Hotel.

Leon was born in 1869 in Winnebago, Illinois, the youngest of five children. Mary Etta was nine years younger, having been born in 1878 in Illinois (city undetermined). Unfortunately, the couple's stay in Prescott was short-lived. Mary Etta died in 1904, a little more than one year after they moved, at age 26 from blood poisoning. Even though Leon was 35 when his wife died, they had no children.

Leon remained in Prescott, and sometime during the next two years, he met Virginia Frances Cox, born November 28, 1881, in Hindsville, Arkansas. They were married on April 29, 1906. A little over a year later, on July 30, 1907, they were blessed with a daughter, Margaret. The following year, they lost Margaret when she succumbed to cholera infection on May 21, 1908, at only ten months old.

Their next child was Ruth, an adopted baby. It isn't known exactly when Ruth came into the family, but it would make sense that the Corbins adopted her sometime following the death of Margaret and before the birth of Virginia.

Frances Corbin gave birth to La Verne Virginia Corbin on December 5, 1911, according to the child's birth certificate. As is the case with so many movie stars as the years wore on, whether it was studio publicity that decided she needed a couple of years trimmed from her age or her own (or her mother's), her birth year ranged from as early as 1908, to as late as 1914. Even her grave marker incorrectly gives her birth year as 1914. She was delivered by Dr. Clarence Edgar Yount in the bedroom of her parents' home at 320 Park Avenue, Prescott, Arizona, at 2:10 a.m. Her father was 42, and her mother was 26. Virginia was baptized by the Rev. Bennett Claire W. Wilms on Easter Day, April 7, 1912.

Both Virginia and sister Ruth had brown hair. At least by the time she was three years old, her mother had decided Virginia should be a blonde, most likely considering it an asset in her ambitions for the child. For the next four years, it is difficult to piece together Virginia's life—except what can be discerned from the sparse bits of information that is available—and unfortunately, these bits of information come mainly from articles and biographies of the child after she became a star, so their trustworthiness is obviously suspect.

For example, it is not known when Virginia, her sister and her mother moved to California or exactly where in the state. It appears Leon moved to California at some point after his wife and daughters arrived there, but the couple did not live together— at least not by the time Virginia's career was in high gear. Why did they move? More than one source claims that, by age three, Virginia was in poor health, and the move was for health reasons. It is quite clear that Frances Corbin had ambitions for both her children, so the move could have been to seek out a movie career for them. Virginia's beauty was evident (she was the more attractive of the two children), and apparently her talent was becoming more evident the older she became. As one fan magazine article noted, "When Virginia was still a wee baby, her mother dreamt about her future and determined to spare no effort to develop her little flower's talent."

The article went on to note, "When this tiny lass came to be three years old everybody started noticing her beauty, and tho she was only a frail little being, her mind was developed far more than one would expect, and when she learnt to talk, she never spoke a baby word. She seemed to have a wonderful memory, also, and easily learnt all kinds of songs, stories and poems by heart."[2]

This article is one that claims the Corbins' move to California was for Virginia's health. Knowing what to believe or not to believe from such sources is difficult at best, especially when it fabricates facts with such statements as Virginia had to leave "her beautiful eastern home" to come to the West Coast. Nevertheless, it goes on to say an artist (unidentified) came to the beach city (also unidentified) where Virginia lived and saw her playing in the sand. "At once touched and inspired by the loveliness of her golden hair, blue eyes and flower-like features, he asked permission to make her portrait to use on an art calendar he was making."[3] Regardless of the veracity of the story about her entry into the modeling business, it is a fact that she posed for artists who used her likeness on calendars, Christmas cards, etc., prior to entering films.

Whether the move to California was for health reasons or not, Mrs. Corbin and her two daughters were in Los Angeles for six months, from approximately May–October, in 1913 visiting Mrs. Corbin's sister, Mrs. Berry, and her husband. Leon had been out to visit them in September. The next available information notes that Leon left for

Virginia's birth certificate gives her birthdate as December 5, 1911. Rarely would her age be stated correctly; usually a year or two were shaved off when she was a child star and years were added when she was portraying more mature roles in the twenties. This photograph of Ruth and Virginia was likely taken around 1915, sometime after their move to California. Note that Virginia's hair, which was originally brown, had already been dyed blonde.

Long Beach, California, in August 1914 to visit his wife and children, where they had been "residents" since the first of the year.

But how did Virginia actually get her start in films? Unfortunately, there is no sure way to know. Publicity departments and fan magazine writers have always dealt fast and loose with the truth—and in many, many cases, simply fabricating stories that will make for more exciting reading. Also, since Virginia Lee Corbin never was a "major" star, documentation of her career is scant indeed, and information is particularly sparse for these first years in the business. Until she began work for Fox in 1917, little about her exists, and her story must be discerned from the bits and pieces one can find in newspapers, fan magazines, trade journals, etc.—some of which is contradictory. As for her appearances in films, some are listed as "unconfirmed"—and as her list of films is discussed here, it must be remembered that the sequence is based on release dates that don't always coincide with the sequence in which films were made.

Regarding her entry into films, one early article noted that Mrs. Corbin wanted to visit a studio. She took her two daughters along with her, and when Virginia was seen, her beauty dazzled a director, and she was "discovered." Another said that her opportunity to enter films came about when she was watching her sister perform at a studio. A director spied her and immediately featured Virginia in her very first picture. It is a fact that Mrs. Corbin was also promoting Ruth for stardom, and Ruth did some acting briefly—however, there's nothing to indicate Ruth was acting in films before Virginia, even though they were four years apart in age. Unfortunately, the only appearance of Ruth that can be determined is a film entitled *The Prodigal Daughter*, a Rex Motion Picture Company production released December 31, 1916, with Allen Hollubar and Jack Mulhall in the cast, but long before this film was released, much had happened to accelerate Virginia's acting career.

Released January 9, 1916, was *Let Katie* [or *Katy*] *Do It*, a five-reel feature starring Jane Grey and directed by C.M. (Chester) Franklin, one of the two brothers (the other being Sidney) who would be responsible for the Fox Kiddie Features during the next couple of years. Although the film is often listed in Virginia's filmography—and there are seven leading kids' roles—Virginia cannot be identified anywhere in the film. In any event, the film does hold an important place in the evolution of the upcoming Fox Kiddie Features.

Jane Grey is the Katie of the title, and she is left with seven children when her sister and brother-in-law are killed in a train wreck. She goes to live with her Uncle Dan (Ralph Lewis) in Mexico in order to get help raising the children. Her uncle's partner is Oliver Putnam (Tully Marshall), her childhood sweetheart. When all of the adults are away, bandits attack the house where the children are staying, yet the children manage to hold off their attackers with a specially-rigged battery of rifles until the cavalry comes to the rescue.

As noted, *Let Katie Do It* is a very significant film because it was the genesis of the Fox Kiddie Features that were so hugely popular and made Virginia a first-echelon star. The sequence of events that led to this feature began in 1914 when Ford Sterling was enticed away from Keystone. Moving to Universal, he formed a partnership with former Keystone employee Henry "Pathe" Lehrman and Fred Balshofer to create the Sterling Motion Picture Company, which quickly failed. The significance of this is that he brought Chester Franklin with him away from Keystone. Also among the troupe was

Chester's brother, Sidney, who had recently tried his luck and failed at being a comedian after leaving the Hobart Bosworth company.

With the failure of the Sterling Company, the brothers decided to try their hand at production, and, starting out on a borrowed $400, they shot a split-reel comedy in Griffith Park called *The Sheriff*. After offering the film to every studio in town and being turned down, as a last resort, they approached D.W. Griffith. To their surprise, he liked the film and signed them up to make a series of one-reel children's pictures. With children brought over from the Sterling Company and some new faces, they began the well-received series of pictures. Commenting on the Franklins' one and only two-reeler in this series, *The Doll House Mystery* (1915), historian Kevin Brownlow notes that the quality of their films was right in line with Griffith's output. He said it "is a close match in technique and content to the best of the Griffith Biographs. The theft of some stock certificates leads to a manhunt in which an ex-convict and his small son are besieged in a lonely shack. The theft turns out to have been an innocent prank by the owner's children. Photographed by Frank Good in the luminous style of the early Triangles— sharp, crystal clear and drenched with sunlight—*The Doll-House Mystery* is put together with exceptional skill. The climax is treated with bold close-ups and spectacular long-shots, and a train-and-auto chase is shot in true Griffith style."[4]

Let Katie Do It was their first feature-length movie under this contract, and the story was suggested by Griffith. Rehearsals were also held under Griffith's supervision. Reviewers liked the film. *Variety* said, "The antics of the children and the battle scenes, and [the] sweetly pretty story make it attractive to folks of all ages."[5] *Motion Picture News* said it "is a finished production. The story is well told; the work of the cast shows excellent judgment in the selection of the players for all the roles, the sets, the locations and the details of costuming all indicate care. Indeed, those responsible for the picture have left nothing to be done on *Let Katy* [sic] *Do It*."[6]

Motion Picture News lists the seven children who form the family in the film as Violet Radcliffe, George Stone, Carmen De Rue, Francis Carpenter, Ninon Fovieri, Lloyd Pearl and Beulah Burns. Most of these are soon to become regulars in the Fox Kiddie Features, but, as can be seen, Virginia was not one of them. A print of the film does exist in the Library of Congress.

The Franklin brothers made five more pictures that featured children in the cast, but only one survives—*Sister of Six* (1916) with Bessie Love in abridged form. No source indicates Virginia was in any of these.

Virginia's next film appearance is also uncredited. Anyone who has seen D.W. Griffith's *Intolerance* may remember in the epilogue, there are two children—both blond— a boy and girl, playing in a field. A close-up of the two children shows the girl playing and laughing. The boy has his back to the camera, but as she starts to run away, we get a quick glimpse of the boy as he tries to grab the girl and give her a kiss.

Virginia is typically credited as the little girl. Since *Let Katie Do It* was a Fine Arts picture under the supervision of D.W. Griffith, it would seem to make sense that Virginia could appear in *Intolerance*, released September 5. It is difficult to confirm unequivocally that the child is Virginia, but, then again, she is very young. If this is indeed Virginia, it is very curious that her personal scrapbook that her mother kept during these early years makes no mention of *Intolerance*.

It is true the little boy in the film is reported to be Francis Carpenter, her costar over the next few years, and, yes, the child in *Intolerance* is almost certainly Francis according to the brief glimpse seen of him when he turns to kiss her. Francis Carpenter's appearance in the film does lend credence to her appearance in it as well. So the question must be asked: Is it Virginia Lee Corbin in *Intolerance* or just another little girl with blonde hair? The facts seem to indicate that it is, but, again, there is no documentation that would prove without a doubt that this is her.

There is no doubt about her next film, though. The short *By Conscience's Eye* was made for the Rex Motion Picture Company (that merged into the Universal Film Manufacturing Company), the same studio that made Ruth's film mentioned earlier. In addition to Virginia, the film starred names that are all but forgotten today—Rex De Rosselli, Marjorie Ellison and Maxfield Stanley. It was released August 11, 1916.

Another unidentified newspaper article also gives a tie to Universal. It states that both Ruth and Virginia are "now playing" with the Lule Warrenton Juvenile Company at Universal City. It goes into detail about Virginia being the "star" of the company. "Ruth and Virginia Corbin, with their mother, Mrs. L.E. Corbin, are at the Broadway apartments for a week. These talented children are members of the Universal Juvenile Photodrama Company. Virginia, only three years old, is the star of the company and is called the most beautiful baby on the film stage. This juvenile company was organized by Lule Warrenton of Honolulu, who is known by everybody as Mother Warrenton.... Her idea of a juvenile film company has worked out splendidly, and she is besieged with talented children and their parents for a place in the company. Beautiful fairy tales and child life pictures, educational and charming, are produced.... Virginia Corbin, the star, is as pretty as she is talented, with great blue eyes and curly golden hair and charm of manner that immediately wins, on the screen or off.... Ruth, the older, is seven years old, and is really beautiful with the deep gray eyes denoting the artistic temperament, fluffy brown hair and perfect features. Two more charming children are rarely seen, and for each is predicted a brilliant future."[7]

Warrenton was a well-known actress, producer and director, well on in age, having been born in 1862, but she was well respected as the leader of films designed for children. One writer noted that "she has no peers in the handling of children,"[8] but a search of film titles both directed and produced by Warrenton doesn't list a film in which Virginia or Ruth are known to have appeared.

Next, Virginia appeared in a two-reel short for Universal produced by Ben Wilson. The film, entitled *The Castle of Despair*, starred Malcolm Blevins who had 48 films to his credit between 1915 and 1918 but has since disappeared into oblivion. Virginia played his character's daughter. Also prominent in the film was Neva Gerber, Ben Wilson's perennial co-star in the films in which he performed. At least three serials that Wilson starred in with Gerber and produced can be seen on home video today: *The Trail of the Octopus* (1919), *The Power God* (1925) and *Officer 444* (1926). Universal released *The Castle of Despair* August 22, 1916. The three-reeler was Wilson's first on the West Coast, and it was described by one reviewer as a "corker." The reviewer went on to say, "Ben has given us in this big three-reeler a new twist on the eternal triangle plot—this time it is two men and one woman. The woman's husband is engrossed in business; his wife is lonely; his friend is obliging. Then the story begins to differ from the original triangular plot because Ben Wilson used his head. The climax is great; the sets are magnificent. The production will please your audiences."[9]

She continued to work for Universal. Her next film was written and produced by Allen (sometimes Allan) J. Holubar. *Behind Life's Stage* was a two-reeler released October 12. In the short, Virginia was the little sister of Flora Parker De Haven. A synopsis says, "It depicts the misfortunes of a little city waif, the sole guardian and caretaker of her little sister. The waif secures employment in a millinery establishment on the day she is ejected from a tenement house for non-payment of rent. She sneaks her sister into the store where they stay all night, or rather until they are awakened by a burglar. The girls' cries bring a friendly policeman, and the children become his wards."[10] The October 20, 1916, edition of *Moving Picture Stories* gives a three and a half page synopsis of this lost film with a charming photo of Flora Parker de Haven as the big sister, Charles Cummings in police uniform, and a small four-year-old Virginia Corbin standing beside him, doll in one hand, what appears to be a blanket with her clothes wrapped up inside in the other, and a cute little cap tied around the chin.

In 1916, a two-reeler could bring as much notice for a star as a feature film, and Virginia's appearance in Allan J. Hollubar's excellent *Behind Life's Stage* (1916) was another good role for her. Flora Parker DeHaven (left) played Virginia's older sister and Charles Cummings was the kindly policeman who took in the two waifs as his wards.

The short was well received, at least according to one reviewer. "There is no wasting words in describing this masterpiece in miniature, for it is perfect in all details of plot, direction, acting and photography. Perfection brooks no praise; it shouts its own laudation."[11]

Released October 27, 1916, *The Chorus Girl and the Kid* starred Marie Empress, a lovely young curly-haired English actress who apparently only has a handful of films from 1916 to her credit. After making these films, she went back to England where she performed on stage for a time. In 1919, as she was sailing back to the United States, she fell overboard and drowned.

The two-reeler was produced by the Balboa Amusement Producing Company. This fits in with the newspaper article that stated the Corbins were living in Long Beach, which is where the Balboa Studio was located. Incorporated for $7,000 in 1913, Balboa once claimed to have the largest glass studio in the industry. *The Chorus Girl and the Kid* was produced by Knickerbocker Star Features. Balboa had just recently contracted with General Film Company to produce films through Knickerbocker.

Although only one other film (to be discussed later) for Balboa is known to include Virginia in the cast, an April 1916 article said, "Balboa is cultivating a kindergarten. The latest additions to the half-portion Bernhardts and Mansfields are Ruth and Virginia Corbin, aged 3 and 7 years, respectively. Both are clever screen actors."[12]

A Franklyn Farnum three-reeler entitled *The Woman He Feared* was released November 14, 1916. In this story, Farnum is a newspaper reporter who has recovered from his addiction to alcohol. The father of the girl he loves has "cast off" his aunt. As a matter of revenge, she gives Farnum alcohol at the wedding feast. A brief mention in the March 1917 issue of *Motion Picture Classic* mentions that Virginia has the part of Cupid in the film. No reference to Cupid or Virginia could be found in any film description, so it is assumed this was a very brief, and likely uncredited, part.

Sometime during the summer or fall of 1916, Virginia was signed to a contract with Yorke-Metro. The Yorke Film Corporation was formed by producer Fred J. Balshofer to produce the highly popular Harold Lockwood-May Allison features. The two stars actually were players for the Metro Company. With the formation of Yorke, Balshofer became president of the Yorke-Metro Company.

Signing Virginia to a contract and the formation of Yorke Film Corporation took place at approximately the same time, and the first feature for the Lockwood-Allison duo would be entitled *Pidgin Island*, based on the popular 1914 novel of the same name by Harold McGrath, and released December 25. *Pidgin Island* would be the 19th pairing of the lovely blonde and the handsome leading man, who, by the way, were not husband and wife. Unfortunately, Lockwood died young, one of the thousands of victims of the influenza plague in 1918.

The company immediately embarked for Monterey, about 500 miles away, for the movie's thrilling water scenes; however, there is no indication that Virginia was among those making the trip. According to *Moving Picture World*, "The five reels embrace many surf scenes, and these have been photographed with a fine eye for the artistic. The action is not allowed to suffer, however, through their amplitude. There are also some good Chinatown scenes, photographed at night. Mr. McGrath's story is one of smugglers, customs inspectors and romance, and the cast for the picture has been selected with care enough to have suited the author himself. The underworld types are convincing. Mr. Lockwood and Miss Allison are seen at their best in the more romantic scenes."[13]

A synopsis tells us that Lockwood is a customs agent who arrests Allison's father. It turns out that Allison is also a customs agent. When her father escapes and plans another smuggling attempt, she has to arrest her own father. Unfortunately, it is not clear what Virginia's role was in the film. *Variety*'s cast list and synopsis do not mention her or a child's role in story, and the American Film Institute's catalog makes no mention of a child either, but a December 1916 newspaper article notes that there are 35 acting roles in *Pidgin Island*, and, in addition to Lockwood and Allison, states, "prominent in the cast are Lester Cuneo, Lillian Hayward, Philip Gastrock, Virginia Corbin, Steve Barton, Elizah Zerr and Yon Foune."[14] The film does exist today.

One can only imagine, with the success this child was experiencing in her first year in the movies, what Christmas was like for her, but true to her trade, the top request on her list was to make a movie with the real Santa Claus. An article titled "Believes in Santa—Baby Virginia Corbin Wants to Play With Santa Claus," said, "Virginia Corbin, the famous four-year-old star of the motion pictures, is a strong believer in Santa Claus and is bubbling with enthusiasm in anticipation of the many nice things the bewhiskered old gentleman is going to bring her. The little star recently wrote a letter to Santa Claus asking him to pose in a one-reel picture for her. That her request may be realized is indicated by the fact that 'Big' Ed Sedgwick, the 300-pound comedian, has volunteered to disguise himself as Santa, and Lee Bartholomew, the well-known cameraman, has agreed to make the film."[15] It is not known if such a film ever was made.

Even at the tender age of four years old, Virginia was very self-confident, articulate and comfortable in front of an audience as evidenced by some appearances she made that year. An unidentified article from her personal scrapbook notes that she was the featured attraction for a Saturday event at the Broadway Department Store at the corner of South Broadway and Fourth Street in Los Angeles. The event was tied in with her recent signing with Yorke-Metro since May Allison was also on hand to introduce her. She also recited a descriptive poem entitled "Tears" written by Harold Lockwood. Aimed at the youngsters, the event included a play, directed by Miss Bertha Wilcox, folk dancing, pantomime, songs and music. "All of the favorite Mother Goose characters are scheduled to go through their various stunts," the article said. "After delivering [the poem] in an admirable manner, she [Virginia] was applauded most enthusiastically. For an encore, the talented child actress related the story of *The Three Bears and Goldylocks* [sic] who was lost in the wood." It goes on to say, "This young child, noted for her beauty, is very versatile and is a descendant from the French and English nobility."[16] Obviously to promote her new star status with Yorke-Metro, she had 1,000 photos to hand out to children in the auditorium on the eighth floor of the building. The landmark nine-story department store had been constructed just three years earlier.

On Saturday, December 30, Virginia was a featured part of a Christmas program at the Hotel Granada. The article gives four unknown names as directors of the program but doesn't mention the program being associated with any group or organization. Nevertheless, in addition to several other numbers, it said, "Mrs. Emma D. Locke opened the programme with a piano reading entitled *Yuletide*, and Baby Virginia Corbin, the youngest and highest salaried screen star, so they say, delighted the audience with an interpretive act with angelic finesse."[17]

The year closed out with Virginia at the center of a huge New Year's Eve celebration. The 1916 New Year's Eve program for the B.P.O.E., Elks No. 99 of Los Angeles, featured M'lle Tuffee as "Modiste," the Bob Burns Orchestra and 24 other acts or numbers. Number 17 on the list was Baby Corbin. Her portion was labeled simply "Selected." She also closed out the program "reclining on a bank of flowers" and "personifying infant 1917."[18] Beside her name in parentheses was "4 years old." Actually, she had just turned five years old earlier that same month.

Much later, in January 1918, one journalist took a look back at events leading up to Virginia's first year in films, although the article seems to be leaning more toward fiction than fact.

Writing for *Sunset Magazine*, literary journalist Rose Wilder Lane noted that Virginia's mother was an actress, although it is difficult to determine when and where she was an actress—the article never indicates that. Lane also implies that because Virginia Cox Corbin was an actress, Baby Virginia was engaged to play the "big time" for three seasons in *Human Hearts*. *Human Hearts* was a popular melodrama. It was written by Hal Reid, Wallace Reid's father, and filmed in both 1912 as a two-reeler with King Baggot in the lead and as a feature in 1922 with House Peters in the lead. Lane notes that for Virginia's tour in the play, "She memorized a part of eighteen pages, and faithfully performed it every night," and all this was before she was three years old! Adding some bathos to the interview, Virginia's mother said, "She used to get so tired between acts that I'd make a bed of coats on a trunk to let her sleep. She was always remarkably bright. She is naturally a great dramatic actress."[19]

The article stated that she did this for three seasons. According to Mrs. Corbin, they then found themselves at Long Beach where Virginia attracted the attention of Ellen Beach Yaw. Yaw was a concert soprano and is not known to have produced any movies, so it is unclear what role she may have played in Virginia's career.

Mrs. Corbin then noted, "Virginia wasn't doing anything at all then but posing for artists and entertaining at hotels. Everyone told me to put her into moving pictures. So I took her to Pathé Fréres, and they put her to work right away."[20] Of course, this does not coincide with earlier articles that said Mrs. Corbin visited the studio one day, and a director discovered Virginia—or that she was discovered while watching her sister perform. Lane relates that after Pathé Western, she went to Mack Sennett, "and now at five is a Fox star." Her time at Fox will be covered in detail later, but some of the information in this article makes it very suspect for fabrication, apparently on the part of Mrs. Corbin from whom Lane is getting her information.

For example, it is interesting that if Virginia spent three seasons performing in *Human Hearts*, her personal scrapbook, kept by her mother during these early years, would contain at least some clippings of referencing this play or Virginia's role in it— nor can this author find any publicized reference to Virginia appearing in the play. It must be noted that a season around the turn of the century was generally 39 weeks,[21] so for Virginia to have performed for three seasons by the time she was three years old seems rather impossible. Also, none of the movies in which the child is known to appear are Pathé Fréres or Mack Sennett productions. Additionally, why would Mrs. Corbin mention these two studios and not Fine Arts (and the unconfirmed appearance in *Intolerance*) or the time she spent at Universal?

In spite of the uncertainties surrounding this period, as the new year of 1917 began, Virginia's star began to rise even higher in the heavens giving a clearer look into her life and career.

3. The Road to Stardom

Nineteen seventeen was the year that Virginia realized her entry into true stardom thanks to the Fox Film Company, but before that came about, there were a few more films in which she appeared.

Released on January 22, 1917, *Heart Strings* put her back working for Allen Holubar. Holubar was 28 years old and had been acting since 1913, but directing for less than a year. His most well-known acting role (at least to modern audiences) is as Captain Nemo in *20,000 Leagues Under the Sea* (1916), a film that amazed audiences with its innovative underwater photography. Filmed the previous year, Holubar was actually continuing to both act and direct.

In *Heart Strings*, he stars as Dr. John McLean, left alone when his mother dies. When one of his patients dies, an eight-year-old daughter is left penniless and with no place to go. John, at first reluctant, decides to take her in. The film appears to be lost, so how much screen time Virginia received as the little girl, Johanna, is unknown. The story fast forwards ten years, and Johanna is now played by Francelia Billington. The plot sounds interesting, though, as Johanna falls in love with Gerald, a medical student. Although Johanna is unaware of his past, John knows about Gerald's former affair with a widow, an affair Gerald insists is over, but when the widow reappears, things are once again complicated—even more so since the widow is Johanna's mother who had left her and her father years ago. In the end, Johanna learns of John's love for her, forgets Gerald, and marries John.

Variety wasn't terribly impressed with the movie noting that it was "not a very original idea, but consistently worked out and acceptably acted and directed," adding, "the sort of photoplay that generally entertains the average picture patron, showing one of those 'vampires' with a luxurious apartment, bow-necked gown, etc."[1] No cast member other than Holubar was mentioned in the review.

Motion Picture News was a bit kinder, noting, "The tone of the production given this release is excellent," adding Holubar "has made a good picture from material of familiar weave."[2]

Virginia followed with another film for Holubar entitled *The Old Toymaker*, released January 28, only six days after the release of *Heart Strings*. Holubar directed, wrote the scenario from a story by H.A. Palowsky, and starred. The two-reel short is about an old toymaker who comes to America, gives his money to a broker in a mine scheme, and the broker absconds with the money—and to make matters worse, he has left his wife and ill child behind. The sick child begs for a doll the toymaker has made, and the doctor believes this may help the little girl recover. In spite of the mother's pleas, the toymaker refuses. One night, in his dreams, the doll comes to life and accuses him of being selfish. He relents and takes the doll to the child. At the same time, the broker has had a change of heart, comes home and returns the toymaker's money. Obviously, Virginia would have played the part of the child, but it would also be interesting to see how Holubar chose to bring the doll to life on the screen.

Moving Picture World called it "a pleasing offering of the sentimental type.... The bringing of the doll to life makes an excellent touch. An enjoyable number, particularly for the children."[3] Again, no mention of Virginia in the review.

The next film wasn't under the tutelage of Holubar. Instead, Virginia had the opportunity to work with the yet-to-be renowned director Henry King whose distinguished credits include *Tol'able David* (1921) for Richard Barthelmess, *The White Sister* (1923) and *Romola* (1924) for Lillian Gish, Belle Bennett's signature portrayal in *Stella Dallas* (1925), which also starred Ronald Colman, *The Winning of Barbara Worth* (1926) with Ronald Colman and Vilma Banky, *The Woman Disputed* (1928) with Norma Talmadge, and a host of top-notch sound movies between 1929 and 1962.

At this early point in his career, King was serving as both director and actor, which he also did in this film, *Vengeance of the Dead*. Produced by the Balboa Amusement Company for release by General Film Company, the film was one of a series of four-reel photoplays planned for release by General Film as Fortune Photoplays. Based on stories that appeared in Street & Smith magazines, the company planned to release one a week. *Vengeance of the Dead* was among the first eight releases announced.

Moving Picture World in early 1917 is rampant with announcements about General Films' new Fortune Photoplays and reviews of the first two films, *The Inspirations of Harry Larrabee* and *Mentioned in Confidence*. *Vengeance of the Dead* was to be the fourth release in the series. An April 21 article in the magazine that focuses on King notes, "Henry King, the distinguished actor-director, is featured together with Lillian West in *Vengeance of the Dead* a forthcoming Fortune Photoplay,"[4] but no review of a Fortune Photoplay after the first two releases can be found. As a matter of fact, *The American Film Institute Catalog* (online) questions if the film ever made it to theaters.

Nevertheless, the film was indeed shown theatrically. Numerous newspaper ads from mid–1917 announce the film's showing at theaters around the country, which makes it all the more curious that exhibitors' publications such as *Moving Picture World* did not review the film. There is a print in the Library of Congress, but it is missing a central reel. The plot is another one of those complicated melodramas so characteristic of the time. There is a Russian spy. Then there is a ballerina he controls because he knows that, back in Russia, she killed her brutish, drunkard husband. Now, in the United States, the spy wants a set of plans for a new submarine, and he wants the ballerina to help him. Coincidentally, the man with whom she is in love, David, is the ship's designer. She almost goes through with it, but kills herself rather than be controlled by the spy for the rest of her life. David raises the ballerina's daughter, Mignon, and 15 years later, marries her. Mignon befriends the spy, and David, softened over the years, allows her to entertain him in their home—mainly because the spy is old and dying. Nevertheless, he believes there is an affair that is taking place, and a divorce ensues. The spy dies and leaves his fortune to Mignon. A year later, a letter is delivered that the spy had written before he died. He tells David he arranged the semblance of an affair to get revenge on David for the ballerina's death—and admits there was no affair, only pity for him by Mignon. David goes to Mignon, finds that she has had their child during their year's separation, and they are reunited.

Once again, Virginia played the part of the female lead (Mignon) as a child. Her screen time is brief, of course. As noted, an incomplete print exists, and the reel that is missing is the part that shows the ballerina's attempt to get the submarine plans and then decides to take poison. *Picture Play Magazine* did run a condensed narrative of the film in June, which gives a nice overview of the story.

Since there are no reviews to be found, it is not known how successful the film was, but it really doesn't matter. It was released in April, and by June, Fortune Photoplays, run by the Horkheimer brothers, disbanded due to financial difficulties. *Vengeance of Death*, therefore, is likely the last of the series.

At the same time Virginia's popularity was beginning to grow and the name Virginia Lee Corbin was settled upon, an adult star named Virginia Lee was also active in films. Virginia is sometimes confused with this star by historians today and credited with films in which she never appeared.

H.M. and Elwood Horkheimer had purchased the California Motion Picture Manufacturing Company in 1913. It was the first movie studio in Long Beach. Evolving into the Balboa Amusement Producing Company, it produced more than 1,000 films before its demise in 1918. Virginia's involvement with the company is logical considering its location. An unidentified article in Virginia's scrapbook begins, "Ruth and Virginia Corbin of 'film kid fame,' formerly residents of Long Beach...," verifying their one-time residence there.[5] It is difficult to trace exactly when Mrs. Corbin and the children lived in each city (one article, as mentioned earlier, does confirm their residence in Long Beach in 1914), but other unidentified articles from the 1915–1917 period also give their residence as San Diego, Santa Ana and Los Angeles. Leon and Virginia Corbin lived separately, but it is obvious they did not divorce. Mrs. Corbin was too busy with Virginia's career, and Mr. Corbin continued to work in drug stores in various cities.

One article that was written in the 1917–1918 period said, "L.E. Corbin, who has just taken a position with the Park Drug company [in Santa Ana], is looking forward to a visit from his wife and baby Virginia, who are now located with the Fox Motion Picture Company at Hollywood and will be in Santa Ana tonight."[6] Another stated, "Mr. Corbin was for many years the owner of the Corbin drug store on the corner of Fifth and Broadway" in San Diego.[7] He was also associated with the Oakford Drug Store in Long Beach and Central Drug Company at Second and Broadway in Los Angeles. There are a couple of articles in Virginia's scrapbook that do document visits to her father. For example, "The little folks of Santa Ana, who love the dear old fairy tales, are hoping some time soon to see the little screen star, Baby Virginia Corbin, who, accompanied by her mother, spent Sunday with her father, L.E. Corbin of this city."[8] The reference to "fairy tales" indicates this article dates from the Fox Films period (1917–1918).

The next film found in some Virginia Lee Corbin filmographies is *Somebody Lied*, a two-reel comedy-drama by Ben Wilson. The Internet Movie Database and the usually very dependable resource *The Braff Silent Short Film Working Papers* (McFarland, 2002) list Virginia Lee Corbin among the cast. There was, however, an actress named Virginia Lee just starting out, and *Moving Picture World* correctly lists "Virginia Lee" among the cast, along with the stars Priscilla Dean and Harry Conway, not Virginia Corbin. The film does exist, and a viewing of it confirms that Virginia Lee Corbin is *not* in this film. The existence of a "Virginia Lee" at the same time "Virginia Lee Corbin" was beginning her career in films continues to cause some confusion among film historians.

The Light of Love, a one-reel comedy released May 26 by Universal, appears indeed to have Virginia among its players. *Motion Picture News* gave a brief reference that said, "Just an episode showing the manner in which a superficial wife had created in her the love of children. Well presented and of the sort often described as 'with a moral.'"[9] Fortunately, to confirm her part in the film, the magazine does list "Virginia Corbin" along with three other cast members—Jessie Arnold (the wife), T.J. Crittendon (the husband) and Marjorie Ellison. None of these names are memorable today, but they were recognizable names then. Born in 1885, Arnold has 25 silent screen credits, a mixture of shorts and features. She was more active on the stage than in motion pictures during the silent era. Between 1930 and her death in 1955, she has nearly 150 more screen appearances which include some TV, but virtually all are uncredited. T.J. Crittendon was 39 years old when *The Light of Love* was made and had 73 credits to his filmography between 1915 and 1924. Marjorie Ellison was 32 when she made this film, her last screen appearance after a short four-year career that included 45 films.

Once again, Virginia's name is linked to a film in which she apparently did not have a part. The Internet Movie Database lists her as a cast member in *Three Women of France*, and in parentheses by her name is "as Virginia Lee." Once again, Virginia never went by "Virginia Lee." She was either Baby Virginia Corbin, Virginia Corbin or Virginia Lee Corbin. By virtue of the title, the description and the stars, it seems unlikely this film would have a child's role anyway. With a title such as *Three Women of France* and three women—Irene Hunt, Adelaide Woods and Virginia Lee—listed as the primary stars, it is logical this is the adult Virginia Lee—and the two actresses have been confused once again.

As is expected when films do not survive, documenting with certainty all of a star's film appearances is difficult. One would think that with a scrapbook kept by Viginia's mother during this period, there would be dependable documentation of virtually every aspect of her career at this time, but the absence of any mention of some films casts doubt yet does not discount an appearance by Virginia with certainty. What is certain is that Virginia was getting noticed, which, one must admit, is remarkable since she had not yet turned five years old.

By mid–1917, however, Virginia was about to see a meteoric rise in her stardom due to her fortunate choice as leading lady in the Fox Kiddie Features.

4. A Regular Tear-Shedder

A *sign that a star* is on the rise and being noticed are the little tidbits that appear in publications related to nothing career-wise. A humorous "blurb" recounted, "The mother of Virginia Corbin told a publicity writer the child was 'precocious,' but as the story had 'ferocious'—the writer has taken to the woods."[1]

And the same magazine now felt she was worthy of a biography for the exhibitors. "Virginia La Verne Corbin. Born in Prescott, Arizona. Her father is French-English and her mother Scotch-Irish. She is but four years of age and weighs 37 pounds, but is growing. Light hair, violet eyes. She made her screen debut in December 1916, and before that had posed professionally for artists. A regular 'tear-shedder,' she is in demand for emotional parts and has played with many of the famous screen stars in Los Angeles. Her debut was made with Marie Empress in *The Chorus Girl and the Kid*, and she has played with Universal, Lasky, Metro and others, her present connection being with Fox. She is a versatile little entertainer and in demand in Los Angeles for club and society entertainments, for tear production is by no means the limit of her art, and she is a singer and dancer of merit. Children who can cry without looking as though their grief had come from a recent spanking are in demand, and she is a tragedienne in miniature, though naturally she has a sunny disposition."[2]

Moving Picture World's short bio on Virginia is from April 1917 and contains a couple of supposed facts that can be questioned. As noted earlier, going by release dates, it appears *The Chorus Girl and the Kid* may have been her fourth or fifth film appearance, but, then again, release dates do not always indicate when a movie was made and there doesn't seem to be any indication she worked for Lasky. At this early date, though, it does correctly give her birth name as "Virginia La Verne Corbin." Up until now, she has been referred to as "Baby Virginia Corbin" or simply "Virginia." The middle name of "Lee" would be added during her Fox tenure.

Also, the bio does provide interesting information regarding Virginia's talents. As noted earlier she did perform at a Christmas program and a New Year's Eve program at the end of 1916, so she obviously was comfortable in front of an audience. The fact that she could also sing and dance are testaments to her versatility and talents at such a young age. Her ability to cry on demand was, surely, an asset for the directors of her films, and would be the attribute that would earn her the tag of "Motion Pictures' Youngest Emotional Star" very soon.

It must also be noted that some bios of Virginia claimed she had performed on stage with both Geraldine Farrar and Fannie Ward, but no reference to a stage appearance with either of these stars could be found.

Virginia had worked with a variety of studios up to this time, most often with Universal. Much of her work was in shorts, and the work she did do in features was brief, not leading roles. The Franklin brothers' decision to make pictures starring children—and the fact that they made quality productions with them—was not only timely, but also a godsend for Virginia and a very talented troupe of other children.

It would seem that William Fox's decision to initiate a series of children's movies, starring children and based on children's stories, would have certainly been influenced by these Franklin pictures.

One must also keep in mind that this was early on in the history of the Fox Film Corporation, having been incorporated barely more than two years earlier. Dating back to 1903, Fox began with a theater then a film rental company to distribute films, an enterprise that proved very successful. He had a contract with the Balboa Amusement Producing Company to distribute their films through his company and may have become familiar with Virginia through her work in the Balboa films *The Chorus Girl and the Kid* and *Vengeance of the Dead*.

His distribution business, the Greater New York Film Rental Company, operated from 1904 to 1913 with a name change to the Box Office Attractions Film Rental Company in 1913. In 1914, he went into the production business and bought the old Éclair studio facilities in Fort Lee, New Jersey, as well as some property on Staten Island. Shortening the name to Box Office Attractions Company, Fox was now officially in the production business.

In 1914, he made his first film in California, and in 1915 leased the old Selig Polyscope studios in Edendale to establish his studio there. In 1916, he completed a new studio at the corner of Western Avenue and Sunset Boulevard, which is where Virginia worked while making the Fox Kiddie Pictures.

An all-kid cast in classic fairy tales was obviously an idea Fox had been working on for some time, but very discreetly. According to Brownlow, "Late in '16, the Franklin brothers were contacted by a mysterious character who arranged to meet them at a theatre in downtown Los Angeles. In an atmosphere of secrecy, they were conducted along corridors and into the office of a man who proved to be Winfield Sheehan, general manager of the William Fox Studios. He told them Mr. Fox had liked their pictures, and particularly the children who played in them. Would the Franklins be interested in coming to work for him?"

"'Mr. Fox is prepared to give you $300 a week,' said Sheehan, 'and a firm contract. He will also give you your own stage and your own company, and he will provide a schoolroom for the children.'"[3] Brownlow went on to note that the Franklins felt themselves in a quandary because they were proud of their association with D.W. Griffith, but there was no "solid contract" with Griffith and the salary offer was three times what they were getting with the famous director. Although somewhat reluctant, they accepted the offer.

The veil of secrecy under which this agreement was reached is an indication of William Fox's desire to keep a good idea from being stolen before he could bring it to fruition. Another indication of Fox's desire to keep things quiet until the right time was the fact that his announcement of the series did not come until late April 1917, well after filming had been completed on *Jack and the Beanstalk*, the first in the series, and filming was well underway (if not completed) on *The Babes in the Woods*. Certainly, pictures with kids had been produced before—as the Franklin brothers had done, for example—and there were child stars around such as Baby Marie Osborne, Zoe Ray, Baby Gloria Joy, Kittens Reichert, Mary Jane Irving, Ben Alexander, Dolores and Helene Costello and others, so featuring children was not an original idea. What was original was featuring an all-kid cast and putting them in famous fairy tales aimed at a children's audience. This was also the first time a major studio was to attempt this type of film, investing big bucks and ensuring high production values.

Fox chose to delay the announcement for just the right time. It was about three months before *Jack and the Beanstalk* hit the screens when *The Los Angeles Times* carried the announcement on April 29, 1917. "During his visit to California, William Fox, the celebrated producer of pictures, took steps for the establishment of a company of children, who are to film stories of the land of make-believe and specially-written scenarios on children's subjects. Announcement of this move has just been made by the Fox Film Corporation, with the additional information that it is expected to release a 'Fox kiddie feature' monthly."[4]

As noted, by the time this article appeared, *Jack and the Beanstalk* had been completed, and the kids had been working on *The Babes in the Woods* for about a month. Much was to be learned from that first film, though. The Franklin brothers had never tackled a kid picture on such a grand scale, and the gargantuan task was not without its problems.

"We approached our first production, *Jack and the Beanstalk*, in fear and trepidation," said Sidney Franklin. "We had never handled a picture of this size. Our staff, which once consisted of two or three assistants, blossomed into an army. Locations had to be found, costume sketches produced, sets designed, catering arrangements made."[5] Filming took place at Chatsworth, about 40 miles from Hollywood. Built among the rocks were the fortified Village of Cornwall and the giant's castle.

The Franklins realized one of their most challenging tasks was to locate a "giant" for the picture. They wired circuses in both the United States and Europe. They scored when Ringling Brothers recommended Jack Tarver who stood at an imposing seven feet, ten inches. "By the time the costume department had finished with him, he looked nine foot tall, and against the children, he loomed into the air like a redwood tree," said Brownlow.[6]

Approximately 250 children were used in the picture, all under the age of eight—and all were required to have a chaperone. Therefore, transportation to the location proved to be a daily headache. Chester and Sidney Franklin would get up at two or three o'clock in the morning to check the weather. If the forecast was for clear weather, the Southern Pacific Railroad was contacted, and things were set in motion. "It was winter, and it did rain occasionally," said Franklin. "There was no sight more beautiful than to see the long train on the spur line in Chatsworth with two or three hundred

Jack (Francis Carpenter) has just rescued the princess (Virginia) from the giant. According to director Sidney Franklin, about 250 kids were used as extras in the making of *Jack and the Beanstalk* (1917), and all were required to have chaperones. Franklin said the large number of children and parents made transportation to their location about 40 miles from Los Angeles a daily headache.

kids, and the same number of mothers, sitting in the cars munching away at our box lunches with the rain pouring down outside. Chet and I directed the kids, with not one in sympathy with us, and we ran up and down the hill all day long.... When night fell, we did too, from absolute mental and physical exhaustion. The burden was heavy, but it was a responsibility we had to take. On one of those nasty days when it rained, and we all stood around, a wind accompanied the downpour, and in the hazy distance we watched helplessly as the giant's castle was blown from its mountaintop."[7]

Another problem, according to Franklin, was the mothers, so much of a problem that they had to keep the parents out of sight of their children in a special roped-off area guarded by policemen.

Although the lead children—Virginia, Francis Carpenter and some of the others— fully understood their interaction with the giant was playacting, many of the youthful extras were terrified of him. The situation was helped considerably when the Franklins sat the children down for a chat with Traver, but appeared to have an unwanted effect because, when it came time for an aggressive attack on the castle, many of the children would not cooperate—they refused to throw things at the giant! "So the Franklins had delicately to suggest that, although he didn't eat children, as they had previously been led to believe, he might have taken a tiny nibble occasionally."[8]

Sidney Franklin recounted an amusing story about a kid's "attack" on the castle. "I remember one child trudging up the hill towards the embattled castle. He must have been at least five years of age. He had a lovely flowing beard and he looked like a tired old gentleman. As he came near me, I asked him where he was going. He looked rather surprised and explained, 'I'm going to fight the giant.' And away he went, dragging a wooden spear that was as long than he was."[9]

The interiors were shot at the Fox studio—coincidentally at the same time as *A Tale of Two Cities* starring William Farnum with Florence Vidor also in the cast. She remembered watching the Franklins work with the kids. "Each one would take a group of two, three or four, and they would work with the camera quite close up. They had evidently rehearsed these things, and everything was so beautifully coordinated that they could work at the same time—both directing the children with such quiet voices that nothing was disturbed. I've never seen better acting anywhere than we saw there with these children, and Farnum and I were just transported. I felt that Chester and Sidney Franklin had something that was unique, and they brought a high form of art to the pictures. I don't think it was ever appreciated the way it should have been. To me it was comparable to Chaplin and some of the things David Wark Griffith did, but it was something that was never repeated—and never equaled, I don't think, in any form."[10]

Although William Fox was anxious to get the Franklin brothers working for him—and he respected their ability—that didn't mean he trusted them. He fully intended the Fox Kiddie Pictures to be high quality productions, but this first picture—the first of an unproven idea—was getting out of hand. In charge of the West Coast studio was Abraham Carlos, who would be booted out later when the next studio manager, Sol Wurtzel, came on the scene. Halfway through the making of *Jack and the Beanstalk*, Fox told Carlos to stop the picture—the studio could not afford it. When the situation seemed hopeless, the Franklins' father entered the picture. He was a successful businessman who had contacts and offered a proposition to the studio—he would raise the money already expended if the studio would sell the rights. Fox agreed. However, by the time the money was raised, Fox changed his mind, and filming continued.

Sidney Franklin remembered that the battle with the studio over money was a constant one. Describing a typical day, he said that after filming on location, "the day ended with some charming phone calls from the studio. 'My God, the money you're spending. A few more days like this and you'll break the studio.'"[11]

The movie was eventually completed, and, even though it originally came in at 12 reels, it was shown at ten reels, about two hours at 20 frames per second, at its premiere. Unfortunately, only an abridged version of the film exists today. It is around four reels or 48 minutes long, and, to the dismay of silent film fans, even this version has not been made available to the home video market, but viewing a shorter 18-minute narrated abridgement assumed to have been produced in the 1940s or 1950s demonstrates why the picture was so popular. At the time of this writing, at least two more versions could be found on YouTube—a 19-minute abridgement with original intertitles that includes several scenes not found in the narrated version mentioned above, and 16 minutes of the film's finish.

The first two versions begin by showing Jack (Francis Carpenter) in his small home by the fire with his mother. He must take the cow and sell it so they can have money to eat. Jack meets a man on the road who offers him magic beans for the cow. Jack is reluctant, but we see a hazy figure of his good fairy (who is dressed more like a Biblical figure with flowing robes) telling him, "Take them, Jack. They'll bring good luck." As the fairy tale goes, he takes them home. His mother is angry at the foolish exchange, and she throws them out the window.

The next day when Jack discovers the beanstalk, we get a glimpse of the small village created for the film—stone houses sparsely populating the rolling hills with a bucolic bridge over a stream. During this scene, there are quite a few adults as the village people gather curiously around the beanstalk and watch Jack climb up it with his dog in a sack that he has slung over his shoulder. The viewer doesn't see a large portion of the beanstalk at any time, but it is rather convincingly created with huge leaves covering a somewhat thin stalk.

When he reaches the top, he meets the good fairy again who tells him, "When you were a baby, a giant named Blunderbore killed your father and robbed your mother of her great wealth, which he has in his castle today. He lives up here, hard by the village of Cornwall, whose little inhabitants he steals and devours. I command you—slay the giant, thus restoring your mother's riches, avenging your father's death and freeing Cornwall."

Jack goes to Cornwall to announce to the King that he has come to slay the giant. There he meets Princess Regina, and they fall in love. The next morning, the Princess, the King and the people of the village "bid him Godspeed" as he embarks on his mission.

The violent scene where the giant kidnaps the princess is included in the narrated abridgement. When he arrives outside

Francis Carpenter proved to be the perfect leading man for Virginia—leaping, fighting, raising his fist in defiance and ready to lead his men "into the jaws of death." Francis was just a year and a half older than Virginia and apparently relished playing the hero in their films together.

her room at her castle in the village, he breaks through the stone walls of her room. She has hidden in a closet. His huge figure appears massive as he towers above the small furniture in the Princess' room and searches for her. He discovers the terrified Princess hiding in a closet. Pulling her from the closet, he lifts her high, like a leaf, with one hand and then carries her off kicking and crying. One can see why a scene such as this could have been rather intense for a young child in those days.

Back at the giant's castle, he gives the child to his wife (who is normal size) to lock away in a room so that he can eat her later. It is interesting to note that at the door of the room, we see the "steam" from the wife's breath indicating how cold the temperature must have been when they were filming this scene. As Franklin noted earlier, it was winter when the movie was made.

Tarver was indeed a perfect choice for the giant—his imposing figure towering above the furniture in the Princess' room—and when he lifts little Virginia high in the air, she appears to be a doll in his hand. The bulky fur coat, long hair, beard and large, false teeth add much to the effect.

Of course, Jack does arrive at the castle to save the Princess as the fairy had instructed him. He sees her in a high window of the castle. In order to gain entry, he goes to the door and asks the wife for food. She allows him to come in but warns him of the giant who is out at the moment.

When the giant returns with two small boys under his arm for his pantry, Jack hides. In addition to the Princess, the story does include the fairy tale's hen that lays golden eggs, which Jack takes back down the beanstalk to his mother.

He returns the next day to the giant's castle and gets inside by wearing a beard and pretending he is a hungry, old man. In this scene, there is also a magic harp, per the fairy tale, on the table with the giant. Unfortunately, the abridgement is missing a significant portion because it jumps here to Jack leading an army of children to storm the castle. Several are on horses and many are on foot, confirming that Franklin's estimate of 200–300 children taking part in the film is accurate.

As the children are on their way to the castle, the wife brings the Princess out for the giant to eat. Here we see why viewers of the time were so impressed with the "emotional star." The tears flow freely and the terror is convincingly portrayed in what must have been a very frightening scene for children in the audience. The immense giant has this diminutive, weeping Princess on a chopping block, holding her down by her neck while he raises a huge knife high in the air.

Virginia was reported to be afraid of the knife, as any small child should be, but as a means of encouragement, she was told that Sarah Bernhardt "had died a thousand times as Cleopatra at the bite of an asp, and that every time she imagined she really was dying." The report said, "The child was fired by a desire to do likewise—to be like the great Bernhardt, the idol of her profession; so she proudly and realistically went through the scene, forgetting all about being afraid."[12]

Outside the castle, there is an impressive long shot of hordes of children approaching on a stone walkway up the hillside. This leads to two long sets of stone steps curving as two arms and leading farther up the hillside to the giant's castle.

The hordes of children stand ready down below with bows and arrows and catapults to throw stones. Jack announces, "I want fifty men who will follow me into the jaws of death!" and leads them up the castle steps. Inside, he walks in just as the giant is about to bring the knife down on the Princess. He throws a rock, knocking the knife from the giant's grip and retreats quickly as the giant pursues him.

The giant then appears along the wall on the castle, and the children pelt him with rocks and arrows. Inside, the wife sends the Princess quickly to her room, telling her to lock the door.

Coming back inside the castle, the giant wants to know where the Princess is hiding and kills his wife for refusing to tell him. He finds the Princess locked in her room and begins to knock the door down. Meanwhile, Jack and the rest of the men are holding a net in which the Princess may jump from the high window.

The scene is intense with the Princess terrified, crying and looking back at the door in horror as the giant begins to break in. With this towering figure in scenes such as the potential beheading of the Princess and breaking into the Princess' room, the giant should have sent a large number of children home with nightmares. There was, however, a photo circulated around with the movie's publicity that showed the towering giant, in costume, holding Virginia high in one arm and Francis in the other—possibly as a way to reassure children this was all "play acting."

At any rate, just as the giant breaks open the door, enters the room and charges toward the Princess, she jumps from the window into the net.

Two of Jack's men have watched in the hallway as the giant enters the room. They quickly close the door and lock it so he can't get out. Then several of the men set fire to the door with the giant trapped inside. Although it seems they have him secured, he succeeds in breaking down the door.

Outside, the men have greased the steps and placed a net at the bottom. The giant runs out, slips on the grease and lands in the net. Jack and the Princess run for the beanstalk as the giant frees himself and pursues them. When they get to the bottom, Jack takes an ax and cuts the stalk down. The giant falls to the ground, and, while he lies there stunned, Jack jumps on top of him and stabs him several times with his dagger—a rather gruesome scene. The production values are impressive, particularly for the time. The shot of the huge castle on the hilltop and the extensive steps leading to it, the interiors of the castle (showing several rooms), and the sheer number of children and their costumes all contribute to a quality production.

Motion Picture News praised the creation of the village where the Princess lived. "Even their conception of the miniature village of Cornwall has been reproduced in all its wonders. 'Long shots' taken from an elevation disclose a wondrous work of artistry in revealing the village of Cornwall. And when the 'close-up' is employed, so fascinating are the miniature bungalows that the children who see it are to be closely watched else they will run down the aisle of the theatre and see entrance to the ideal play house."[13] A long shot of the village does impress with a stone wall stretching around possibly 20 or more dwellings, and a long straight road leading from the gate to the Princess' castle at the far end. Another article described the setting. "Here in a tract five acres in extent, a complete medieval city was erected. Its tiny schoolhouse, church, palace, windmill, prison and dwellings were tinted in bright reds, oranges, blues, purples and greens."[14] Obviously, the colors were impressive to the writer; however, they really didn't make a difference in a black and white film.

The modern opening to the film is lost. It showed Virginia and Francis being read *Jack and the Beanstalk* by their nurse. Later, their mothers go to a tea and leave them alone. The children decide they want to go out in search of the enchanted forest. They agree to meet at the crossroads at three o'clock, and, although Francis is late, he eventually arrives in his little motorcar to find an impatient Virginia, and the two set off on the road to adventure.

What most certainly ensured the success of the film were the performances of Virginia and Francis Carpenter. There could not have been two more enthusiastic portrayals than these. Carpenter jumps and runs and expresses excitement, anger, passion and fortitude as well as any adult thespian. Reviewers and magazine writers commented regularly on Virginia's beauty, and one can see why in this film. She truly is a beautiful child, and the tears that she sheds so readily tug strongly on the heartstrings.

In his article on the Fox Kiddie Features, Brownlow said, "The children enter so much into the spirit of the story that one is never quite sure whether they are sending it up or taking it seriously. Francis Carpenter, the hero, is stern, tough and unconquerable, and one can watch him grow from three in *Let Katie Do It* to five or six in the Fox pictures. Virginia Lee Corbin, she of the blonde tresses and lustrous lips, obviously reveled in her parts—invariably Princesses."[15]

Francis Carpenter and Virginia are shown in a scene from the modern opening to *Jack and the Beanstalk* (1917). In this part of the film, the two children are being read the story of "Jack and the Beanstalk" and decide to go off in search of the enchanted forest. Unfortunately, the modern prologue doesn't seem to have survived.

In early July, William Fox had announced, "In response to a general demand throughout the country from women's clubs, editors, educators and others interested in the welfare of the young, I have staged a series of children's fairy tales. The first, *Jack and the Beanstalk*, will be shown at a New York Broadway theater not later than September. In the children's pictures, all parts will be enacted by juvenile artists selected with great care, and the plays are intended for the young and old."[16]

Actually, the film premiered just 21 days after the publication of Fox's comments— on July 30 at the Globe Theater in New York.

5. The Most Consummate Little Actors in the World

*V*irginia had garnered a fair amount of recognition for her work prior to the Fox Kiddie Features, but when *Jack and the Beanstalk* premiered in the summer of 1917, her star rose in the heavens like a rocket.

The premiere at the Globe Theater was the beginning of a ten-week engagement there. It "was received by the audience and the newspaper critics among it with impressive enthusiasm. The critics were unanimous in lauding the picture as a remarkable novelty in the silent drama."[1]

Praise for the movie and its two principal players came from every corner. In 1917, *The New York Times* was only reviewing a small number of movies, and the reviews were more often bereft of any significant praise for a film, but the premiere of *Jack and the Beanstalk* at the Globe on Broadway did catch its attention and gain the reviewer's approval. Calling it "Fox Films' most spectacular movie," the reviewer went on to say, "The fairy tale, as a piece of workmanship, was admirably clear and varied, with the constant shift of scenes quick as thought, and a well-sustained climax of interest in the little hero."[2]

Variety criticized the two-hour length as "a trifle wearisome," but also exclaimed that it was "admirably visualized in the form of a huge, spectacular production," adding that it "brings back your childhood days in a manner to send you scurrying in search of the manager of the show to wheedle a pair of complimentary tickets for the juvenile members of your family.... It is the sort of feature that should pay an annual visit to every town in the country."[3]

According to *The New York Tribune*, "*Jack and the Beanstalk* is the most artistic picture William Fox ever has produced, and this is said with due apologies to *Neptune's Daughter*, *A Daughter of the Gods*, and *The Honor System*."[4]

Motion Picture News noted that the movie was still drawing crowds at the Globe in its second week there and emphasized the film's attraction for both children and adults. The publication told exhibitors that it "will prove as strong an attraction for the older generation as it does for the kiddies.... The children will enjoy every scene. The elder ones will be attracted by curiosity and once attracted, will be held spellbound by the revelation on the screen."[5]

One unidentified article described this scene. "Nobody knows who enjoyed *Jack and the Beanstalk* most at the Strand yesterday, 5-year-old Johnny who perched on the edge of his seat for the whole ten reels or grandpa, who had gone to 'take the children.' Johnny, on the way out, shrieked ecstatically at Tommy across the street that it was 'O-oh, just splendid!' and grandpa told father that it was 'some picture' and he'd better go."[6]

Hyperbole seemed to be the order of the day for *Jack and the Beanstalk* with adjectives such as "wonderful," "mighty" and "marvelous," and descriptions exclaiming "ten reels of the best picture you have seen in some time," "the most artistic picture William Fox has ever produced," "more beautifully produced than one would believe possible," and "an original turn in the road leading to new and greater things in the art of motion pictures."

No one expected the praise that Francis and Virginia would receive for their acting after the release of *Jack and the Beanstalk* (1917). One writer said Virginia "expressed emotion with the artistic touch of a Bernhardt," and another referred to her as a "junior Marlowe," a reference to the famous stage actress of the time. Francis was given high praise when he was called "a miniature William Farnum," one of the most popular stars of the day.

But as much praise as the film itself received, Virginia Lee Corbin and Francis Carpenter were elevated to a level of talent equal to any star on the screen at the time. One said Virginia "expressed emotion with the artistic touch of a Bernhardt."[7] Another called her the "junior Marlowe of the screen" (referencing Julia Marlowe who was a well-known stage actress at the time, especially for her Shakespearean roles).[8] Francis received a special compliment from one writer who called him "a miniature William Farnum."[9]

A syndicated piece that appeared in many newspapers across the country said, "Two marvelous children, Francis Carpenter and Virginia Lee Corbin, play the leads. Not only are they the most beautiful children on the screen, but they are the most talented. The acting of Virginia, as the Princess, in her love scenes with Jack, who has come to slay the giant, is simply away ahead of anything that any other child has ever accomplished. Virginia is four and a half, and Francis is a year older."[10]

A writer in Kansas said, "These children are the most consummate little actors in the world. They simulate joy, grief, love, hate, disappointment, indignation, fear, despair, and the many other passions with amazing fidelity. Small wonder that audiences are gripped as they see these young marvels play such difficult roles."[11]

Two other children who were also to become regulars in the Fox Kiddie Features were Carmen De Rue and Violet Radcliffe. As stars, Virginia and Francis obviously received the lion's share of the publicity, and more often than not, they would be the only names mentioned in a review, but Carmen and Violet were also extremely talented and lent much charm and enthusiasm to these films.

In *Jack and the Beanstalk*, both play male parts. Carmen is the King in a long black beard and gives a passionate, animated performance. Violet is Prince Rudolpho who is vying for the Princess' hand. Although Prince Rudolpho is introduced in an intertitle in one of the versions viewed, the competition between him and Jack for the hand of the Princess is never referenced again in the abridgement. One review did praise the two youngsters with "Violet Radcliffe … gives the cutest interpretation of Prince Rudolpho, the villain who upbraids Jack in a frenzy of jealousy, and there is Carmen De Rue whose King of Cornwall should make history."[12]

Prior to *The Birth of a Nation*, no one, at least in the United States, felt a lengthy film held appeal. Actually, most felt it was a detriment to audience appeal. Griffith changed all that when his three-hour epic was such a big hit. Just two years later, when *Jack and the Beanstalk* appeared in theaters, the length of a finished film and the amount of money spent were indications of a higher quality product. Therefore, it's not surprising that promotion for the film played fast and loose with the facts to enhance the enormity of the film.

For example, in his interview with Kevin Brownlow, director Sidney Franklin said they used 200–300 kids. Viewing the abridgement available today seems to confirm Franklin's estimate as accurate, but 1,300 was the more common figure being quoted to the public. It is not known exactly how much was spent on the making of *Jack and the Beanstalk*, but publicity quotes ranged from $300,000 to $800,000. As a matter of fact, Fox himself quotes the cost as $500,000. These figures would equate to between $6 and $16 million today, so it's safe to assume the cost to make the film was inflated for publicity purposes. The film's giant, who is regularly put at eight and a half feet tall, was actually between seven foot three and seven foot six, according to Franklin and biographies on him today.

Finally, publicity will regularly note that the film took a year to make, sometimes whittling that down to eight months. One article in which the writer visited the location said the cast was in their fourth month of filming. Unfortunately, this too was a clipping from Virginia's scrapbook, and, since her mother never wrote a date on any of the snippets, no date could be determined for the writer's visit. It is a fact, however, that filming began on *Babes in the Woods* in late March, so *Jack and the Beanstalk* would have begun filming in July 1916 if it took even eight months to film—not likely in this time in movie history.

Promotion obviously included personal appearances. Miller's Theater in Los Angeles was at the juncture of Spring and Main streets, a section that closely resembled a smaller version of New York's Times Square, and the large marquee at the juncture of the triangle was for Miller's. A 1917 photo of this intersection shows the marquee reading, "Make Miller's a Weekly Habit, There's Miller Over There, Read Our Ad Here Tonight, We Show Wm. Fox Photoplays."

A large newspaper ad announced that the four principal stars—Francis Carpenter, Virginia Lee Corbin, Carmen De Rue, and Violet Radcliffe—would be making personal appearances there "starting tonight," September 4. Only one star appeared each night, though, with Francis on Tuesday evening, Virginia on Wednesday, Violet on Thursday, and Carmen on Friday. As the week began, the film had already been playing at Miller's for two weeks, and the theater reported that it had drawn "the biggest crowds of any picture ever seen"[13] there and had "broken all attendance records" there.[14]

One ad for the film at Miller's carried a not surprising disclaimer, considering the immense popularity of the film. Within a large newspaper display ad, a boxed in warning declared, "THE PUBLIC IS BEING DECEIVED, Owing to the sensational popularity of our big Fox Standard Picture—*Jack and the Beanstalk*—unscrupulous small picture shows are foisting upon their patrons cheap 'imitations'—old one and two reel pictures, made over five years ago, bearing the same title. Do not be deceived by these imitations. The genuine *Jack and the Beanstalk* that has electrified Los Angeles is in 10 big spectacular reels and is now showing ONLY at Miller's Theater."[15]

Another brainchild, no doubt from a Fox publicist, was to offer $500 in prizes for the best reviews written on *Jack and the Beanstalk*, but the reviews had to be written by boys and girls under the age of 14. The contest, announced in September, would offer $100 each to five lucky writers.

Fox had no way of knowing just how popular his first Kiddie Feature would be. For a man who had wanted to stop production midway through the making of the film, this must have been more than just a relief, but an indication that he had a goldmine on his hands with this series. However, even before Virginia and Francis were being acclaimed by critics around the country in terms typically reserved for the biggest stars of stage or screen, Fox knew he had something big on his hands. It's no surprise that he knew he had to lock in his little star before being snatched up by one of his competitors, so he signed her to a year-long (some sources say five-year) contract in the spring, more than two months before the first Fox Kiddie Feature hit the screens. Although the terms of the contract are lost to time, one article noted that she was signed "at a good round weekly sum."[16] Another article said Francis and Virginia had been signed to a five-year contract, along with their dog, Sport. "All sorts of salaries and advantages are provided for the children, while Sport gets a home for life at the Hollywood studios, and all he can eat, providing of course, it is deemed wise to permit his appetite to get the better of his judgment."[17] The article added that both Francis and Virginia had been given a pony and cart for their work in the movie and were promised a new automobile as a part of the new contract.

It also didn't hurt to "butter up" Mrs. Corbin and her daughter as well as gain a little free publicity by throwing a party for his new star. The headline read, "William Fox Entertains 'Baby' Corbin," which was "in celebration of the event of the successful completion of her notable work in the Franklin Brothers' $300,000 fairy story spectacle entitled *A Modern Jack and the Beanstalk*. William Fox ... recently tendered 'Baby' Virginia Corbin, the four-year-old emotional star, a luncheon at the Hotel Alexandria, and a box party at Clune's Auditorium afterwards. Favors were miniature old-fashioned china dolls. The place cards were daintily hand painted. Twelve people made up the party, which included Virginia's sister, Frances Corbin, Mr. Carlos' daughter, Mr. Farnum's daughter, Carmen del [sic] Rue, Violet Radcliffe and their mothers."[18] (Note at times Virginia's mother may be referred to by her first name, Virginia, or at other times by her middle name, Frances.)

Virginia was also making the transition from "Baby Corbin" to "Virginia Lee Corbin." Even the previous year, when she was starting out and working for other companies, there was rarely an instance when her full, given name of Virginia La Verne Corbin was ever used. In cast listings, she was usually just "Virginia Corbin," but as can be seen from the headline of the aforementioned article, she had not yet totally shed the "Baby" label, which is not surprising considering her young age. It is difficult to determine when "Virginia Lee Corbin" first began to be used or even why—it certainly sounded better than "Virginia La Verne Corbin." However, with the starring roles in the Fox Kiddie Features, "Virginia Lee Corbin" began to appear on a regular basis.

And, speaking of her age, publicity surrounding *Jack and the Beanstalk* regularly quoted her as being four and a half. Actually, she had just turned five the previous December, but the practice of trimming a year or so off her age had already begun and would continue through most of her career.

Yet, five years old is still very young, and one article emphasized this with a headline, "Wants to Be a Baby Occasionally." It told a charming story that took place as *Jack and the Beanstalk* was nearing completion. Virginia "became enamored with a little extra girl ... and seemed much more interested in playing with her than in acting in the next scene. Finally the extra girl was sent away, and then little Virginia settled down to work with the remark, 'You've got to let me be a baby once in awhile.'"[19]

6. Emotional Star

*E*ven though Virginia's popularity was increasing before *Jack and the Beanstalk*, this "A" class picture from a major studio solidified her place among the most recognizable names in Hollywood in the late 'teens—and suddenly her new-found fans throughout the country wanted to read about her while others saw dollar signs in her name.

No doubt the work of a press agent, articles suddenly appeared around the release of *Jack and the Beanstalk* claiming that Virginia was of royal lineage—very fitting for someone who had just portrayed a princess onscreen. Although the announcement appeared in several forms in newspapers throughout the country, *Photo-Play Journal* in August 1917 carried a two-page article with photos that explained, "Recently, she has received an ancient necklace from her grandfather who lives in Philadelphia, Lyman Jerome Corbin, which embodies a finely executed coat-of-arms of the Corbin family, and bears the date of 1015. This coat-of-arms has been handed down from ancestors of the present Corbins from generation to generation for nearly one thousand years."[1]

According to the story, it was worn by the first Corbin who came to England with William the Conqueror. The distant relative had been knighted on the battlefield at Windsor and the necklace was worn by a variety of distinguished family members over the years. She was reportedly surprised by the gift which made her feel as if she was a "really truly princess."

After Virginia learned that one of her ancestors had been knighted, a vignette that was circulated to newspapers said, "One of those kindly men who pride themselves on making friends with children, patted Virginia on the head and asked her name and age. Virginia told him, adding a few details of family history. 'One of my grandfathers was knighted by William the Conqueror,' she said, 'but I can't remember that.'"[2]

There is one problem with the story, and that is that Lyman Jerome Corbin died in 1892 in Huron, South Dakota. He was a native of Massachusetts, had lived in Rockford, Illinois, and was considered to be one of the pioneers of Huron. Not only had he been dead for 25 years at the time of this story, there is no record that he ever lived in Philadelphia.

The remainder of the article, of course, focused on the talents and charms of little Virginia as well as the benefits of photoplays by children and for children. It was accompanied by a bust shot of Virginia in her robe and crown from *Jack and the Beanstalk*, and the writer gushed, "The illustrations herewith show better than words can tell the royal splendor of this little star in royal robes, and we can hardly blame her directors when they claim that no child could look and act so natural in royal roles who was not born that way."[3] Regarding children in motion pictures, the typical saccharine pontification continued for several paragraphs and ended with "Let there be no cessation in the commendable work of bringing forward and developing more children who show sufficient Thespian ability! The photoplay is enriched by the inspiring efforts of the little ones, and the photoplay fans are immeasurably pleased to watch young America equal and surpass their seniors."[4]

Using movie stars as a successful means of product endorsement was discovered early in the history of cinema too. An article promoting Goodrich tires shows a dainty Virginia Lee Corbin sitting on the front fender of a period car talking to Ezra Meeker who was famous for traveling in a prairie schooner from Oregon to Washington, D.C. As if to endorse Goodrich tires, it was noted that Meeker made the same trip in his Pathfinder—an automobile that was produced between 1912 and 1917.

She also endorsed Palmer tubes. "Now that summer is here, she plans to make many trips when she is not working," the article said. "Realizing that many a short jaunt is spoiled by tire trouble, she has equipped her car with Palmer cord tires. Little Virginia said ... 'My car is so big, and I am so tiny that I cannot always see everything in the road before me, and I sometimes run over sticks and boards and get punctures in my tires. In order to prevent a lot of these happenings, I was told that Palmer cord tubes should be used.'" An accompanying photo show Virginia posing with a tire almost as tall as she and captioned, "She drives, or rather owns, a big King eight equipped with Delion tires and Palmer cord tubes."[5]

In 1917, Peggy Jeans were a

Virginia's growing popularity was evident from the attention she was receiving in newspapers and film-related publications. One story that circulated among numerous publications was that she had received an ancient necklace that once belonged to the first Corbin who came to England with William the Conqueror-supposedly proving that Virginia was a "really truly princess."

popular brand of clothing for young girls, and Virginia was the perfect age to endorse the product. Designed for kids aged two to 14, the one-piece "jump suits" were described in advertisements as being "made of pink and blue chambray—and gingham—with pockets, belt and all."

The Peggy Jeans photos in Virginia's personal scrapbook are a charming and nostalgic window in time as Mrs. Corbin kept several snapshots done by photographer Paul Greenbeaux in a photo shoot for the product. Virginia is dressed in a cute little jumper that has a white square collar and three-quarter sleeves. The sleeves and pants legs are cuffed in gingham, as is the large buttoned belt while the outfit itself is a light solid color. A newspaper ad shows her wearing this outfit with a billed cap, holding a tin bucket and shovel with one leg propped on a low concrete wall. The photos show various poses on a sidewalk in front of a house with Virginia looking back at the camera while pushing a baby stroller. One photo that wasn't used in advertisements has Virginia standing in a small pond, or possibly a fountain area at a park, up to her knees in water. However, she is holding her hands together at her chest and crying, so it's obvious she wasn't happy about this particular pose.

A couple of years later, she was still being used for promotions. An ad had her posing in her "Billy Boss Dress" made in Los Angeles by Cohn-Goldwater Co.

And there were other ways businessmen tried to cash in on the little star's name. An article headlined "Have You Tried the 'Baby' Corbin Special?" said, "Little 'Baby' Virginia Corbin, the four-year-old emotional star of the Fox studios, has recently granted the request of a large Los Angeles confectioner for permission to name a new fountain concoction the 'Baby Corbin Special.' There's more than one angle to being famous!"[6]

In 1917, the country was in the midst of its heaviest involvement in World War I, and the drawing power of Hollywood stars to support the war effort was quickly realized. Much has been said over the years about the success of bond tours by Douglas Fairbanks, Mary Pickford, Charlie Chaplin and Marie Dressler, who, as a team, raised huge sums of money as they toured the country. The value of little Virginia Lee Corbin's name was also put to good use. Although her youth did not lend itself well to a bond tour, she did contribute to the war effort in other ways.

Sometime during the summer of 1917, the Stage Women's War Relief conducted a drive with the slogan "Everyone must have a flag by the Fourth [of July]." The object of the drive was to sell flags and raise money for war relief. Mentioned first among those mentioned as "aiding" the drive was Virginia. Others were Mrs. Charles Ray, actresses Eugenie Ford, Gladys Brockwell, Juanita Hansen, Bertha Mann, Grace Wilson, and Adele Clifton, plus some unrecognizable names to silent film fans today.

In another event, Virginia was joined by Baby Marie Osborne and Ben Alexander. It was noted that the "juvenile stars of the film play world are still receiving congratulations for the notable parts they played on the Red Cross Shop program last Friday. The children, in solo entertainments, made tremendous hits and helped swell the Red Cross Shop funds considerably."[7]

An article headlined "'Baby Corbin' Gets Letter of Thanks from Belgium" said she "has just received a letter from the Belgium Red Cross Society in Antwerp, signed by seven prominent 'relief work' officials, thanking her for the active part she took at the bazaar held by the Los Angeles American Red Cross Society for the benefit of the Belgium relief work in Central Park last fall. At this time, 'Baby' Corbin appeared on the stage every half hour from eleven to five, and her name proved a very strong drawing card at the ticket office. Little Virginia has received scores of requests for her picture from Belgian and French soldiers and has granted every one."[8]

In December, she was among those assisting with the Needlework Guild's war benefit bridge party in Los Angeles. Along with Virginia, other stars who took part were Kathlyn Williams, Francis Carpenter, Winifred Kingston, Mary Miles Minter, Louise Lovely, Louise Glaum, Fay Tincher, Dolly Dare, Dorothy Davenport, Louise Huff and Gail Kane.

Virginia continued her personal appearances to support the war effort in 1918. In April of that year, the city of Manhattan Beach held an official opening of its new municipal pavilion. The "grand military ball" was used as a means to raise funds for the Manhattan Beach Red Cross Society. "An interesting entertainment preceded the ball, which was ushered in by a promenade led by Miss Olive Thomas and William Desmond, motion picture stars, the music being furnished by the jazz band from the submarine base at San Pedro. Thomas Berkivie of Los Angeles delivered an address on behalf of the third Liberty Loan, Miss Margaret Salinas sang two solos accompanied by Mrs. Clara Weimer, Miss Virginia Lee Corbin, the well-known child motion picture actress, presented an emotional act entitled 'Tears,'" and, in a rare mention of Virginia's sister, "Miss Ruth Corbin gave several exhibitions of fancy dancing."[9]

On June 1, she took part in a children's festival at the Majestic Theater in Los Angeles. The program was entitled "Poster Folk" with proceeds going to the Juvenile Red Cross fund. Announcing the upcoming event, *The Los Angeles Times* said, "Many of the costumes the wee people will wear stagger the imagination. Marie Louise Larkin, a 6-year-old, will wear a dress composed of thirty valuable ostrich feathers costing $300. Virginia Corbin, the Fox star, James Bush, Gloria Joy and Marjorie Heck are but a few of the precocious little performers who will take part."[10] Virginia's part on the program was to give "interpretive numbers."

Her appearances for this cause were not relegated to the Los Angeles area. One unidentified clipping notes that she and Francis Carpenter were to appear in person at the Sedalia Theater, in Sedalia, Missouri. Although it was for the purpose of helping the Sedalia Red Cross raise funds for their Canteen Division, it also served to publicize *Jack and the Beanstalk*—with photos from the event showing the children in their costumes from the movie.

A charming photo found in Virginia's scrapbook shows Virginia beautifully dressed in doily sleepwear with a doily cap tied around her chin, kneeling at her bedside, hands clasped with elbows resting on a pillow and looking up the heavens praying. Inserted in a cloud above her head is a large contingent of soldiers marching with their guns. It is not known how the photo was ever used, but the snapshot in the scrapbook shows an adorable child who, by implication of the image, prays for her country's soldiers every night.

Virginia also appeared to be enjoying the beginnings of the lifestyle of a movie star—even at five years of age. A tidbit entitled "Prosperity Note" said, "Virginia Corbin has ordered a motorcar in baby blue, with white wheels, white enameled leather trimmings, and cushions and furnishings of rose color. Miss Corbin finds this color scheme tones best with her hair and complexion."[11] It makes for good reading, and there are references from this period indicating Virginia's fascination with cars. However, even if a five-year-old wanted a car, it's difficult to imagine one being purchased for her. The purchase of an (assumed to be) expensive car in 1917 sounds more like the beginnings of the financial troubles she would have with her mother regarding her earnings ten years later.

With fame also comes recognition. Because of this, Virginia didn't regularly visit the theaters. However, she begged her mother to let her watch *Jack and the Beanstalk* with an audience. Mrs. Corbin acceded.

At the theater, Virginia was seated beside a young man about her age who "was intensely excited over every scene.... When the point in the picture arrived at which it seemed certain that the Giant would dispatch the heroine, the lad's courage almost oozed out. Virginia became greatly concerned. 'Perhaps I better tell him that I am all right,' she whispered to her mother. Her parent gave consent, and she leaned over to her neighbor and said, 'Don't worry. I am the Princess and came out of it safely.' The effect was electrical. The boy recognized the heroine of the play in an instant, and his feeling could not be restrained. Two small arms flew around Virginia's neck, and a loud kiss was posited on her cheek. Thus it happened that the scene of the leading lady being embraced by one of her own audience was enacted. Be it recorded, also, that Virginia Lee Corbin is quite capable of blushing."[12]

Virginia was a popular star now, and her name was used by the Belgium Red Cross, the Liberty Loan Drive and by other benevolent efforts. How this photograph was used is unknown, but it does provide a charming picture of a child praying for the troops during World War I (Virginia Lee Corbin's personal scrapbook).

Another omen of things to come was a court case that occurred around this time in which a man named Don Meaney claimed he obtained a contract for Virginia with Fox for $75 a week. He alleged the child's parents failed to pay him a commission to which he was entitled. However, the report noted, "since the Meaney contract was made, the Fox people have given the child's parents a new contract covering two years and running from $100 to $175."[13] The report did not mention the outcome of the case. This seems to be the first encounter for Virginia with a court, but it wouldn't be the last. As a young adult, she would find herself standing before a judge more often than she ever imagined.

With stardom also comes nicknames, and the realistic crying and range of emotions Virginia portrays in *Jack and the Beanstalk* earned her the sobriquet of filmdom's "Youngest Emotional Star." She noted to one interviewer that acting was easy because it was just "play acting." One story from the set said director Sidney Franklin was directing a scene in which Virginia was to cry, "but the best he could get was giggles, and a broad smile." He had never encountered any problem coaxing tears from the little star, so he was quite puzzled. "Finally he said, 'Come on, Virginia, why don't you cry; you have never acted this way before?' Pointing her finger, Virginia said, 'I can't. Every time I try to cry, I see him, and then I have to laugh.' Turning in the direction indicated by the child, Mr. Franklin saw standing to one side Charles Conklin, the clever little Fox comedian in one of his ludicrous make-ups. The diminutive comedian was ordered off the set, and Virginia cried copiously."[14]

When and who first coined the phrase "Youngest Emotional Star" is unknown, but what is known is that the title stuck. It came about after reviewers and the rest of the nation had seen her performance in *Jack and the Beanstalk*. Although the adjective "youngest" may vary, "emotional star" didn't. The ads for the movie and articles on Virginia regular refer to her "the miniature emotional star," "four-year-old emotional star," "Fox's emotional star," and more.

Actually, "emotional star" wasn't a term used exclusively to describe Virginia. Alla Nazimova was called the "Russian Emotional Star," and ads referenced Olga Petrova as "the emotional star." The lesser-known Florence Reed who was popular in the 'teens was called "the great dramatic emotional star."

A label that appeared to have been given to Virginia even before "emotional star," but didn't catch on as well was "the Dresden Doll of the movies." One writer said of the nickname, "That's better than any name I could think of because it really suits her. Her pretty little doll face is so perfect that you hope she'll never, never grow any older. A slender little figure, with a stateliness derived, perhaps, from her English-French ancestry, which is fascinating, supports her flower-like face."[15]

A Dresden doll, also known as a parian (referring to the fine white marble of Paros, Greece) doll, was manufactured in Germany between 1860 and 1880 and was very popular in the 19th century. Although it may appear to be a china doll, it differs in that it is made of white porcelain, and the head is not dipped in glaze before firing, making it look very similar to bisque dolls. Again, Virginia was not the only one to whom this label was given—Mary Miles Minter was also referred to as "the Dresden Doll of the Movies."

With so much attention being given to this first Fox Kiddie Feature, and the unimaginable popularity of its two main stars, Fox knew the next in the series needed to be released while the wave was riding high.

7. The Magic of Aladdin

laddin and the Wonderful Lamp was chosen as the second film to be released in the series, and it too, just as its predecessor, premiered at the Globe Theater in New York September 24 and was released to the open market October 14.

It appears from comments made by William Fox on more than one occasion that *Aladdin* was not the second fairy tale to be filmed—and it is very likely four films in the series had been completed by the time *Jack and the Beanstalk* was released. In early July, three weeks prior to the first release, he was announcing, "*Aladdin and the Wonderful Lamp* from the *Arabian Nights*, Stevenson's *Treasure Island*, and *Babes in the Woods* are among the children's pictures already staged."[1] "Already staged" would seem to indicate they were already filmed and completed—and clues to their filming dates confirm this.

Fox also commented that after completing filming on *Jack and the Beanstalk*, "Immediately we started *Babes in the Woods*, and then *Treasure Island*, and then *Aladdin and the Wonderful Lamp*. With these in our pocket, we knew there was no end to what we could do."[2] Obviously, Fox was naming the films in order of their production which indicates *Aladdin*, although the second to be released, was actually the fourth to be filmed. As already mentioned, newspaper articles have confirmed that filming began on *The Babes in the Woods* immediately after the filming of *Jack and the Beanstalk*, and *Treasure Island*, the third to be filmed, was being shot on location at Balboa in May.

It can be surmised from these clues that these pictures were being made over a two-month period because in late July, it was reported, "The Fox kiddie company, which is directed by C.M. & S.A. Franklin, has finally started production on *Aladdin and His* [sic] *Wonderful Lamp*." It goes on to say, "A number of unusual settings were required for this fairy tale, and, consequently, production was delayed."[3] About a week later, an article said, "Economy in transportation of children has been made possible by Los Angeles traction lines running special cars for motion picture companies. The first organization to use this method is that of the Franklin Brothers of the William Fox studio. For the past two weeks, they have been making scenes for *Aladdin and His* [sic] *Wonderful Lamp* at Los Angeles harbor."[4]

It would make sense, then, if *Jack and the Beanstalk* was filmed during the winter, and *The Babes in the Woods* was being filmed in March and April, and then *Aladdin* went into production in late July and early August, *Treasure Island* must have fallen somewhere between the filming of *Babes* and *Aladdin*. For some unknown reason, Fox chose to release *Aladdin* second, which must have been very soon after its completion, although he had both *The Babes in the Woods* and *Treasure Island* in the can.

More appropriately, *Aladdin* was released in eight reels, putting it not much over an hour and a half rather than the two-hour length of *Jack and the Beanstalk*. The premiere at the Globe Theater on Broadway was, just as its predecessor, "a huge success." Reports noted that during its first week, it was shown twice daily to "well-filled houses." *Motion Picture News* headed a second week review with "Second of Kiddie Series Surpasses Even *Jack and the Beanstalk* in Popularity."[5]

Reviews were almost universally positive. *Motion Picture News'* review said, "William Fox presents a wonderful visualization of this old fairy tale, so delightful, so faithful to the illusion that those of us who are acquainted with it have painted in our mind's eye that it is like greeting an old friend to see it on the screen," adding, "it can safely be acclaimed [the Franklin brothers'] best effort."[6] Another said, "Most of us believe that we knew the story of *Aladdin and the Wonderful Lamp*, but the new screen version of it has shown it with power and a beauty that was hidden in the written words."[7] Yet another said it has been "beautifully and effectively picturized," adding, "The production is gorgeous ... 'Aladdin' is destined to be the most talked about picture this town has ever seen."[8]

Variety's lack of enthusiasm is evident and somewhat puzzling. The reviewer seems to be criticizing both the spectacular settings and tempo of the movie at the same time. "As a spectacular production, it is little short of stupendous, the mammoth scenes following in rapid succession with almost bewildering frequency," adding, "the scenic investiture represents a wealth of time, thought and expenditure of coin of the realm."[9] While the reviewer was struggling for a legitimate criticism, he/she at the same time admitted that the movie was shown "to the huge delight of gown-ups, as well as children," then concluded with "But whether the antics

Once again Virginia was given the opportunity to display a range of emotions in *Aladdin and the Wonderful Lamp* (1917). She continued to get high praise from reviewers too. One said, "There is very much of the attractive woman of experience in the way Virginia Corbin acts the role. Nevertheless, she has all the charm and grace of a child of her actual years."

of precocious children 'playing theatre' will entertain those old enough to vote is the only question at issue. Judging by the Monday night audience, it may."[10]

As for the acting of the children, *Variety* said, "their acting, naturally enough, savored of the travesty variety, and could not for one moment be taken seriously."[11] Was it supposed to be? At any rate, the *Variety* reviewer was in a very small minority, if not all alone, in his assessment of the film and the children's performance. For example, "There is very much of the attractive woman of experience in the way that Virginia Corbin acts the role. Nevertheless, she has all the charm and grace of a child of her actual years. But the rapid change of emotion, the swift fluctuations of sentiment that marked her earlier work in *Jack and the Beanstalk* is seen in this play, only magnified a score of times. Francis Carpenter has a new phase of tragedy to add to his previous work, and the brilliancy of his acting can only be seen to be appreciated."[12] Or, "These children [Virginia and Francis] are the most consummate little actors in the world. They simulate joy, grief, love, hate, disappointment, indignation, fear, despair, and the many other passions with amazing fidelity. Small wonder that audiences are gripped as they see these young marvels play such difficult roles."[13]

Even though *Aladdin* came in two reels shorter than *Jack and the Beanstalk*, it is still unfortunate, as with the first Fox Kiddie Feature, only an abridged version exists today. *Aladdin* has been made available for home video and comes in at 40 minutes, less than half its original length. It is fortunate that the abridgement works as a complete story, but, at the same time, silent film fans can bemoan the fact that some obviously great scenes are possibly gone forever. For example, there is a scene where Francis struggles in the desert, parched, dry and clutching his throat—and a huge sandstorm develops—but, alas, these do not appear in the abridgement. In another scene, the evil Magician has the Princess far off in the desert in a palace that has been erected by the spirit of the lamp. This too does not seem to have survived.

But what does survive is a wonderful telling of the fairy tale with sumptuous sets, elaborate costumes, and utterly delightful acting by the children. It opens with a shot through the gates of Bagdad with hundreds of Arabs in the street bowing toward Mecca. One of these is Aladdin who seems more concerned with a pretty little veiled girl than praying. His father beats him and runs him back into their home.

The scene moves quickly to the palace with the throne room elaborately decorated and filled with dancers and others who are watching. Violet Radcliffe is the evil Magician, complete with turban and curled mustache, who craves the beautiful Princess. The Princess, of course, rebuffs his gifts and recoils at his touch, but the Sultan (played by an adult, Alfred Paget, who was Prince Belshazzar in *Intolerance*) tells the Magician to bring him a rich gift and he may have the hand of the Princess.

A new face was introduced in this film, Buddy Messinger (who, if he did appear in *Jack and the Beanstalk*, it was in an uncredited role). Buddy's younger sister, Gertrude, was Yasmini, the Princess' handmaiden in the movie. In *Aladdin*, Buddy is the Magician's Evil Spirit, or, more accurately, his evil advisor. The Evil Spirit tells the Magician of the magic lamp that can bring him riches and the hand of the Princess, but it is in a cave and can only be accessed by someone "innocent of heart," that is, Aladdin.

The meeting of Aladdin and the Princess is played in a very cute scene as she is carried through the streets in her palanquin. She sees Aladdin and drops her shoe on

The Sultan has promised the hand of the Princess to the evil Magician (played by Violet Radcliffe) if he brings a rich gift. Back in her room, the Princess (Virginia) vows that she will never marry the Magician despite her father's wish. Bowing at her feet is Gertrude Messinger, who played the Princess' handmaiden in *Aladdin and the Wonderful Lamp* (1917).

the road. He quickly gets it, and begs, "Beautiful Princess, may I give you your little slipper?" and she responds, "Yes, and you may even put it on my little foot."

Observing this scene, the Magician and his Evil Spirit realize Aladdin's love for the Princess. The Magician approaches him, tells him if he secures this magic lamp, he can get all he desires. The cave, which is accessed through a hole in the ground and covered with a large stone, is entered by Aladdin. He secures the lamp but refuses to give it to the Magician until he helps him out of the hole. The Magician instead covers the hole with the large stone. Of course, Aladdin escapes by using the magic of the lamp. By the way, the Genie is played by barrel-chested Elmo Lincoln who, the next year, would become famous as Tarzan.

Aladdin brings riches to the Sultan and is promised the hand of the Princess, but as the fairy tale goes, the Magician poses as a trader in lamps ("new lamps for old") and gains possession of the magic lamp. He wishes poverty on Aladdin once again and then he, himself, wins the promise of a marriage to the Princess by bringing great riches to the Sultan.

While the Magician is petitioning the Sultan for the Princess' hand, Aladdin is able to go to the Magician's room, overpower the Evil Spirit, and regain possession of the lamp. He tells the Genie to turn the Magician into a fish peddler. Right before the Sultan's eyes, the Magician's clothing changes to that of a fish peddler, and all the riches he had brought turn into fish. The Sultan orders him away.

At this point, the abridgement shows a few shots of Aladdin, then the Princess in her room, and then to the marriage of Aladdin and the Princess—but the most thrilling part of the movie is missing here—all is not over with the Magician. Synopses of the movie tell of a palace in the desert that the Magician has erected with the help of the lamp. He has kidnapped the Princess and taken her there to force her to marry him. If she refuses, he threatens to throw her to the lions if she does not marry him. There is a last minute rescue by Aladdin and his soldiers, and the Magician is killed. Obviously, Aladdin's regaining the lamp and turning the Magician into a fish peddler is not the end of the story as the abridgement goes.

Virginia was interviewed about the movie, and, unlike most interviews, this one sounds as if the writer was actually taking down the comments of a child, with maybe a little adult help. Plus, it gives some insight into what is missing from prints today. "*Aladdin* is a wonderful play," Virginia told the writer, "and I have one of my very best roles in it. Of course, you know that I am a princess in the play, and I have all sorts of wonderful adventures ... but I think that one of the best scenes is the one with the lions." She continued, "You see, the lions are not small ones at all, but very big, and I am very near them in the way that it is arranged—and it does look very serious and perilous for me. No, I am not really afraid, but, in the play I am and surely I ought to be ... and just at the moment when all seems terrible for me, two people—children, you know—reach down into the cage and make a seat for me with their clasped hands and lift me out—and then what do you suppose happens? I faint. It is very thrilling, and the scene is beautiful, and I am sure everybody will like it. Remember, these are real big lions, not little ones. I know."[14]

Another story regarding the lion said Virginia and Gertrude Messinger were watching the lion pacing back and forth in his cage and pawing the ground, Gertrude said, "He is sweeping the cage with his paws." "Nonsense," says the leading lady with an air of superior knowledge as far as lions are concerned. "He is doing the one-step."[15]

Still another said, "Virginia ... did some real acting while riding on the camel during the making of the picture. Her placid face doesn't tell the real fears she experienced every time she sat on the back of the jogging animal."[16] However, at no time in the abridgement can Virginia be seen riding a camel.

8. Fairy Tales, Fox and Friction

irginia's hometown newspaper was justly proud of their famous progeny, noting, "Prescott has produced a motion picture star—small in size and age but quite a luminary in the world of make-believe. She is no other than the daughter of Mr. and Mrs. L.E. Corbin, the former for many years in the drug business here with A.W. Bork and for a time connected with the Owl Drug & Candy Company as a working stockholder." It goes on to quote the bio previously mentioned from *Moving Picture World.*[1]

With the astounding critical success of the first two Fox Kiddie Series features—and singling Virginia out for acting honors—her star had definitely risen higher than most of the adult stars in the second half of 1917.

The third of the Fox Kiddie Features, *The Babes in the Woods*, was originally set for release on November 18. However, in October, exhibitors' magazines were announcing the release date had been moved to December 23, cashing in on the higher attendance during Christmas season, especially due to children being out of school. However, other justifications were also given. Theda Bara's *The Rose of Blood* was set for release November 4, and this impacted the decision for the later release. The other reason given was the huge success of *Jack and the Beanstalk* and *Aladdin and the Wonderful Lamp*. These were still enjoying excellent attendance around the country and allowed for a slight delay in getting *The Babes in the Woods* out to theaters. Fox also re-labeled it as a "Special" feature rather than a "Standard" feature. This required a higher rental and was a logical thing to do based on the popularity of the first two Fox Kiddie releases.

It was later decided that, in order to take full advantage of the Christmas season and ensure that more of the country would have access to the film during this time (theaters outside of the cities may not get a film until weeks or even months after its release), the official release date was changed to December 2.

As with the first two Fox Kiddie Features, all that survives today is an abridged version. The 36-minute abridgement, though starting out abruptly, does provide a complete storyline. How much of the film is missing is difficult to pin down. The 36-minute abridgement would equate to less than four reels. The *American Film Institute Catalog of Feature Films* lists it at five reels. In *Moving Picture News* exhibitors' magazines from the second half of 1917, the length is listed at five reels and eight reels. In one article, it notes, "is several reels more than ordinary feature length."[2] Other sources give the length as seven reels. Some of these lengths are given prior to its official release, so it is possible Fox was still editing the film, and a final length could have not yet been determined—although a change from five to eight reels or the other way around would seem unlikely.

It opens with Hansel and Gretel's father dying. The evil stepmother and uncle are plotting to get rid of the children—who are heirs to their father's fortune—and get the riches for themselves. Two men are hired to take them to the woods and kill them. One of the hired men turns out to have a conscience and ensures the kids are not harmed but leaves them in the woods.

Asleep under a tree, they are set upon by the Robber Prince and his band of men. Once again, Violet Radcliffe plays the villain and once again grimaces, scowls, flails her arms and twirls her mustache in Victorian melodramatic style. Obviously, Sidney Franklin (although both brothers are usually credited, Sidney was at the helm of this one) knew the humor adults would find in the acting while children would be enthralled by this animated villain.

Francis Carpenter was also very animated in his acting—as some have suggested, portraying himself as a miniature Douglas Fairbanks. In each of the films, it is very humorous to see him push up his sleeves every time he is about to engage in a fight. Also, anytime he and Virginia are threatened, little Francis enjoyed kissing his co-star, which he does whether they are portraying terror or joy.

This is one of a set of 8" × 10" lobby cards that was issued along with the movie and would have been displayed either outside the theatre entrance or in the lobby, as its name implies. Fox spent less on the making of *The Babes in the Woods* (1917), and, coincidentally, the movie wasn't quite as good as its two predecessors, although critics continued with their praise of Virginia and the series.

Of course, Virginia's trademark was her crying, and, of the three main stars, she actually turns in the most underplayed performance, if you could call it underplaying. She cries naturally and at the right times. Her only calling card is constantly shaking her head from side to side violently each time she is threatened.

The hero and heroine, though, with the help of the fairy queen, escape the Robber Prince. He goes to the wicked witch who lives in a gingerbread house and says he will pay well if she can find Hansel and Gretel and deliver them to him. Sending out a magical white dove to find them, the children are brought to the witch's house. Hansel is locked in a small room outside to fatten up so the witch can eat him. Gretel is forced to cook for Hansel.

True to the original story, Gretel tells the witch that Hansel will not fit in the oven. The witch crawls in the oven to show her that even she can fit in it. Gretel shuts the oven door, and, after the oven explodes, that's the end of the witch.

The gingerbread men outside are actually the King's soldiers on whom the witch cast a spell. Hansel is able to release them from the spell with the witch's wand. They leave but come in handy later in the story.

The two are once again captured by the Robber Prince and taken to his lair in a huge Redwood tree. He promises to release Hansel if Gretel will marry him. She refuses, Hansel is about to be killed, and the King's soldiers arrive just in time to save the day.

A significant portion that is left out of the abridgement is the framing of a story-within-a-story. The Fox film actually begins with a modern segment—the father of the two children, John Hamilton, marries a second time, but his new wife does not like the children. She does like her husband's brother, Mason. Hamilton has suspicions about the pair and goes off on a trip. However, before he does, he draws up a will leaving the major portion of his estate to the children. The will also stipulates that, in the event of the children's death, the money goes to his brother.

With his manservant watching the pair, Hamilton gets word out that he has died. Soon afterward, the manservant reports to him that his wife and brother are plotting to kill the children. Of course, the wife and brother are astonished when Hamilton returns. Mason is sent from the house, and Hamilton gathers around him his wife and two children to tell the story of *Hansel and Gretel*. Supposedly, as a result of the story, the wife repents of her ill intentions.

However, the story of *Hansel and Gretel* is pretty much intact in the abridgement, and, from what is seen in it, the film is very visually appealing. Most of it is shot outdoors in the woods, and the gingerbread house is very well done. "The house itself is a wonderful structure of gingerbread, stick candy, hot cross buns and such delicacies," one reviewer said.[3]

An interesting story, the kind newspapers love, was circulated regarding the filming of the scene where Hansel and Gretel ride a swan across a river. "To photograph it, a huge stuffed swan was mounted upon an invisible float and launched into the water. Desiring to test the buoyancy of the tiny craft, the director asked a number of small boys in the cast to volunteer as a trial passenger, but each refused to take the risk. 'I'll ride it!' cried little Virginia who was standing near.... Director Franklin ordered the camera trained upon the little 4-year-old girl who had out-dared her larger brothers, and the swan set sail. All went well until the graceful craft reached the center of the lake, and then the towing wire broke allowing it to drift helplessly toward the lower rapids. No boat was available for the rescue and horror was involuntarily registered upon the faces of the spectators. Little Virginia kept her head, however, and by kicking the water vigorously, she managed to propel the swan near enough to the bank to enable her to catch the rope thrown out to her. By this time, too, one of the Franklin brothers was on his way to the rescue."[4]

Reviewers gave no less praise to this entry in the series than the previous two. "Virginia Lee Corbin, the dainty maiden who can weep to order and continue indefinitely, is tragically charming, with Francis Carpenter as a pocket edition of Francis Ten Bushman. Any adult who cannot enjoy these pictures as much as the youngsters do should hasten to be shrived for his sins."[5] Another said, "The greatness of the photo fantasy ... can only be appreciated by seeing the picture ... the Fox kiddies are the most wonderfully talented children in the world. The old, old story of *Babes in the Woods* is told in a new and fascinating manner in this wonderful photo spectacle."[6] Still another commented, "The Fox production of this famous story is one that will never be forgotten to those who see it, because of its splendor, with all its youthful romance and wonders of fascination that it lays before your eyes."[7]

Silent film historian Kevin Brownlow felt this entry was not equal in quality to the other filmed fairy tales. "*Babes in the Woods* is the only kid picture to fall short of the remarkable standard. The Fox company made the mistake of splitting the team [the Franklin brothers] up, and evidence exists which proves that Sidney Franklin was forced to do a rush job. For the first half, *Babes in the Woods* is as brooding, violent and gruesome as Grimm's Fairy Tales themselves; Hansel and Gretel are fattened for the oven, but the witch is cooked instead. The second half, all action, is rousingly handled, and as exciting as a western."[8]

The anticipation of a new entry into the series that had been created by the success of the first two was evidenced by its opening at the Globe Theater in New York. Reportedly, for the first two weeks it was shown there, it played to capacity attendance each night.

Of course, advance publicity for the film abounded, especially in exhibitors' magazines. Certainly circulated by the Fox publicity department was the claim that the movie was filmed at the Grand Canyon of Colorado (that's what the publicity says), the mountains and valleys of California, Hawaii, and at the Fox studio in Hollywood. Filming at the Fox studio is understood; however, the Grand Canyon (be it Colorado or Arizona) and Hawaii may leave room for doubt. There is certainly nothing in the abridgement that shows scenes of the Grand Canyon or Hawaii.

Based on letters from William Fox (who, during these years remained in New York) to his production supervisor Sol M. Wurtzel in Los Angeles, expenditures for location shooting such as this would not have been permitted. It must also be noted that Wurtzel, although given complete control of the West Coast studio, came along late in the game for the Fox Kiddie Features. He arrived in Los Angeles in October 1917, and, by that time, at least four, if not five, films in the series had been completed.

In a letter dated December 27, 1917, to Wurtzel, Fox writes, "I soon learned when I was in Los Angeles that the Franklin Brothers were working for the Franklin Brothers and for the reputation they had in sight rather than the Fox Film Corporation. However, I was able, with my presence there, to get Mr. Sid Franklin to make a picture for half the cost he made any of the children pictures, and in a period of five weeks. He showed me conclusively that he can work rapidly if he wants to, and in my opinion, *Babes in the Woods* is a better picture than *The Mikado* [later released as *Fan Fan*] or *Treasure Island*, both of which cost twice the money, or, from what you said about *Ala Baba*, it is better than *Ala Baba*."[9] (Note: *Ala Baba* (*sic*) is not *Aladdin and the Wonderful Lamp* but another Fox Kiddie Feature that will be discussed later.) If Fox was in Los Angeles at the time overseeing expenditures, and *The Babes in the Woods* was made at half the cost of the other stories in the series, location shooting in the Grand Canyon, much less Hawaii, is more than questionable and almost certainly publicity hype.

However, the filming in the mountains and valleys of California is not only borne out by what has survived of the film itself, but articles that tell of the filming—specifically in the Santa Cruz area. In a March 26, 1917, newspaper article, 13 children from Fox had checked into the Casa del Rey Hotel and would begin filming the next day for *Babes in the Woods*. (Note that the title is sometimes referred to as *Babes in the Woods* or *The Babes in the Woods*, although *The Babes in the Woods* is the title given by the Fox studio.)

Virginia Corbin (the "Lee" was quite often left off in publications even at this late date) and Francis Carpenter were singled out in the article along with Violet Radcliffe and Carmen de Rue. Interestingly, the article noted that Ruth Corbin, "professional dancer and sister of the leading lady," was among the troupe. The article went on to say, "The children are having a splendid carefree time today surf-bathing, and, inasmuch as they are the same as all other kids in their strong leanings toward elephants and peanuts, they will probably be extended all professional courtesies by Al G. Barnes this evening and take in the big show."[10] Barnes had a show called the "Big Four Ring Wild Animal Circus" that traveled the country, so this must have been a treat extended to the children on that first day of arrival before beginning work the next day.

A reporter for the local newspaper recounted her visit to "the powder mill" about a week later where the children were filming. The powder mill was used to dissolve and purify the crude potassium nitrate from Chile, which eventually led to the production of explosive powder. The facility is at the location of the present Henry Cowell Redwoods State Park near Santa Cruz.

The writer's description fits perfectly in the scenes that can still be seen in the surviving portion of the film today. "Did you ever realize how beautiful the powder mill site is? Majestic wonderful redwoods stand guard over millions of wild flowers, ferns and shrubs.... The two little babes in the wood, Virginia Corbin and Francis Carpenter, were fast asleep under a beautiful tree in their cunning old-fashioned frocks of blue and old rose. While from the forest sprang forth the imps of the wood, the great big starry owls and canary birds, and then the children—for the most part our own little daughters, sisters, nieces, etc."[11] Another article described the filming and stated that 55 children, not counting local children used, were employed and taken to "the Big Redwoods in the mountains to the north of that city." It said the children rose at 5 a.m. each day and "motored twenty-eight miles up into the Santa Cruz mountains to a location among the big redwoods that has never before been photographed by a motion picture camera. Here they found hollow tree trunks big enough to shelter a motor car, mysterious rocky caves, tiny waterfalls above deep bathing pools, and altogether an ideal fairy-land for elf-like film folk."[12]

The writer who visited the powder mill also noted that a good number of local children were used in the filming, and one article even listed many of them by name for local residents to recognize. It said the company would be leaving that night, April 3, at 7 to return to Los Angeles.

Looking at the amount of footage that was obviously filmed in this forest, and considering the fact that the children began filming in this particular location March 27 and wrapped up filming April 3, it is easy to see that these pictures did not take months to complete, making expensive trips to the Grand Canyon or Hawaii difficult to believe.

Virginia was receiving nothing but positive press as a result of the popular Kiddie Features, and an article that appeared the next day by the same reporter who visited the powder mill site is indicative of this. "Yesterday out at the powder mill site, [I] met this doting mother and her daughter, called the 'Dresden Doll of the Movies.' That's better than any name I could think of because it really suits her. Her pretty little doll face is so perfect that you hope she'll never, never grow any older. A slender little figure … supports her flower-like face. It must be wonderful to be ALL beautiful—not only in face, but in exquisitely molded hands and feet." And, as one would expect, Mrs. Corbin added to this description by saying, "She is lovely, isn't she?"[13]

One columnist said, "Since I saw Virginia Lee Corbin in *Babes in the Woods*, I now know who will be the logical successor of Mary Pickford. Virginia looks like Marguerite Clark, but she is as dramatic as Little Mary."[14]

9. New Star in the New Year

*N*ineteen *seventeen had been* a life-changing year for Virginia. She had risen from a virtual unknown to the most popular child star of the year. Praise for her acting came from every direction, and her personal appearances were a hit as she proved that she had talent—many talents—reciting, acting, singing and dancing.

Her popularity among children, especially little girls, was far beyond any other child star that year. To these little girls, she was a princess. The discovery—or publicity department hype—that she truly was of royal lineage, the distant relative of someone who had been knighted by William the Conqueror—only affirmed in the children's minds that, not only was she playing a princess on the screen, she truly was a princess in real life.

Mrs. Corbin claimed to one reporter that Virginia couldn't walk down the street without being recognized and approached by other children—and that she received several fan letters each day. One can't help but wonder why Mrs. Corbin decided to keep one of these letters in Virginia's scrapbook, but the charming sentiment is likely representative of the type of fan mail she was receiving. Glued at the top back to the black album page, the letter is fragile and separating at the seams, but the hand-written, pencil note is still very legible. "Dearest Miss Corbin, I am a little girl twelve years old and I wanted to tell you how wonderful you are. You are one of my favorites and I like your acting very much. Want [sic] you please send me your photo? Wishing you more success, I remain ..." and she signed her name, Elma Elliott, along with her mailing address in Hooperstown, Illinois.

As the new year began, Virginia and the Fox Kiddie Features were still riding high with the newest film due for distribution in January. The ever-changing release date for *The Babes in the Woods* has been related; however, there was one Fox Kiddie Feature that was released just prior to *Babes*. November 24, Fox sent out *Ali Baba and the Forty Thieves*, but Virginia and Francis Carpenter were curiously not among the cast. Some regulars in the film from the previous fairy tales included Gertrude Messinger, Buddy Messinger, Lewis Sargent and Raymond Lee, but the star of the film was Georgie Stone who had appeared in none of the previous Kiddie films.

Stone started working in shorts in 1915 at about six years of age, and co-starred with Thelma Salter earlier in the year (August 1917) in *In Slumberland*, a "fairyland" story produced by Thomas H. Ince. Fox filmed *Ali Baba and the Forty Thieves* in the fall of 1917 and finished up sometime in November. Therefore, a November 24 release date would have been an amazingly fast turnaround. Although it was also directed by the Franklin brothers, the film did not garner the attention of the Virginia Lee Corbin-Francis Carpenter vehicles, nor did it afford Stone the level of stardom these other children enjoyed. As a matter of fact, Stone never starred in another picture but did work regularly supporting major stars such as William S. Hart, Tom Mix, Shirley Mason, Blanche Sweet, Bessie Love, Thomas Meighan and others before making his last picture in 1923.

Unfortunately, the next Fox Kiddie Feature to be released with Virginia and Francis Carpenter, *Treasure Island*, appears to be a lost film. Not even an abridgement is known to survive today.

It premiered in New York January 25, 1918, and went into general release two days later, even though, as noted, it was the second of the series to be filmed. An original release date of November 18 was planned, but reportedly there was an order by the fuel administrator to close down all industrial establishments for five days. The Fox printing plant at Fort Lee, NJ, was affected by this causing the delay. Fox announced that "to meet this situation and provide a picture for the week of January 27, the Fox management has taken *Treasure Island* and *Troublemakers* [starring Fox's other child stars, sisters Jane and Katherine Lee] from the Standard Pictures and placed them on the special features calendar, giving exhibitors their choice. Either production which is desired by those holding Fox Special Features contracts will be furnished for the last week of the month."[1]

The previous May, Chester Franklin took between 25 and 30 children to Balboa (Sidney Franklin told Kevin Brownlow that his brother directed *Treasure Island* alone) where one article noted there was "a veritable fairyland peopled with fairies, gnomes, sprites and other fanciful beings created for the special delight of the little ones." The troupe set up camp at Newport Beach where the same article pinpointed the picture making to be "at the extreme east end of the sandspit opposite Rocky Point."[2]

Robert Louis Stevenson's story of pirates and buried treasure first appeared in serial form in the periodical *Young Folks* under the title *The Sea Cook or Treasure Island* between July 1881 and June 1882. The story, considered a classic not only today, but equally well regarded in Virginia's lifetime, was very familiar to the children of the day. As one would expect, Fox took some liberties to make it more appealing to the young ones and keep the two stars at the forefront.

The story begins true to the Stevenson tale with seaman Bill Bones arriving at the Benbow Inn. He is attacked by men who want the treasure map he possesses that belonged to the notorious pirate Flint. In the midst of the melee, Jim Hawkins gets the map and flees to the home of Squire Trelawney. Virginia's part in the movie was not in the original story. She plays Squire Trelawney's daughter, Louise.

At Squire Trelawney's home, Jim goes upstairs and falls asleep while the Squire studies the map. To more appropriately insert children into all parts of the story, the film from this point forward is a dream sequence. So Jim (Carpenter), with Virginia in tow, goes Treasure Island, there encountering Long John Silver, a former Flint shipmate named Jim Gunn, whom he befriends, and a host of pirates.

She Fears Pirates

"TREASURE ISLAND"
WILLIAM FOX PRODUCTION

Treasure Island (1918) was the fourth of the Fox Kiddie Features and, along with *The Babes in the Woods* (1917), made it clear critics' praise was waning. William Fox had decided even before *Treasure Island* had hit movie screens that the series was not profitable and no further pictures would be made. This newspaper clipping shows Francis as Jim Hawkins and Virginia as Louise Trelawney. The child between them is believed to be Lloyd Perl as Black Dog.

While Jim is on the island, Louise stays on board the ship with Captain Smollett. However, fearing mutiny by the crew, Louise and the Captain flee to take refuge in a stockade on the island. There are plenty of fights between the good pirates and the bad pirates, and, of course, in the end, Jim rescues Louise, finds the treasure, and sails for home.

Once again, Violet Radcliffe got to play the villain portraying Long John Silver. Buddy Messinger was there again as Captain Smollett, and Lewis Sargent was back for his second Fox Kiddie Feature as Ben Gunn. He had previously appeared in *Aladdin and the Wonderful Lamp* in a minor role.

Variety said, "The Fox kiddie cast is much more successful in playing fairy fantasies which permit of wide liberties in visualization. The sophisticated villainies of old Flint's pirate crew are beyond the reach of children. Thus, where *Jack and the Beanstalk* was amusing to grown-ups, *Treasure Island* isn't. Yet it will provide genuine entertainment to children." The reviewer did point out that at the Stanley Theater in New York there were "shrieks of glee" from the children, so, he admitted, it has accomplished its purpose. Interestingly, of the cast, Virginia was the only one the reviewer singled out for praise. "The kiddie cast does interesting work, particularly little Miss Corbin, who gives a quaint touch to the role of the squire's daughter."[3]

One source noted that the director had placed much more emphasis on humor in this entry. The humor may have been inserted to alleviate the seriousness of the original story.

Although *Variety* may have found some small aspects of the film to criticize, Fox had scored another hit, and praise emanated from every corner of the country with such grandiose statements as "a magnificent picturization of a great novel" or "rich in scenic effects and telling."

Advance publicity for these films was done in a number of ways, one of which was to send to newspapers humorous and/or human interest kinds of stories during the filming. One story recounted an incident in which Jim (Francis Carpenter) and his mother (Eleanor Washington) are going through Bill Bones' sea chest. They pull out clothes, tobacco, a quadrant, pistols, silver and other odds and ends. Suddenly, Washington shrieks. There is a gray mouse in the trunk with her four babies. Francis came to the rescue, though. He picked up the mouse, took it to his director, and it, along with the baby mice, were put in a cage and hauled away.[4]

In another, "Virginia and others of the Fox forces were playing in the 'lot' at Hollywood, California, where *Treasure Island* was made. Two of them got into a squabble. One of them told the other that she was 'a bad little girl.' The other answered, 'How can I be good when you torment me?' Then up piped Virginia. 'You can't be good unless you pray.' A woman standing near asked, 'How do you know, Virginia?' 'Because I've tried it.' The woman was astonished and complimented Mrs. Corbin on the wisdom of her daughter. 'Oh,' said Mrs. Corbin, 'that's not original with Virginia. I read that in Robert Louis Stevenson's works and commented on it. Virginia just remembered it. She has a wonderful memory.'"[5]

The first four Fox Kiddie Features did indeed receive positive press, and from all indications, were attended well—at least when first released. However, a letter from Fox to Wurtzel in February indicates the pictures, as a series, were not profitable. Fox said, "*Jack and the Beanstalk*; This was successful. However, in carrying out this idea of fairy tales, the net result of the combined fairy tales gave the company a loss. The company should have made a handsome profit if it had stopped at the conclusion of *Jack and the Beanstalk*, but it ruined its chances by insisting on a series of these fairy tales."[6]

Actually, Fox had already decided to cancel the series back in November. In a letter to the Franklin brothers, he said, "When we showed *Jack and the Beanstalk* to the trade, they were enthusiastic about it, and of course it encouraged us to go on with this type of picture. The second release was *Aladdin and the Wonderful Lamp*. The exhibitor felt that we offered him this picture too soon. I am of the opinion that the exhibitor is mistaken in his attitude, and that in the near future he will realize his mistake. To continue to make this type of picture would only make these pictures a drug on the market, which we don't want to do. I felt that it is your ambition to direct such pictures as the company can readily sell and make a profit on. I am sure you fully realize that the basis of your earning capacity is formed on how much money is earned on the pictures you direct, and that you are anxious to direct such pictures for which there is a popular demand."[7] The Franklins, surprisingly, were somewhat relieved noting that the making of the kiddie pictures was both "tiresome" and "nerve-wracking." They did express regret that Fox did not want to continue the series and felt that any failure to profit from the films was due to ineffective advertising. The plan, then, was that the Franklins would direct "grown-up" pictures but incorporate children into the stories.

It is likely that all of the kiddie pictures, including the last, *Fan Fan* (original title *The Mikado*) had been completed by the time Fox made this decision in November. Fox's loss of faith in the series may also have been part of the reason *Fan Fan* didn't go out to theaters until almost ten months after the release of *Treasure Island*, but before *Fan Fan* hit movie screens, Virginia was in two more movies with a very popular cowboy star.

10. The Cowboy and the Last Fairy Tale

ox wanted to separate the two brothers for financial reasons. Writing to Sol Wurtzel, he said, "I have not examined the Franklin brothers' contract. I am under the impression that that contract provides that they are to separate if the Fox Film Corporation desires and to work individually.... If the contract provides that we can combine these two directors again, you can do so, although it is my opinion that it will be a waste of time, for each one of these men has proven that he is capable of direction by himself, and there is nothing to be gained by having them work together, thereby causing a double expense of two directors for one company."[1] The West Coast studio needed four directors, and up to this point, the studio had been utilizing the Franklins, Frank Lloyd, Edward LeSaint and Bertram Bracken who had been directing one of Fox's biggest stars, Gladys Brockwell. Fox, though, preferred having the Franklins direct separately, "leave Bracken out," and thereby still have four companies working at once.

Apparently that is what happened. First of all, Bracken only directed one picture for Fox that was released in 1918 (and, of course, this could have been filmed months earlier), and Virginia's next film, *Six Shooter Andy* starring Tom Mix, was directed by Sidney Franklin without assistance from brother Chet.

Mix had started back in 1910 making shorts for the Selig Polyscope Company. His background is varied, although it's been fictionalized numerous times. He did serve in the Army as an artillery sergeant during the Philippines campaign, but he never saw action and was actually a deserter, a fact that was kept secret over the years. He had been a bartender and a sheriff/marshal before joining up with the Miller Brothers Wild West Show that was very popular traveling around the country in the first ten years of the century. Since these cowboys were sometimes borrowed for movies, that is what led Tom into a career in films.

He stayed with Selig until 1917 when he joined Fox. His first films for Fox were shorts, but then he began to make five-reel features, and, although his shorts had been very popular, his real fame was now on the rise as he entered the feature-length market.

Six Shooter Andy was only Mix's third feature for his new producer. Unfortunately, it appears to be a lost film, so how much Virginia may have contributed to the picture is unknown. Actually, this film appearance seems to be a distinct comedown from her starring roles in the Fox Kiddie Features. She is one of eight children, many of whom were her fairy tale co-stars, in the film's cast—Georgie Stone, Lewis Sargent, Buddy Messinger, Raymond Lee, Violet Radcliffe, Beulah Burns, Vivian Plank and Virginia.

All eight were the brothers and sisters of Enid Markey who played Susan Allenby, the love interest for Mix. Markey is best remembered as Jane in the first Tarzan movie starring Elmo Lincoln, which she had just finished before this film. The actor who plays the bad guy in this film is one of the best to grace the silent screen—Sam De Grasse. De Grasse can be seen in several silent films that survive today, and he was a particular favorite of Douglas Fairbanks who used him as a bad guy in such films as *Wild and Wooly* (1917), *Robin Hood* (1922), *The Black Pirate* (1926) and others.

Trade magazines noted in late December Tom Mix and his company were in Victorville, about 86 miles from Los Angeles, filming location scenes for *Six Shooter Andy*. By early February, reports were that the filming was wrapping up in anticipation of a February 24 release. The date was later pushed to March 3.

In *Six Shooter Andy*, De Grasse plays Tom Slade, the town's corrupt sheriff. Slade and his men stage a robbery and kill Susan's father, and Andy (Mix) and his father kindly take in the orphans. When Andy's father is killed by Slade's deputy, he vows to clean up the town. Andy demands the deputy's arrest, but to no avail. The deputy is eventually killed by Andy in a duel. A newspaper review gives some idea of the role of the children during the film's climax. "The sheriff is confronted with the number of killings that have taken place.... Slade defies the committee. Just at this time, the Mexican brings things to a climax by going to the girl's [Susan's] room and carrying her to a room over the town saloon. The children try to prevent him, but are beaten by him. The Mexican is discovered by the sheriff who kicks him out and then claims the girl. She indignantly repulses him, and he gives her a few minutes to decide. But some of the children have reached [Andy]."[2] And, of course, Andy rescues Susan and kills Slade in the process.

The story was set in a historical background. "A new street depicting the town of Bannock when it was at the highest of the mania for gold and when viciousness and organized lawlessness was [sic] rampant as it was at no place on this continent at any time, is being used by Tom Mix in making his new play for William Fox."[3] Gold was discovered in Bannock, Montana, in 1862 creating the biggest western gold rush since the great 1848 Gold Rush. The town actually did gain a reputation for lawlessness, as many of the new inhabitants were Civil War deserters, outlaws or just plain business profiteers. So, for those in 1918 who knew the history of this famous town, *Six Shooter Andy* would have an added interest. However, several newspaper accounts mention the story as taking place in Bannock, Nevada, which also had a gold strike in 1909 and was essentially nothing more than a camp that played out by the next year. Therefore, it is much more likely that the location chosen for Mix's story would be the infamous Bannock, Montana.

Variety wasn't impressed, though. "Typical western; rather of the old picture school in its idea ... just ordinary, helped a bit by its star... could have been vastly helped by better written and brighter captions."[4] One newspaper review headlined "It Will Stir

Enid Markey (in the center of all the children in the wagon) plays Susan, Tom Mix's love interest, in *Six Shooter Andy* (1918). The corrupt sheriff has killed her father, leaving Susan and her siblings in the care of Mix who vows to bring the sheriff to justice and clean up the town. Virginia was one of Susan's seven siblings in the story and can be seen at bottom left on the wagon.

You as You Have Not Been Stirred Before" *was* impressed. "Six *Shooter Andy* is a production that will appeal to those who have plenty of red blood in their veins and who like an abundance of gunplay.... The acting of Tom Mix will be most pleasing to say the least. He not only looks the part of a young Westerner of the early days, but he acts it as well, and his ability as a horseman will not be denied."[5]

As for Virginia, at least one review singled her out noting that she would have a "prominent part in the play." One wonders if it may be an indication she was given a bit more to do in the film than the other children in the cast. What appears to be a canned release from Fox that appeared in a number of newspapers singled out Virginia among the children mentioning two of her most famous kiddie films. Another write-up said several of the children have been seen before in *Jack and the Beanstalk* and *Aladdin and the Wonderful Lamp*, adding that Virginia Lee Corbin was "one of them." A typical display ad announced, "Tom Mix assisted by Enid Markey, Virginia Lee Corbin." Obviously, the name-drawing power among the children belonged to Virginia.

By the way, Francis Carpenter was not among the children supporting Mix because he was busy working in *The Girl with the Champagne Eyes* starring Jewel Carmen and directed by brother Chester Franklin.

Virginia's next film, another Tom Mix vehicle, would take her away from either of the Franklin brothers' tutelage, an association she had enjoyed on the last six pictures she had made (one of which has not been discussed yet.) *Ace High* was directed by Lynn Reynolds. This was his second Mix feature, and he would go on to helm 17 of Tom Mix's films over an eight-year run. Reynolds was most adept at westerns and directed several of Hoot Gibson's films before his untimely death in 1927 at age 37. At a welcome home dinner party following a location shoot, he and his wife, actress Kathleen O'Connor, got into a heated argument accusing each other of infidelity. With guests trying to calm the situation, Reynolds went into another room and shot himself in the head.

Filming for *Ace High* was scheduled to begin in late February. According to exhibitors' magazines, it was reported to be wrapping up in early May and was released June 9.

This was one of those pictures where Virginia played the part of Annette Dupre as a child. Reynolds future wife, Kathleen Connors, was Annette as an adult. Mix is credited with the story and Reynolds with the scenario.

In the story, Jean Rivard (Lloyd Perl at age ten, Lewis Sargent at 15, Mix as the adult) finds Annette and her mother in the snow, but the mother is dead. The child is adopted by a notorious saloon owner and sent East to be educated. That's the end of the child's part. The rest of the story has Annette return, but her adopted father plans to put her to work in the saloon. It's up to the adult Rivard, now a Canadian Mountie, to rescue her and beat the bad guys. Rivard gets her back to her real father, a railroad president, and marries her.

Variety liked the film. "The title of this Fox production ... which stars Tom Mix, may be used to characterize the picture. It is above the average in every way. In beauty of scenic effects, in atmosphere, in photoplay and direction, it is all that could be desired. It moves with a snap from start to finish until the spectator is brought up breathless when the end finally comes."[6] *Photoplay* called it a "thrilling melodrama."[7] Interestingly, exhibitors commenting in *Moving Picture World* said it was a "very fair picture," "regular program stuff—action too slow."[8]

Even though Virginia's part was small, at least one newspaper included a "blip" to acknowledge her presence in the film. "Virginia Lee Corbin who scored such success in *Jack and the Beanstalk, Aladdin and the Wonderful Lamp*, and other classics, is one of the supporting cast in *Ace High*."[9]

Lobster Films (Paris) has a fragment of the film, about a half reel. This seems to be all that has survived.

November 17 saw the release of the last of the Fox Kiddie Features, *Fan Fan*. This was almost a full year after the film's completion. Reports in exhibitors' publications from September 1917 said filming started that month immediately after the completion of *Aladdin and the Wonderful Lamp*, which would make it the fifth fairy tale to be filmed in the series. In November, Fox reported to the media that the last scenes for *The Mikado*, the original name for *Fan Fan*, were being filmed. Labeled as a "Fox Extravaganza," *Fan Fan* was released one week before Fox's other "Extravaganza," *Ali Baba and the Forty Thieves*, which starred Georgie Stone. *Ali Baba* is also one of the Fox Kiddie Series, although Virginia and Francis Carpenter are not in it. However, both were being filmed in the fall of 1917, and no explanation has been offered for the nearly one-year delay in their release.

The Mikado is a comic opera by Gilbert and Sullivan that had its first performance in 1885 and immediately became a success. Gilbert later adapted it into a children's book. This is what the Fox Kiddie Feature was based on. The name change to *Fan Fan* was not mentioned until pre-publicity appeared for its release in the fall of 1918.

Photoplay magazine ran an article in their January 1918 issue that talked about *The Mikado*, other Fox Kiddie Features, and Virginia in particular. It began, "Forming a semicircle around an urn filled with incense, a group of Japanese children sat on their heels, their heads bent low, and prayer beads in their hands. Little streams of smoke curled from innumerable joss sticks in a jar in front of an ancient altar. There was no sound except the slow steady ringing of a gong and the voice of a yellow-robed Japanese priest monotonously intoning a chant for the dead. The children looked very dejected and sat very still, because they knew that all this was a matter of business as well as of make-believe. This was a game and they were naturally playing it with childish thoroughness. The Fox kiddies were making a scene for *The Mikado*."

Later in the article, it noted Virginia's remarkable ability to conjure up tears when

Fan Fan was released in the fall of 1918, a full year after it was filmed, probably because Fox had given up on the series well before this time as being an unprofitable venture. The story was based on the Gilbert and Sullivan comic opera *The Mikado* with Virginia, as seen here, minus her blonde curls and, instead, wearing a dark wig and Oriental garb. The movie received less advance publicity than the previous Fox Kiddie Features, a shorter run, and less notice from the media, although Virginia continued to receive praise for her performance.

called for in a scene. "There as another scene in *The Mikado* where Yum Yum—little Virginia—left alone next to the room in which lies the body of her father, realizes for the first time how utterly alone in the world she is. She has been separated from Nanki Poo [sic]—Francis Carpenter—and there is nobody near who loves her—nobody at all. It was explained to Virginia that under these circumstances, Yum Yum would naturally feel very sad. 'And when people feel sad,' said this little five-year-old baby, 'They always cry.' She sat for awhile with her face turned away from the camera, her head bent, her shoulders drooping. Yum Yum was feeling sad. Then Virginia began to swallow back and seemed to be trying with all her might to keep from crying.... As the baby turned her face to the camera, the tears were streaming own her cheeks. She looked so utterly miserable that nearly everyone around cried with her. A minute later, she and The Lord High Executioner [Violet Radcliffe] were playing tag."[10]

The story tells of Hanki Pan (Francis Carpenter, incorrectly identified as "Nanki Poo" in the above-mentioned article), the emperor's son, who is in love with Fan Fan. His father, though, wants him to marry Lady Shoo (Carmen de Rue). Hanki Pan and Fan Fan elope. They are later caught by Lady Shoo and the Chief Executioner (Violet Radcliffe) who plan to behead Hanki Pan. The emperor learns of the plot, intercedes, and Hanki Pan and Fan Fan remain together while the Chief Executioner and Lady Shoo are married.

Except for the lead parts, Fox employed a number of Japanese children for the film. The canned release sent to exhibitors stated that it is "a lavish production from first to last. The settings made to represent the Japan of old form background of the finest atmosphere for the actions of the little people who portray the principal roles. This collection of children is, without doubt, the brightest group that ever faced a battery of motion picture cameras."

Virginia was once again praised for her performance. "Little Miss Corbin in her tiny kimono and high chignon of shiny black hair is utterly delightful. Her acting is natural and full of grace, and the expressions she can manage with her microscopic little face would do credit to one far older in years and experience. She seems capable of 'registering' almost any emotion, and her artless smiles can change to real tears in no time at all."[11]

It is obvious that *Fan Fan* had less advance publicity, a shorter run, and less notice from the media than the previous Fox Kiddie Features. The series had run its course, and, most importantly, Fox was losing money on them. The relationship with the Franklin brothers had deteriorated from the beginning. Fox was disenchanted with their seemingly lack of concern for company profits and bristled at their wanting to go on location, excessive costs and long filming times. For example, when a normal shooting schedule should run from 18 to 24 days, *Fan Fan* had taken 65 days to film.

Fox had great faith, though, in the beginning that this series was just what the public needed and had four of the movies completed by the time the first was released. *Jack and the Beanstalk* came out in July of 1917, and filming was already begun on the fifth feature by September. So, by the time Fox realized that his idea was not producing the anticipated results, he was deeply into the series.

In a letter to Sol Wurtzel complaining about the Franklin brothers, he said of the Kiddie Features, "You remember how anxious and urgent I was to consummate their [the Franklins] contract, for I felt then that the children pictures would be a sensation all over the world. I have since learned my mistake."[12]

In spite of all the positive publicity received for the Kiddie features, the first, *Jack and the Beanstalk*, was the only one of the films to actually show a profit for Fox. Back in the summer of 1917, he had actually announced more stories than those that were released—*The Brownies*, *Pinafore* and *Alice's Adventures in Wonderland*, to name a few. As noted, he had made other Kiddie features that did not star the Corbin-Carpenter team such as *Ali Baba and the Forty Thieves* with Georgie Stone and *Troublemakers* (1917) with the Lee sisters, Jane and Katherine, as well as others that starred the Lee sisters. However, the series fell flat at the box office, which likely had something to do with Fox's decision to delay the release of *Fan Fan*, possibly feeling the market had been glutted and needed a break.

Fox biographer Vanda Krefft offered one explanation for the series' failure. "In fact, because Fox never had a childhood, he didn't understand children at all. His movies portrayed them as small adults in an often terrifying world. In a letter to the editor of the *New York Tribune*, one woman protested that at a recent screening of *Jack and the Beanstalk*, children throughout the audience were sobbing desperately: 'the realism in many places struck terror in their souls' ... a *New York Tribune* critic wondered, 'Do these babies really understand such emotions as love, jealousy and despair?'"[13]

Brownlow, in his praise of the films, said, "The pictures were lavishly mounted. Children's films, over the years, have tended to receive the minimum of attention from art directors on the basis that 'no one will notice, so why bother?' But the Franklin pictures positively seethed with vast sets, elaborate costumes and hordes of extras.... Frank Good's photography is at its best in spooky caves and sun-drenched forests, although his carefully-lit interiors have occasionally suffered in the reduction to 16mm. In a way, the films are reminiscent of the dreams one has as a child—full of unmotivated terror from giants and witches, but offsetting this with an exhilarating element of superhuman power. Aladdin, chasing the culprit who has stolen his lamp, is confronted by an insurmountable wall. He has to climb it, and there are not footholds. So he does what any child would do in a dream—he takes a short run and literally flies to the top."[14]

Regardless of the lack of financial success for Fox, the films had made Virginia a star and solidified her place in the cinema world for several years to come.

11. From Star to Supporting Roles

efore Fox realized the kiddie films were not going to be the success that he imagined, he was investing money in the children's comfort and care and—to his credit—ensuring they were happy and treated properly. In fact, in the fall of 1917, he built a new stage exclusively for use by the Franklin brothers in filming the fairy tales. A new bungalow was constructed at the studio that would serve as the children's "home" while working which included a nursery, dressing rooms, shower baths and a fully equipped "modern" schoolroom. One article noted, "The children are given five hours a day in school, but it never seems that long to them. Naturally, the time must be broken, an hour or two in school, off to the set for the making of a scene and then back to lessons again. They never sit still long enough to become restless, and so give all the attention to the occupation of the moment. The teacher has only a few children in the room at a time, and, as they belong to all different grades, she is able to give them an amount of individual attention they could never receive in a public school."[1]

Virginia was very happy working at Fox, and the media adored not only her beauty, but also her bright mind and sunny disposition. Actually, they fell in love with all of the children in the Fox films, but none of them elicited the attention that Virginia received. Magazines did stories on her—sometimes so trivial one wonders if they just needed to fill space. Newspapers ran tidbits about anything that may be of interest to a fan.

Picture Play magazine ran a full-page story in their October 1918 issue with accompanying photos about Virginia getting all dressed up in clean rompers and then going across the street to the park and playing in the water fountain. The story was obviously fabricated because the photos portrayed of Virginia are those that were taken when she was promoting Peggy Jeans (mentioned in Chapter 6). A part of the photo shoot did indeed have her standing in the water in a fountain, but whether this even took place across the street from her home is doubtful.

She was still in demand for promotions, though, as evidenced by her pose in a newspaper ad sporting a "Billie Boss Dress" for $2.49.

Another piece of fluff is found in the April 1919 issue of *Photoplay* magazine, entitled "E-x-t-r-y! Great Hollywood Disaster!" The writer supposedly wrote to Virginia, "*Photoplay* magazine has asked me to write a page or so about you and your work.

Won't you send us your latest photographs and one or two views of that fine old Teddy Bear?" The one and a quarter page article, with photos of Virginia waving, her damaged Teddy Bear reclining in a chair and another of her and Francis Carpenter with the giant from *Jack and the Beanstalk*, is a correspondence about her Teddy Bear who is missing an arm and a leg. The writer sums up his opus by saying, "Our original idea was to publish just a page about Virginia's life. But, as Teddy Bears are far more important to such little girls than their own life stories, we thought you'd be interested." He did follow up with a few paragraphs about Virginia's entry into films and closed quoting her as saying, "I am studying classic dancing, the ukulele and French and Spanish," adding that she wants to go onto the stage with her sister, Ruth.[2] Again, amazing, yet questionable, endeavors for a child who just turned seven.

Many newspapers latched onto a story about Virginia's purchase of a new automobile in March 1918. Her earnings allowed her to get a new King Eight, which she had painted a "dainty blue" and upholstered in velvet velour. She also promoted Palmer Tires and was quoted as saying, "The tubes are really all that is claimed for them, because since I have used them I have had no tire trouble of any form, and it certainly makes me feel fine to know that I am not going to be bothered with costly blowouts. My advice is to use Palmer cord tubes."[3]

In October, it was reported that she was making house-to-house calls in her area in the interest of the salvage department of the Red Cross.

One magazine ran a piece about stars' sandwiches, and Virginia's sandwich was featured—sliced chicken covered with mayonnaise on toast, with slices of tomato that have stood in French dressing.

In December 1918, she was one of several stars featured in a *Photo-Play Journal* article recounting their last Christmas. She noted that it was her first Christmas in the moving pictures, and she was happy because her movie, *Jack and the Beanstalk*, "would make millions of people happy, and I am glad of that." She said she had lots of presents at home, and "all the members of the company gave each other nice things."[4]

Virginia was one of several child stars featured in an article in March 1918 in *Motion Picture Classic*. Along with Thelma Salter, Georgie Stone, Francis Carpenter, Madge Evans, Jane and Katherine Lee and others, the magazine gave a couple of paragraphs of trivia about each child. Virginia's ability to cry on a moment's notice was, of course, mentioned, and also that she plays tennis and aspires to be a champion player.

June 1918 had Virginia and Baby Marie Osborne featured in a two and a half page article in *Motion Picture Magazine*. It told of her career in movies up to that point, how she entered pictures, and praising her beauty, talent, modesty and refinement. And, as most fan magazines ran a rotogravure of several full-page photos of stars, Virginia was often among them in charming photos, holding a flower, about to powder her nose as she gazes into a hand-held mirror, or peeking through the brush at the edge of a lily pond.

In a popularity contest conducted by *Motion Picture Magazine* over a period of several months in 1918, Virginia fared very well. As of July 20, 1918, she ranked 110th with 12,482 votes. The top vote getter was Mary Pickford with 127,832. While 110th may not sound impressive at first, she still outranked stars such as Roscoe Arbuckle, Mabel Normand, Constance Talmadge, Corinne Griffith, John Bunny, Enid Bennett,

Jack Holt, Eileen Percy, Elliott Dexter, Roy Stewart, Edward Earle, Milton Sills, Margery Wilson and others—not bad for a child who had not yet seen her seventh birthday (and the only one of the Fox kiddies to appear on the list)!

Still under contract to Fox, one wonders why, with her popularity, Fox didn't find a starring vehicle for her. However, when considering how he felt about taking a loss on the kiddie features, Fox, no doubt, figured he'd stick to the adult stars for awhile. So Virginia's next film was actually a starring vehicle for one of Fox's biggest stars, Gladys Brockwell. *The Forbidden Room* was released March 2, 1919, and was directed by Lynn Reynolds, who had also directed Virginia in *Ace High* with Tom Mix.

She and Francis Carpenter were the children of an unscrupulous contractor in the movie. Brockwell works for an unscrupulous police chief and leaves him when he makes unwanted advances. Co-star William Scott is the district attorney—not popular with the police and out to get a certain crooked contractor. The police chief makes unwanted advances—she goes to work for the district attorney—the DA takes her on a fishing trip as a working secretary, and they fall in love—photos taken by the police chief and contractor make it possible to get a trumped up white slavery charge against the DA. The DA thinks Brockwell was in on the plot and fires her. The film ends in a big courtroom drama where Brockwell slickly manipulates things (she actually commits perjury) so that the contractor, on threat of losing his children (Virginia and Francis), admits the truth.

Because the film is presumed lost, once again it is difficult to tell the level of Virginia's and Francis' participation. Obviously, though, they were not the stars, and the days of seeing their names at the top of a marquee were at an end. The film was not received well. For example, *Variety* called it "a story with tremendous possibilities, but which has been directed into mediocrity."[5] As for Virginia and Francis, what few reviews there are just mention "the children," if mentioned at all.

Three months after the release of *The Forbidden Room*, Virginia was continuing to be in demand for personal appearances for all types of fetes. In June, she was present at a celebration for World War I flying ace Capt. Eddie Rickenbacker. He had 26 aerial victories during the war, was a Medal of Honor recipient and received more medals for valor than any other American in the conflict. Rickenbacker rode in an airplane that was towed down Broadway in Los Angeles. A photo of him on the reviewing stand shows him lifting Virginia up on his arm and flanked by such personages as Douglas Fairbanks, Roscoe Arbuckle, and a host of military dignitaries. Prior to the aforementioned photo being taken, Virginia was "nestled" in a tall basket surrounded by flowers, and the basket was presented to Rickenbacker.

The next month she was at the automobile races at the Ascot Park Speedway in Los Angeles where numerous stars and directors appeared, some participating in the race such as Marshall Neilan, Tom Mix, Carter De Haven, Douglas MacLean, Roscoe Arbuckle, Al St. John, Larry Semon, Henry King and more. Virginia participated in the fashion parade along with such stars as Blanche Sweet, Anita Stewart, Peggy Hyland, Bessie Barriscale, Priscilla Dean, Enid Bennett and others.

And in September, she was at a boxing demonstration. "Baby Virginia Lee Corbin … is to be the guest of the *Evening Express* tonight when the regular Friday night boxing show will be staged in the gymnasium on Hill Street. Baby Virginia has always been a sort of a pet of the newsies, and they have yet to show how clever they are with the padded mitts, and it has been arranged so the little actress will witness her first exhibition of a fistic contest. After the show is over, a sort of a reception will take place with the kiddies all seated about having a heart-to-heart talk with the smallest of movie queens, who will relate to them some of her experiences while working before the camera in the making of the kid pictures."[6]

Virginia was self-confident and at ease in her personal appearances. She had talent, with both singing and dancing ability. She was approaching eight, even though she typically had one or more years trimmed off her age in the media. Although eight is very young, studios typically turned their backs on child stars as soon as their miniature cuteness begins to disappear—even in these early days of the movies—and films such as *The Forbidden Room* wouldn't really provide Virginia the opportunity to keep her star's bright light before the public as she, or her mother, would want. So, with her talent and stage presence, Virginia's next endeavor not only seemed logical, it also proved to be a very smart move.

12. Vaudeville Lights

"*Virginia Lee Corbin is the* latest actress to be lured by the footlights. And her mother, Mrs. Corbin, claims that she is the youngest motion picture star to leave the screen for the speaking stage. Little Virginia is preparing a sketch for vaudeville called 'Tears.' Many of the little kiddies who saw Virginia in *Jack and the Beanstalk* and *Babes in the Woods* will be sorry to see her leave pictures."[1]

A complete list of all of Virginia's personal appearances in vaudeville is impossible to compile, but a pretty good idea of her travels and where she appeared can be determined from newspaper accounts. The aforementioned announcement was dated September 22, 1919. However, the earliest newspaper account that can be found of a vaudeville appearance for her is the next August. A part of the reason may be that she was completing one more picture before beginning her tour.

The White Dove was released March 28, 1920, and starred H.B. Warner, whose most famous role would come seven years later as Jesus Christ in Cecil B. DeMille's *King of Kings* (1927). Virginia played the daughter of Warner's character. The female lead and Warner's love interest was played by Claire Adams.

Several articles announcing the movie referred to Virginia as having been selected for "the lead" in the movie. As one noted, "Virginia Lee Corbin, the child prodigy, has been borrowed from the Fox Film Co. and will play the lead in H. B. Warner's next picture which Henry King is directing for Jesse D. Hampton Productions. She has fallen into good hands, for it was King who brought Baby Marie Osborne to such high favor among American fans and later he directed *Little Mary Sunshine* and Gloria Joy with similar success. Virginia is to be given a part almost, if not quite, as strong as that to be played by Mr. Warner."[2] It must be remembered that Virginia has worked for King once before, in *Vengeance of the Dead* in 1917. It could be possible he was responsible for her appearance in the film.

Considered to be a lost film, it is once again difficult to ascertain the depth of Virginia's part in the film, and the film's synopsis does not indicate a large role for a child. It's all about how a son feels he has led a good life while everyone around him has "deviated from the path of righteousness," including his dead wife, his father, a half brother and the girl with whom he is in love. In the end, he realizes that everyone is not perfect, is reunited with them, and, of course, marries the girl. There is no mention in the description of a child.

Still under contract to Fox, Virginia was loaned out to Jesse D. Hampton Feature Corporation for *The White Dove* (1920). Since it is considered to be a lost film, it is difficult to ascertain the depth of Virginia's role, although one reviewer said her part was "almost, if not quite, as strong as that to be played by Mr. Warner." The star, H.B. Warner, holds eight-year-old Virginia in what appears to be a very dramatic scene from the movie. Co-star Claire Adams is seated on the sofa (image courtesy Hershenson/Allen Archive).

It is also somewhat difficult to find information on the film. It doesn't appear that any of the major fan magazines acknowledged its existence, and *Variety* also did not review it. However, the exhibitors' publication *Harrison's Reports* blasted the film. "A poor picture. Neither interest is aroused, nor sympathy wakened. On the contrary, the effect produced upon the emotions is repellant because the story is based on an unpleasant theme."[3]

In addition to being a "poor picture," another reason the film may not have gotten much attention is the fact that it was released by a minor company, the Jesse D. Hampton Feature Corporation, and released by an equally minor distributor, Robertson-Cole Company. On loan-out from Fox, the experience obviously did nothing to advance Virginia's career.

However, the decision for her to enter vaudeville did help to advance her career simply by keeping her name in front of the public until the right moment to re-enter pictures. The excellent notices she received from her performances also helped ensure her continued popularity as well as good attendance around the country.

Naturally enough, she began her tour in Los Angeles. An August 30, 1920, a newspaper ad announced "Baby Virginia Corbin in Person" for the first week of September at Grauman's Million Dollar Theatre. Her performance "in a musical and dancing turn" was in conjunction with the screening of Douglas MacLean in *The Jail Bird*. She was at the theatre for at least two weeks as a September 10 ad had Virginia declaring, "Hello People! I Want to See You!! Everybody enjoyed my act at the Grauman's Million Dollar Theatre, Los Angeles, and I hope you'll like me, too.—Virginia Lee Corbin."[4]

Virginia's mother had contracted her to tour the Pantages circuit. Alexander Pantages had about 30 theatres mostly in the west and middle of the country—none on the East Coast. His wasn't the largest chain, but it did carry prestige, especially for those who may not have been the highest salaried vaudeville performers of the day. So Virginia's next documented appearance, for the week beginning October 18, was in Seattle, Washington, at the Pantages theatre there. As an indication of her star power and ability to draw an audience, the newspaper ad in *The Seattle Star* only mentioned Virginia— no other performers on the bill.

And others could have been mentioned because Virginia was traveling this time with a "troupe"—as indicated in the next ad for an October 23 appearance in Vancouver, British Columbia. It does not give her top billing. Instead, it lists her among other acts such as "The Melody of Youth," The Powell Troupe, Marjorie De Vore, Sally Taylor in "Musical Moments," Austin and Delaney in "The Syncopated Hotel," and singer May Lorimer. The troupe would have had anywhere from four days to two weeks at each location.

In November, she was at Pantages theatres in Portland, Oregon, and San Francisco. The first week in December found her in Oakland, listed third on the bill behind "Melody of Youth" and the Powell Troupe, a "tightwire" act. A December 7 newspaper report claimed that the week of December 5–11 would be Virginia's last week with the Pantages vaudeville circuit after a ten-week tour of the coast. It went on to say that she would be going to New York where she is expected to appear in a Broadway production and would be accompanied by her mother, who also "acts as her manager."

It's easy to understand how Virginia's talents, personality and comfortableness on the stage would have garnered some interest in her appearing on Broadway, and the prestige associated with it must have been very appealing for Mrs. Corbin. Because of the announcement, one can assume that some discussions took place with an agent or promoter, but, unfortunately, a stint on Broadway never materialized. It must also be kept in mind that Mrs. Corbin was not opposed to contacting the newspapers herself and, in later years, very quick to use them to her advantage when she and Virginia were having difficulties. It's possible the story came from an over-zealous mother who saw a glimmer that was, unfortunately, only too quickly extinguished.

In mid–December, she appeared with the same troupe at Pantages Theatre at 7th and Hill in Los Angeles. The December 30 advertisement in Salt Lake City, Utah, listed some different acts appearing with her, such as "Sweet Sixteen: A Musical Comedy," Joe Whitehead, The Original Nut, and Edna Earl Andrews & Co. in "Saint & Sinner."

Nineteen twenty-one began with an appearance in Ogden, Utah, at the Orpheum. With the end of her tenure with Pantages in December, Virginia was able to continue her vaudeville career with a circuit that had been around longer and carried a little more prestige as well as featuring more big name artists. Apparently the previously mentioned December 7 article was correct in saying she was ending her tour with Pantages, but still incorrect regarding a Broadway engagement for the little star.

According to the Ogden newspaper, she would begin her appearances there on Thursday, January 6, and "will perform especially for the kiddies at Saturday's matinee," adding, "Miss Corbin is not the least dismayed by the glare of the footlights and presents comedy and light drama with the skill of a veteran."[5]

The week of January 24 she appeared at the Empress Theatre in St. Louis, Missouri. February 3–4 she was at the Barth Theatre in Carbondale, Illinois. Beginning with her appearance in Carbondale, it can be surmised from the advertisements that Virginia was, at least for some dates, appearing alone since most of her upcoming appearances were in conjunction with a movie being shown, not a vaudeville troupe.

For example, a March 21 article in the *Chicago Tribune* announced "the talented Juvenile Movie Star in Person" at the Lubliner & Trinz Michigan Theatre with the Justine Johnstone movie *The Plaything of Broadway*. As a matter of fact, she spent the better part of the next month in Chicago going from one theatre to the other, no doubt a welcomed respite from traveling.

A few days later it was another Lubliner & Trinz theatre, the Covent Garden on North Clark Street. This time she was on the bill with the movie *Not Guilty* starring Sylvia Breamer. Still in Chicago in early April, she was at the Pershing Theatre with a Thomas Meighan movie, then back to Lubliner & Trinz Biograph on Lincoln with a William S. Hart movie. There was one more appearance in Chicago—Lubliner & Trinz Madison Square with a George Walsh movie.

On April 8, an article appeared in the *Santa Cruz Evening News* that said, "Virginia Lee Corbin, popular child star, recently closed a fourteen-week tour of the western states with the Pantages circuit and has signed a contract with a New York corporation; and after a brief publicity tour will appear in a series of pictures under her own management."[6]

An April 21 article stated that Virginia, "who has been making personal appearances in the various movie and vaudeville palaces of Chicago, will soon leave the metropolis for New York to fulfill a contract to appear at all of the First National houses. She is expected to return to Los Angeles about September first."[7] A series of pictures under Virginia's (that is, her mother's) own management never happened. The contract to appear at all First National houses in New York also did not take place, although Virginia would work for First National in the coming years. This seemed to be setting the tone for Virginia's career in the twenties—lost opportunities and questions as to why they didn't happen and what could have been if they had.

The next record of an appearance was a four-day engagement June 16–19 at the Orpheum in Madison, Wisconsin, with the usual reception for children on Saturday. A reviewer said of her performance, "Virginia Lee Corbin, the headline act at the Orpheum, is a winsome little youngster who won her well earned fame in the movie world. She is a good-looking miss who assumes a number of novelty juvenile roles in an unaffected manner that sustained her reputation as a versatile junior actress."[8] Obviously, Virginia's vaudeville tour was being received well and reaping positive publicity.

By the end of June she could be seen in person at the Junior Theatres Orpheum

Circuit Grand Opera House in St. Louis. This time the ad gave her top billing (and in all caps) ahead of such acts as The International Nine—World's Fastest Acrobats, Wiesser & Reeser—Tan Town Follies, Madame Bedini and Her Horses, Billy Broad with Original Songs and Sayings, Princess Nai Tai Tai—the Original Lark, and Charles & Helen Polly—Genuine Versatile. Virginia, the ad noted, was to appear "in an act of songs, dances and chatter entitled "A Distinct Novelty."

With an unexplained gap from early July to late October, the end of that month found Virginia back in Chicago at the Julian Theatre, then Thielen's Majestic Theatre in Bloomington, Illinois, in mid–November, the Orpheum in Green Bay, Wisconsin, a week later, and then closing out in December at the Pantages in Minneapolis, Minnesota. Interesting that the ad placed her name above and in much larger type over Mary Miles Minter's latest movie. Of her appearance there, an article stated, "Little Virginia Lee Corbin, dainty child actress from movieland, headlines this week's bill at the Pantages. Her winsome personality wins the audience from the rise of the curtain. Unlike so many stage children who effect an air of sophisticated smartness before the footlights, this little girl relies on her baby smile and actions for her appeal. Her singing and dancing is [sic] good. She appeals also to the children in the audience."[9]

Virginia was back on the Pantages circuit at the beginning of 1922 with two weeks at the Pantages Theatre in Vancouver, BC. She was not the headliner

Virginia took a break from movies to tour in vaudeville from approximately August 1920 until early 1922. Newspaper accounts indicate she was received well and was often the headlining act among a troupe of various performers. This typical ad from November 1921 in Bloomington, Illinois, indicates how talented the little star was, both singing and dancing in her appearances (for which she received praise in reviews) as well as giving recitations.

this time, but did get favorable notices. By January 22, she was in Portland, Oregon, at the Pantages there and was headlining. "The headline attraction for the week will be pretty little Virginia Lee Corbin known all over America by followers of the silver screen. Dainty Miss Corbin is appearing in person, offering a program which promises much laughter, bits of pathos and some singing and dancing,"[10] all of which makes the young actress sound very versatile!

By the second week of February, she was appearing in Los Angeles, which seems to be the last of her vaudeville days. Interestingly, her father's name appeared in the newspaper a couple of weeks later, something that was rarely seen. From Azusa, the article said, "Mrs. L.E. Corbin and daughters, Ruth and Virginia Lee of Los Angeles, spent the weekend with L.E. Corbin. Mrs. Corbin and Virginia Lee have just returned from the East where little Virginia Lee has been on the Pantages circuit which covered various points in England, France and the Eastern States."[11] Virginia's father continued to be removed from his daughter's career and seemed content to continue working as a pharmacist in various locations in California, and, obviously, the relations between he and his wife were congenial as he continued to stay in contact with his daughters. The part of the article that was obviously fabricated was Virginia's touring of England, France and the Eastern States. Virginia's touring never took her farther east than Chicago.

As 1922 got well underway, Virginia's and her mother's thoughts turned back to Hollywood where the days of being referred to as "Baby Virginia" and playing child roles would soon be coming to an end. Although she had just turned ten years old in 1921, Virginia would be moving to juvenile parts and then onto a role that would define her in the twenties as a flapper.

13. Back to Hollywood

Although 1922 started off with several vaudeville appearances, they came to an end within the first two months, and the rest of the year was somewhat of a lull before getting back in to pictures. This may have been by design to allow Virginia to age a bit more or simply an absence of offers for work. At any rate, Virginia would continue to be in the news, even if it was a love affair with another movie star.

Newspapers were obviously having fun with a tidbit coming out of Hollywood about Virginia and Jackie Coogan, a natural pairing considering Coogan's recent meteoric ascent to fame as a result of his co-starring role in Charlie Chaplin's *The Kid* (1921). Headlined "New Movie Scandal," the article read, "A new scandal shook the movie colony today. Jackie Coogan transferred his affections from seven-year-old 'Patsy,' living next door, and is feeding lollypops to Virginia Lee Corbin."[1] A month later, Jackie was denying the rumor, saying, "That's a big fib. There ain't nuthin' to it. Patsy's my girl. Virginia's awful pretty, all right, but she isn't my girl."[2] It was noted that both Patsy and Virginia were guests at Jackie's home the previous week, and all three had a good time playing hide and seek.

Virginia's purchase of a car back in 1918 was apparently not a passing whim. While on tour in Portland, Oregon, she had spotted a new Hudson automobile—referred to as a "coach." She dragged her mother into the dealership demanding that they purchase the car. "But, Virginia," her mother said, "you already have a nice car, and this one will cost a great deal of money." "I don't care," calmly retorted the child. "We can sell the other one if you think we should, but I'm going to have this coach—this one right here."[3] However, territorial sales rights prohibited her buying it in Portland. She would have to purchase the car in Los Angeles where she resided. She warned her mother she wouldn't forget, and, sure enough, shortly after returning to Los Angeles, Virginia asked to go to the Hudson dealership—and the car was purchased. The article was accompanied by a photo of Virginia standing in front of the car and pointing to the Hudson emblem on the grille. What is striking about the photo is how much Virginia had grown since the Fox days. At ten years old, she had gained height, slimmed down, and was quickly becoming a beautiful young lady.

It must be assumed the story is basically true, and it sounds as if it is—with maybe some embellishment by a newspaper writer. Virginia seemed, even at this early age, to be developing a strong and sometimes demanding personality. Considering the problems that would come later, this interaction was a clue to their personality differences.

As indicated by such an automobile purchase, the Corbins were in better shape financially than they had been in their lives, and both Mrs. Corbin and Virginia enjoyed the social scene that came along with money—something that would be more a part of Virginia's life as the years went on.

Friday, January 21, sister Ruth entertained with a dinner party at the Foothill Inn. This was only for a few children and their mothers, none of whom are recognizable names. Of course, Virginia and her mother were present, and "after the dinner party, the young people, chaperoned by Mrs. Corbin, motored to Pomona, where they enjoyed a pleasant dancing party."[4]

In August, Virginia was in San Francisco. The Café Marquand at Geary and Mason Streets was advertising "Theatrical Night" listing "Miss Virginia Lee Corbin, the World's Most Famous Child Artist" as the guest. Outside of the ad, there was no other mention of the event.

Virginia had been off the screen for a while. Her last picture was released over two years earlier. To her good fortune, vaudeville had kept her before the public and her name in the newspapers as well as some occasional tidbits such as the Coogan "scandal." It showed that Virginia had made an impression, people had not forgotten her, and her personal appearances proved she had real talent. No doubt, Mrs. Corbin was champing at the bit to get her back in pictures, especially after the lack of work she was getting in 1922. Thankfully, that opportunity was to come along, albeit from a minor company that was just starting out.

Announcements began appearing in September 1922 that Virginia had signed with Fisher Productions who were establishing headquarters in San Francisco and, as of September 18, 1922, would begin actual production within six weeks. The report said, "This young lady upon whose shoulders San Francisco may expect to lay hopes of the development of the production industry is just 12 years old, blue-eyed, blonde and perhaps the only emotional child actress on the stage." Notice the burden of success seemed to be on Virginia's shoulders and there is never any consistency in stating her age. Usually it's a year or two younger than her actual age, but this time the article said she was 12 when she actually would not turn 11 until almost three months later.

The report goes on to say, "But as the company itself is being financed by San Francisco capitalists, who have long worked quietly to develop the film industry in San Francisco. Their first action was to reach out and find Victor B. Fisher, internationally known film figure, to manage their enterprise. Before coming here, he was general manager of the Associated Photo-Plays, Incorporated, with offices in Los Angeles and New York. So Fisher has started by specializing in a big dramatic production featuring Virginia Lee Corbin. Once the operations start, famous film stars from Los Angeles and New York will be brought to this city for general pictures…. To date, Miss Corbin is the only actress to arrive in San Francisco for the first story."[5]

Another report said, "The company is to make from three to six super-pictures yearly, using only the best stories and players. Fisher … is now selecting the story for his initial production. The Pacific Studios at San Mateo will be used as headquarters, and production activities will commence during mid–November. Evidencing great foresight, the new concern has signed the young Miss Corbin for leading parts for a five-year period, certainly a mark of faith in her already proven screen ability."[6]

Film production for Fisher would not happen by mid–November or in the next six weeks as promised, but Virginia would eventually make a film for the company. Unfortunately, the five-year contract would prove to be overly ambitious.

In the meantime, she received a distinguished honor from the International Photographers' convention in London designating her as the most beautiful child entry among the pictures exhibited in Ransome Hall. Lillian Gish won first honors for adults.

Personal appearances continued to provide income in the absence of movies. In October, Virginia appeared at the Granada Theatre in San Francisco. "Virginia Lee Corbin, a pretty youngster with fluffy golden hair, eyes of vivid blue, peaches and cream complexion, will be one of the features today and all week at the Granada theater.... In her act at the Granada, she will sing, dance and talk. The young actress has been engaged by the Fisher Productions, Inc., a local company, to make pictures for them for the next five years. Work on the first will be started in about three weeks. Virginia and her mother are making their home in San Francisco where the Fisher pictures will be made."[7]

Virginia was essentially inactive during the first half of 1923. Part of the problem could have been waiting on Fisher Productions to get underway. Another delay was due to an operation for appendicitis that Virginia had in May. She was, however, "back at work" in late May.

The newspapers and exhibitors' publications were giving coverage to Fisher's activities and quoting his grand promises—which all sounded well. He had already announced that his first picture would be *Youth Triumphant*, a George Gibbs novel that had been serialized in *Green Book Magazine*. His biggest coup, however, outside of signing Virginia, was the signing of the popular Anna Q. Nilsson for the picture. The blonde, Swedish beauty began in films in 1911, and she was one of the most popular stars of the silent era. Although she did not enjoy star status in the sound era, she worked steadily in films until 1954.

Fisher had also acquired other notable names for the picture including Raymond Hatton, George Siegmann, Claire McDowell, Lucy Beaumont, Ward Crane, Eugenie Besserer, William Boyd, and Kate Price, among others—quite a distinguished list of names. Filming took place over the summer and wrapped up by the first of September. The picture had been renamed *Enemies of Children* and, according to a September 8 article, the picture "was finished last week at the coast studios of Fisher Productions, Inc., and prints and negatives were rushed to New York."[8] However, it would be three more months before the picture was released to theaters—December 13—barely more than a week after Virginia's twelfth birthday.

Although it is presumed to be a lost film, Virginia played the lead as a young girl. Nilsson then took over when the lead character became an adult. It concerns a street waif who is taken in by a wealthy family and cared for until the day comes for her to consider marriage—then her questionable parentage and mystery of her birth come under scrutiny. *Variety's* best comment on the film was that it was a "mediocre" presentation. "The celluloid version is jumpy in the telling besides demonstrating a lack of attention to detail," the reviewer said, and the following comment could be interpreted as a "dig"

Virginia's first film after her vaudeville stint was *Enemies of Children* (1923) starring Swedish beauty Anna Q. Nilsson. The caption accompanying this photograph says, "Anna Q. Nilsson helps Virginia Lee Corbin with her lessons between scenes of *Youth Triumphant* (the film's working title), a Fisher Production." Virginia was a couple of months away from being 12 years old when she made this picture.

at Virginia's performance, as the reviewer said, "If playing before an audience which is prone to kid dramatics, *Enemies of Children* probably will prove the source of some entertainment, but for other assemblages, it will more than likely remain as simply 'another picture.'"[9]

In spite of the hullabaloo the previous year that Fisher was going to bring film production to San Francisco, *Enemies of Children* was filmed in Los Angeles, and by early 1923, Fisher was already announcing he had engaged studio space there. Instead of the three to six productions a year he had previously predicted, by April he predicted the company would film three productions each year. In June he was teasing exhibitors and the public with an announcement that production on his second feature would begin immediately—although he never announced what that story would be. In the end, for whatever reason, *Enemies of Children* proved to be Fisher Productions' one and only release and faded more quickly from the movie industry scene than it had appeared.

Although filming may have ended as the fall season approached, Virginia was not done with Fisher. As early as late August, newspapers were carrying a story that Virginia's mother had filed suit against Fisher Promotions, Inc., for approximately $11,500—or about $300 a week in back salary that, Mrs. Corbin claimed, had not been paid. The suit would also help explain some of Virginia's inactivity in early 1923. Mrs. Corbin claimed that a contract was signed on August 21, 1922, although the company had not been formally organized. It was organized on October 1, though, and she claimed in the suit that Virginia had sat idle for 45 weeks waiting for work. Fisher Productions had paid $2,000 leaving $11,500 still unpaid.

No reference can be found to the settlement of this suit, so an out-of-court settlement must have been reached. There is also no reference to Fisher producing a film in the coming years, but a curious article did appear in May 1925. It was an announcement that 18-year-old Virginia Lee Williamson had been signed by Fisher Productions, and it was Virginia Lee Corbin and her mother who had recommended the young lady to Fisher! This would certainly indicate that some sort of amicable agreement had been reached by Mrs. Corbin and Fisher regarding Virginia's back salary. As for Virginia Lee Williamson, no further reference can be found on her.

In spite of only one film being made in 1923, which was marred by a salary dispute, Virginia was still of interest to the press for other things. Over the years, photos would appear of her modeling clothes. For example, in June, a picture of her was published wearing a white basket-woven flannel sports costume, embroidered in green and gold with a gold silk cord about the waist in place of a belt. Knickers of the same material and gold leather sandals completed the outfit. In the October issue of *Picture Play* magazine, she is shown modeling a serge kilt-pleated skirt with a Peter Pan blouse of white silk, very attractive and appropriate for the growing pre-teen.

In August, Tilden Dakin, who was a famous California landscape artist, painted a variety of poses of Virginia while he was visiting Los Angeles—an event that also made it into the newspapers. It is not known if the paintings still exist today.

Mrs. Corbin was very good at generating publicity too—usually self-promoting. For example, a June article stated, "Explanation of the daughter's achievement lies in the mother, Mrs. Virginia Corbin, 39, who has combined motherhood and professional managership [sic] to rare degree. Unlike many mothers of screenlings [sic] who immolate them on the celluloid altar from sheer mercenary motive, Mrs. Corbin has completely subordinated her own social and one time promising, professional life to that of her daughter. 'I can truthfully say,' she explained, 'that I haven't had a selfish impulse in cultivating Virginia's native talent. I simply hoped that she might be as a woman and actress all that I wanted so much to be and missed. While she was still a babe, my husband and I separated. It was in an effort to win back his love that I set out to make something extraordinary of our child; to show him that I could do something worthwhile. Love was not to be salvaged, but laying the foundation for Virginia's career soon became even more compelling. I pawned a diamond ring for $35 and with that we launched her in the movies at the age of three."[10] So goes the kind of saccharine babble that readers of the day relished.

14. One of the Few to Survive

*T*he press liked Virginia and welcomed her growing up and playing older parts. Again, the absence from the screen was well timed—long enough to let her mature both physically and mentally for awhile, yet not long enough for the public to forget her. One writer astutely noted that Virginia, "who made her first appearance eight years ago with many other precocious youngsters, is one of few to survive. Most film prodigies 'break' and are forgotten between the years of 6 and 9. To pass beyond this threshold of a picture career, children must, of course, develop something more than curls and cuteness, girls especially. And parents, no matter how gifted their offspring, must demonstrate shrewd managerial ability, until the fledglings can shift for themselves."[1]

As the promises of a five-year contract and stardom with Fisher Productions fizzled out, Virginia and her mother must have been very concerned about the future. The concern, though, would be short-lived.

No long-term contracts were being offered, but she was approached by Universal for a one-shot deal in a series starring Jack Dempsey. Dempsey, who was only 28 at the time this series was made, had been the heavyweight boxing champ since 1919, a title he held until 1926. Even back in the silent days, movie producers saw the box office value of celebrities from the sports world.

Universal announced that Fight and Win would include ten two-reel "features," each a complete story, with one issued every other week. The series (Universal did not refer to it as a "serial") carried a boxing theme throughout with titles such as *Winning His Way*, *The Society Knockout*, *The Title Holder*, *K.O. for Cupid* and other names that would clearly convey the theme. The first installment was released June 21 while filming on the remaining stories continued into the early fall.

With a few exceptions, exhibitors gave positive reviews saying they were impressed with Dempsey's acting and the quality of the stories. Esther Ralston was the love interest, however, Virginia's part in the series is unknown, as none of the entries are believed to have survived—and apparently no synopsis was published in trade publications. Since Virginia was advertised as one of the six main actors, it can be assumed she appeared in more than one installment.

Exhibitors were happy with the series and claimed excellent attendance. One the-

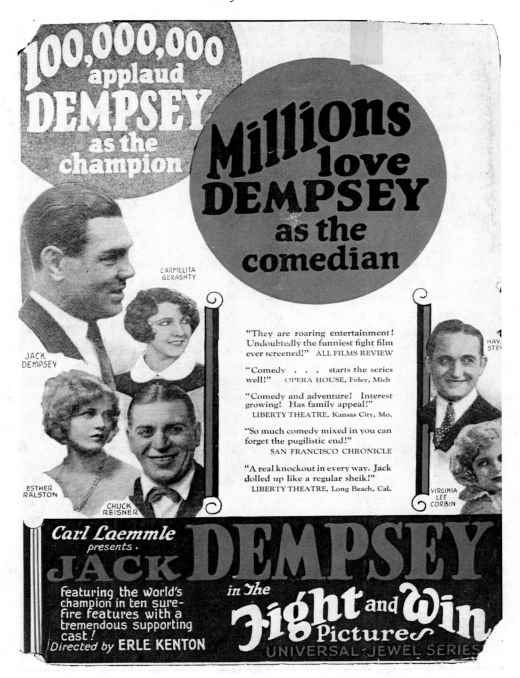

Fight and Win (1924) was a series, not a serial, each installment constituting a complete story with a conclusion—no "cliff-hanger" endings. Jack Dempsey's prowess in the ring made him a household name in the 1920s, so it was only logical that moviemakers would want to cash in on his name. Unfortunately, none of the 10 entries in the series appear to have survived, so Virginia's role and how many of the entries in which she may have appeared is unknown. However, as can be seen here, she was one of six featured players in the series.

ater owner exclaimed, "A great bet. Has comedy, romance, sport and drama, well directed. If balance as good, they're a safe booking." Another said, "Each one a complete story. A favorite with any audience. Tone, good." Still another said, "Boy! Here is a knockout! Better than 'Leather Pushers' and 'Fighting Blood.' Jack can retire from the ring and make a good living making pictures."[2]

Dempsey had a limited career in films making one feature in 1925, appearing in several shorts during the remainder of the silent years, and then making appearances, sometimes uncredited, in several films during the 1930s.

One interesting side note—*Moving Picture World* included an ad for exhibitors displaying various styles and sizes of poster that could be obtained to promote the series. The largest of these, a six-sheet poster, shows only two of the cast—Jack Dempsey and Virginia. Apparently, she still had drawing power.

While Fight and Win was picking up speed at the theatres, Virginia was winding up her work on her next film—*Sinners in Silk*, released September 1. Participation in this film must have been particularly pleasing to Virginia and her mother. Metro-Goldwyn-Mayer had been formed in April 1924, just a few months earlier, and *Sinners in Silk* was the studio's seventh production. Virginia was in very good company on this film with such stars as Eleanor Boardman, Adolphe Menjou, Conrad Nagel, Jean Hersholt, Hedda Hopper, Dorothy Dwan and other well-respected names in Hollywood.

With such a large cast of notables and Virginia's part listed simply as "flapper," it's likely she wasn't much more than a glorified extra in the film, but it is noteworthy that, not yet 13 years old, she was given a role that portrayed her as significantly older than she actually was—and it was the first, but certainly not to be the last, time she portrayed a flapper in a film.

A newspaper article helps to understand the maturing Virginia Lee Corbin who was now back in the movies. "It is a different Virginia Lee who graces the screen today. Gone are the curly locks and the round baby face and the chubby little hands. Instead, there is a stately and more mature wisp of a girl."[3]

Again, assumed to be a lost film, all one can do is surmise from the description what was on the screen back in 1924—and it sounds as if it was a "fun" film, although a somewhat trivial story. Menjou plays an aging roué who meets a flapper (Boardman) on a ship. Desiring to enjoy life again, he undergoes rejuvenation surgery. Afterwards, he has the flapper up to his apartment, but soon learns she is a "good girl," her flirtations being a bit misleading. The flapper's old beau (Nagel) enters the picture, and it's soon discovered he is the old roué's son. Menjou's character then decides it's best to go back to a more mature way of life.

Flaming Youth with Colleen Moore had set the jazz age flapper theme in motion the year before, so *Sinners in Silk* was another entry in this genre with wild parties, drinking, smoking, and generally doing silly things (in one scene the young people play quoits with diamond bracelets for missiles and a champagne bottle for the pin). As for Virginia's part, it sounds as if the party scene would have been the most likely sequence in which she would have screen time.

The exhibitors' trade publication *Harrison's Reports* was generally positive about it. "There is nothing to the plot, but it has been produced so well, the direction and acting being of a high standard, that it manages to keep the interest pretty tight all the way through…. The picture impresses one as being magnificently made."[4] *The New York Times* said the film started off promisingly but ended up being a let-down. "Nevertheless, there is no denying the entertainment value of this picture, as it is equipped with lavish settings, excellent photography, novel and amusing situations, and the excellent acting of Adolphe Menjou."[5] *Variety* simply didn't care for it. "It's an old, old theme, done countless times before and ever so much better."[6] Outside of the three leads—Menjou, Boardman and Nagel—other cast members weren't getting noticed in reviews. *Movie Weekly* gave it an 80 percent and called it "quite entertaining." The photo accompanying the review shows Menjou and Virginia in the back seat of a car, Menjou looking rather pensive and Virginia smiling at him—dressed in dark turban, large fur-collared fur-sleeved jacket and a long, dark dress. Photos such as these just arouse the curiosity even more regarding her role in the film.

And she continues this type of role in her next film, another entry for Metro-Goldwyn Mayer, *Wine of Youth*. Again, Virginia was finding herself in a prestigious picture with the added perk of one of the silent era's most capable directors—King Vidor—and a cast that was equally as impressive as her previous picture's. *Wine of Youth* also offers glimpses of future sound era stars Jean Arthur and Anne Sheridan in uncredited roles.

Adolphe Menjou played an aging "roué" in *Sinners in Silk* (1924) who has undergone rejuvenation surgery to enjoy life again—with a younger woman, Eleanor Boardman. In the cast listings, Virginia is simply identified as "flapper." This photograph of her in the back seat of a car with Menjou leads one to wonder if she was one of his "flirtations" in the film.

Fortunately, *Wine of Youth* does exist today, and it's an excellent film. There are six principals with Eleanor Boardman taking the main lead. She's supported by William Haines, Ben Lyon, Pauline Garon, Bobby Agnew, and William Collier, Jr. Also key to the picture are Eulalie Jensen as her mother, E.J. Ratcliffe as her father, and Gertrude Claire as her grandmother.

Tish (Garon) hosts a wild, Jazz Age party at her home while her parents are gone. There's plenty of drinking, love-making, dancing, etc. The first time Virginia is seen, she jumps up on a table and starts dancing. Mary (Boardman) is being courted by Lynn (Lyon) and Hal (Haines) who almost come to blows arguing over whose girl she is. Tish and Max (Collier) are in love—and both girls have a "modern" view of their role in life—unlike their mothers and grandmothers, their first priority is *not* finding a husband. Bobby (Agnew) is Mary's 18-year-old brother. His goal at the party is to kiss as many girls as he can.

He spies Virginia when he comes into the party, and, while dancing with her, asks her if she's ever gone 60 miles an hour. Of course not, so they rush out to his car—his father's car, by the way, that he sneaked away from home. When the car starts going fast enough that Virginia gets nervous, he heads toward a tree. She buries her head in his shoulder, and he stops the car just in time. The idea works, and she kisses him.

As a side note, it is interesting that *Motion Picture Classic* devoted a full page entitled "The Immemorial Pastime" with four photos from the movie in their September 1924 issue. One features Lyon kissing Boardman. Two show Agnew's conquests in his car—Virginia and Gloria Heller. The fourth shows Collier and Garon snuggling on the floor.

Back at the party from her car excursion with Bobby, Virginia wants to hang on

Virginia's part in *Wine of Youth* (1924) was brief. She was one of two girls Bobby Agnew entices into his car for a wild ride and a kiss, after which he takes her back to the party— mission accomplished.

to him, but he's no longer interested—now looking for his next conquest. He spies another girl (played by Heller), asks her the same question, they go for a ride, and he pulls the same routine—garnering him his second kiss of the evening. Bobby's car routine and her attempts to hang on to him at the party are the last views of Virginia in the film.

After the party, Mary, Tish, Lynn, Hal and Max are in the kitchen getting something to eat and hit upon an idea. Unlike their parents, they agree couples should get to know each other better (in a non-sexual way, of course) before marriage—not wait until after the wedding. Max suggests they spend a couple of weeks at a campground, and the plan is agreed upon. Unfortunately, Mary thinks her mother will approve of the idea, but she does not, so Mary sneaks out and the group goes camping.

Prior to leaving on the trip, Mary had both Hal and Lynn promise they would not try to "make love" to her on the trip. Keep in mind that in 1920s lingo, "make love" meant hugging and kissing—not sex. However, on the first night, Tish, Max and Hal are continuing the party spirit with drinking and an evening swim. Lynn, the quieter, more sensitive of the three boys, is in his tent, and Mary is in hers—both trying to go to sleep. While his companions are swimming, Hal sneaks back up from the lake, a little intoxicated, goes inside Mary's tent and tries to force his attentions on her. She runs outside where he continues to pursue her, but then she faints.

As the scene changes, they are bringing Mary back to her house and placing her, apparently still unconscious, on the sofa. At the height of their worry, Mary wakes up and tells them she was faking in order to get back home. She further tells them she has decided that the ways of her parents and grandparents are not so outdated. Bobby rushes in and warns that her mother is up and her father will be home soon. The others leave hurriedly, and Mary and Bobby hide.

When her father comes in, he and Mary's mother enter into a violent argument. The father blames the mother for failing in the raising of their children. Both claim if they had it to do over again, they'd never marry each other. She tells him she can't stand him thinking he's right all the time—she also can't stand the sound of his voice or being in the same room with him. He tells her she's been a disappointment to him—and on and on and on. The children hear all of this and are devastated.

The parents are taken off guard when the children appear and say they've heard it all. In spite of the parents' protestations that they love each other, Mary tells them it's all a lie. How could they possibly go on living together? The mother, barely able to stand from the ordeal, says she's leaving home and goes upstairs. In the bathroom, she takes a bottle of poison from the medicine cabinet. Downstairs, the father, Mary and Bobby hear something and rush to find the mother on the floor. The grandmother comes in, and all are scurrying around getting the mother to a bed and calling a doctor.

As they all hover over the seemingly unconscious mother, the father cries and begs his wife not to leave him. Mary suddenly realizes how much her father really loves his mother. Her faith in their marriage is restored—and the mother wakes saying she never did take any poison—only fainted from the emotional trauma.

Although it's five o'clock in the morning, Mary, happy again, rushes out of the room, picks up the phone, calls Lynn to come over, and they agree to get married.

The film was based on a successful stage play entitled *Mary, the Third* by Rachel Crothers. The introduction of the film shows the grandmother sitting on a sofa with her suitor back in 1870 being proposed to at a party—where they dance the polka—and claiming, "There never has been a love as great as ours." It moves to 1897 at a party where they are dancing the waltz, and Mary's father proposes to her mother on the same sofa—and she too exclaims, "There never has been a love as great as ours." So, not surprisingly, after Mary and Lynn agree to get married at the end of the film, they kiss, then hug, and Mary exclaims, "There never has been a love as great as ours."

According to an original script of the movie, the title *Don't Deceive Your Children* was once considered as was the play's title, *Mary, the Third.* As a side note, Ben Lyon performed in the stage play in his same role as Lynn.

Harrison's Reports panned the picture calling it "a poor entertainment," adding, "There is hardly any human appeal to it."[7] *The New York Times* was a little kinder, saying, "Those with whom the recent series of flapper films found favor will be entertained.... It is not bad as a warm weather show," and it noted, "Were it not for the weakness of

Wine of Youth (1924) is the first film available for viewing today since *The Babes in the Woods* in 1917. Virginia had matured quite a bit in the intervening seven years (although she was only 13 years old) and was already establishing her talent at playing a flapper, a role in which she excelled throughout the twenties. In this photograph, she is dancing on a piano as the band plays in the opening party scene.

the last chapter, this film would be quite a bright, frivolous affair."[8] *Variety's* reviewer was more pleased with it than the other two. "...it holds a strong story with several definite punches and, moreover, offers several legitimate excuses to show a few flapper and sheik petting parties and gin contests in full swing." The reviewer added, "...it is intelligently handled and made interesting."[9]

It should be noted that a pre-release showing of *Wine of Youth* took place in late July in New York. *Sinners in Silk* did not get its first showing until late August. This would seem to indicate that *Wine of Youth* was filmed first. However, official release dates state that *Sinners in Silk* was the earlier release on September 1 with *Wine of Youth* following two weeks later on Sept. 15.

In viewing *Wine of Youth*, what is particularly interesting for the Virginia Lee Corbin fan is the transition she has made since the Fox Kiddie Feature days. It is unfortunate that there are eight films between *Babes in the Woods* and *Wine of Youth that* are unavailable for viewing. The six-year-old in *The Babes in the Woods* has happily changed from a little girl to a very pretty young lady in this most recent film, though just 12 years old when it was made, but as will be seen in her upcoming films, Virginia was usually cast as older than her actual age. It's also interesting that a year or two was always trimmed off her age during the Fox days. Keep in mind her scene in the car with Bobby Agnew included a rather lengthy, somewhat passionate kiss. While Virginia was only 12 at the time, Agnew was 24 years old! So it goes in the movies!

Virginia was freelancing with no studio contract to give her that kind of security, but, to her credit as a performer, she was working steadily. Certainly, the contract with Fisher Productions had turned out to be a disaster, but working for Metro-Goldwyn-Mayer in 1924 on a per picture basis was better for her career than being under contract to a second-rate studio. In addition, 1924 was continuing to be a good year for her with another picture for a major studio, a notable cast, and a first-rate director.

15. A Former Child Star Grows Up

*J*ames Cruze was at the top of his game in 1924. With the huge success of *The Covered Wagon* the previous year, films with his name underneath "directed by" were almost guaranteed box office. He had been at the helm of seven features since *The Covered Wagon*, and he was still highly revered among silent film directors.

In the first half of 1924, he was given the task of bringing *Mother O'Day* to the screen, a very popular melodramatic tale first published in *McCall's Magazine*. *Mother O'Day* was never considered to be the title. Instead, *The Café of Fallen Angels* was chosen as a more intriguing one. It was later changed to *The City That Never Sleeps*, the title under which it was eventually released. Some sources list two separate movies with the titles *The Café of Fallen Angels* and *The City That Never Sleeps*. This is obviously a mistake, as there never was a film released under the title *The Café of Fallen Angels*.

With this film, Virginia was beginning to be recognized more as a "star," not simply one of the cast members. In announcing the film as early as June, a *Los Angeles Times* article headlined "Virginia L. Corbin Given Lasky Role" singled her out among the cast. It notes that she signed with Paramount on June 11, 1924, to do the picture. "Cruze is enthusiastic over his find. Miss Corbin's friends, by the same token, are enthusiastic over her good fortune in being placed under Cruze's direction. His wide and sympathetic knowledge of human nature, coupled with his ability to fathom the depths of human hearts is expected to give the screen a new and glorious personality in Virginia Lee Corbin grown up."[1]

And it was only right that Virginia should be receiving such notice in the press since she portrays one of the two central characters in this film. The other is Louise Dresser who is her mother. The story begins in 1905 on the Bowery where Mother O'Day and her husband run the Café of Fallen Angels, a saloon. When the husband is killed in a fight one night at the saloon, Mother O'Day decides this is no place to raise her two-year-old daughter, Molly. She is brought up in the society home of Mrs. Kendall, ignorant of her parents' identity or where the money comes from to support her. Time passes to present day (1924, that is), and she has become a snobbish flapper who frequents the former saloon, now a cabaret, that her real mother owns. It is there she meets Mark Roth (played by Ricardo Cortez). Mother O'Day knows Roth is a crook and, with the aid of a reporter, sets out to expose him to Molly. As the story ends, she is saved from Roth and is reunited with her mother. How unfortunate that, again, another of Virginia's films is assumed to be lost.

The City That Never Sleeps was released September 28, making it the third film to hit the theaters that month with Virginia among the cast, and, as noted earlier, she was receiving more of the star treatment in publications and getting good reviews. "Virginia Lee Corbin is delightful as Molly. She seems like a delicate miniature, too exquisite to be touched, and you'll like her in spite of the anguish she causes her mother,"[2] one reviewer said. The following review is a bit cryptic indicating someone made a misstep in setting type, but the point is still to be understood. Repeated here as it appeared in print, it says, "Virginia Lee Corbin, just grown out of pinafores, in this picture shows decided personality as ingénue. She is one of the child prodigies of the screen who has to forge ahead in a promising weathered the gangly, awkward age career."[3]

Virginia's ability to cry real tears on demand continued to serve her well as an ingénue. "'That's the finest thing I ever saw,' exclaimed James Cruze referring to Virginia Lee Corbin ... grown up into glorious blonde young womanhood.... Miss Corbin, without any external aid like music, soft lights, or sympathetic conversation, had wept real tears. She was facing Louise Dresser who plays the part of her mother in the story...."

In *The City That Never Sleeps* (1924), Louise Dresser is Mother O'Day and runs the Café of Fallen Angels. At an early age, she arranges for her daughter, Molly (Virginia), to be brought up in a society home. Molly becomes a snobbish flapper who, ignorant of her mother's identity, snubs her when they meet.

But suddenly, a climax of the story brings a shooting affray and instantly recalls the moment of her babyhood when her own father was slain—and she recognizes her mother."[4]

Moving Picture World gave her a positive review as well. "[She] gives a good performance of the unsympathetic role of the unappreciative and snippy flapper daughter."[5]

It is equally interesting to see how some reviews not only don't agree, they take a completely opposite stance. *Movie Weekly*, for example, complimented the cast "with the exception of Virginia Lee Corbin who presented as annoying an ingénue as it has been our luck to see."[6]

Nevertheless, the role of Molly in this movie may have been her best role since the Fox days in terms of establishing her stardom—and she was only 13 years old at the time!

The remainder of the year continued to be good to Virginia. Although she wasn't enjoying a contract, she was still working steadily, although moving about a bit from studio to studio.

This lobby card shows Molly (Virginia) with Mark Roth (Ricardo Cortez), a suave crook from whom she must be saved in *The City That Never Sleeps* (1924). Most reviews were complimentary of Virginia's performance, although one referred to her as an "annoying ingénue."

Moving next to the F.B.O. (Film Booking Offices) studio in a film produced by Mrs. Wallace Reid (Dorothy Davenport), Virginia was given another plum role in *Broken Laws*. Since the death of her husband, Wallace Reid, from drug addiction the previous year, Davenport set out to make socially conscious films with some relevance to issues of the day. Her first and most famous was *Human Wreckage* that she made in 1923, which brought to the screen the dangers of drug addiction. *Broken Laws* was her second effort that warned of the dangers of overindulgence in raising children.

The story, written by Adela Rogers St. Johns, concerns a mother (Mrs. Reid) who overindulges her eight-year-old son, Bobby, and never spanks him. At 16, she buys Bobby (now played by Arthur Rankin) a car. When he and his flapper girlfriend (Virginia) are out one night, he runs into a wagon and kills an old woman. Bobby is convicted of manslaughter, and his mother begs the judge to let her serve his term since it was her overindulgence that led to the disaster. In the end, it all was a dream, Bobby is still eight years old, and the mother changes her parenting tactics drastically giving the boy a good spanking.

Filming for the movie began sometime in late September or early October. It was

Virginia plays Arthur Rankin's girlfriend in *Broken Laws* (1924). At 16 years old, he and Virginia are out in his new car one night when he runs into a wagon and kills an old woman. The film, produced by Mrs. Wallace Reid and intended to be a lesson in overindulgence for parents, was received well by critics.

announced in early September that Percy Marmont had been selected to replace Ramsey Wallace as Richard Heath, Virginia's father in the story.

The New York Times liked it calling it "a thoroughly sincere effort with a strong lesson for overindulgent mothers. It is produced with earnestness and restraint; the scenario writers, the director and the players having all contributed their part in making it a successful photoplay."[7] *Harrison's Reports* said it was "a wonderful production ... it keeps a tight grip on the spectator's attention all the way through."[8] Other than referring to "the players," Virginia was not singled out in available reviews for recognition—somewhat of a letdown after all the favorable comments about her work in *The City That Never Sleeps*. An unrestored nitrate print of *Broken Laws* exists in the Cinémathèque Royale (Brussels).

The Chorus Lady was released November 23 and provided one of the few starring vehicles for Margaret Livingston. Although a very popular star, she was more often relegated to supporting roles, many of them in "bad girl" or "other woman" parts. She made approximately 50 films during the silent era, but her most famous role was that of The Woman from the City who beguiles George O'Brien away from wife Janet Gaynor in F.W. Murnau's *Sunrise* (1927).

The Chorus Lady was directed by Ralph Ince for Regal Pictures, a minor, short-lived studio, and distributed by PDC (Producers Distributing Corporation). Livingston is Patricia O'Brien, the chorus lady of the title, and Virginia is her younger sister, Nora. Alan Roscoe is Dan Mallory, Patricia's fiancé. Philo McCullough, in one of his typical villainous roles, is Crawford. Dan races horses, but when his prize horse is blinded in a fire, the wedding is postponed. Returning to New York, Patricia and Nora find work in the *Follies*. Dan eventually races his horse, wins $20,000, and goes to New York to finally marry Patricia. Unfortunately, he finds her in the apartment of Crawford. Things are settled, though, when Dan learns that Patricia had gone there to rescue little sister Nora from the villain. (In the next chapter, when *Headlines* [1925] is discussed, there will be seen a coincidentally similar plot line.)

The story, written by James Forbes, goes back quite a few years. It was a successful stage play starring Rose Stahl, and the Jesse Lasky Company made a film of it in 1914 starring Cleo Ridgely.

In one review, the 1924 version was described as "an entertaining drama with a lot of amusing comedy and a generous sprinkling of heart interest." The same reviewer said Virginia was "attractive as the silly younger sister."[9] Another called it "an excellent drama. There are situations in it that move one deeply."[10] In contrast, *Variety* blasted the film saying it "must be ranked as one of the most poorly acted, insipidly directed and generally all-around exasperating films in some time." What must have really stung for Virginia was the last sentence of the review. "Margaret Livingston in the title role seemed intermittently colorless and ridiculous. The remainder of the cast contains few names of any box office worth."[11] Ouch!

What a shame viewers can't judge for themselves today, as this too is assumed to be another lost film.

Although both *Broken Laws* and *The Chorus Lady* have official release dates in November 1924, reviews did not appear in major publications until in January 1925. It is known that the historic Mission Theater in San Diego, CA, opened its doors Novem-

The Chorus Lady (1924) starred Margaret Livingston (left) as a chorus girl and Virginia (on the telephone) as her sister. The movie received fairly good reviews, and one reviewer said Virginia was "attractive as the silly younger sister." The caption for the photograph says, "The girls listen in while Pat O'Brien (Margaret Livingston) and her sister, Nora (Virginia Lee Corbin) are 'dated up' for an after-the-show party."

ber 26, 1924, with a showing of *The Chorus Lady*, and advertisements for screenings around the country can be found in newspapers throughout December. It apparently opened in theaters in New York in January, which is the basis for reviews in publications such as *Variety* and *The New York Times*, of course. However, why there was an apparent delay in New York screenings of the two movies is unknown.

A November 1 article in *Moving Picture World* talked about the more than 30 productions that are planned by William D. Russell's five companies. One of these productions was *Battling Bunyan* under his Crown Productions company. The adolescent, freckle-faced Wesley Barry was announced as the star, and among those listed to be in support of Barry was Virginia Lee Corbin. *Battling Bunyan* is available for viewing today, but, unfortunately, Virginia is not in it.

Human interest type tidbits and photos continued to appear about Virginia in newspapers and fan magazines. Publications noted how the former "baby" star had grown up. One fan magazine devoted a full page to her with one photo from her Fox days and another recent photo with the title "A Baby Star Who Has Become a Leading Lady." Another magazine said, "How the real 'baby stars' are growing up, to be sure! Virginia L. Corbin, who used to play baby roles in Fox pictures, is a young lady now. You can't say that she has lengthened her dresses and done up her hair, because young ladies don't do those things any more.... While Virginia was growing up—she is sixteen now, I believe—she left pictures for a while and went into vaudeville."[12] In an article entitled "Growing Up with the Stars," she was featured with other former child stars such as Wesley Barry, Ben Alexander, Madge Evans and Lila Lee.

In a photo from *The City That Never Sleeps*, she and Ricardo Cortez were one of seven couples pictured under the title "Offering a Few Lessons in the Art of Make-Up." The magazine caption said, "When he says he'll die if he can't kiss you, coldly offer your hand." At least one fan magazine acknowledged that she was still school age and pointed out that she did "attend school" every day, regardless of which studio she was working for.

In April, the Hollywood Women's Club hosted an Easter fashion pageant. A leap-year wedding was the closing feature of the revue, and bridesmaids included Alberta Vaughn, Lucille Rickson, Clara Bow, Mary McAlister and Virginia.

A beautiful photo of Virginia in a parade shows her sitting in the back seat of a large automobile, dressed very prettily with hat and fur stole about her shoulders. On the side of the automobile a sign reads, "Virginia Lee Corbin. Greater Movie Season. Paramount Pictures." With her is an attractive, unidentified woman, and two women

The Greater Movie Season in Los Angeles was a month-long series of activities during August that highlighted the work of the movie industry. Virginia appeared in the parade August 1, 1924, accompanied by her mother in the front passenger seat and two unidentified ladies. The appearance helped promote her role in *The City That Never Sleeps* (1924) as indicated by the sign on the side of the car noting her association with Paramount Pictures.

are in the front seat—the passenger seat being occupied by Mrs. Corbin. Paramount is indicated on the sign because, at the time of the parade, Virginia was working on *The City That Never Sleeps.*

The Greater Movie Season was a month-long series of activities during August in Los Angeles to highlight the work of the movie industry. The month was kicked off with a parade through the streets of the city on August 1. In 1924, the parade began at 11 a.m. at 18th and Hill streets and proceeded through the business district to Hope and Ninth Streets where it disbanded. Reports noted that there would be more than 200 cars carrying stars through the streets for fans to see.

One syndicated newspaper article highlighted Virginia and Marguerite Snow as two former stars who are making a "comeback" after being absent from the screen for a few years. The article also served to highlight her upcoming appearance in *The City That Never Sleeps.*

In October, she attended the opening of Paulais, described as a "confectaurant." Several Hollywood notables attended the opening with Bryant Washburn behind the counter serving ice cream while Syd Chaplin "sampled the soup" dressed in chef's attire. The Paulais Venetian Players entertained on their stringed instruments from a balcony, and Robert's Golden State Band played jazz on the rooftop. Film stars who assisted with the reception of guests were Carmelita Geraghty, Lillian Rich, Dorothy Dwan, Virginia Gilbert, Clara Bow, Priscilla Dean, and Virginia, among others.

An article that appeared in August could have been another subtle omen for the problems that Virginia and her mother would have in the not-too-distant future. In a column of "ramblings" entitled "Strutting Oolong Lane with Lounge Lizzie" by Grace Kingsley in *The Los Angeles Times*, she said, "'Well, I haven't seen that child since her mamma used to spank her when she let some other child take the scene away from her!' I exclaimed. 'My isn't she pretty!' 'Oh, well, her mamma spanks her once in a while yet,' explained Lizzie. 'But Virginia Lee says she isn't going to be spanked ever again!' 'I understand Mrs. Corbin would just love a cigarette once in awhile, but Virginia Lee won't let her have it. She says it will reflect on herself.'"[13]

Although trivial on the surface, this may be seen as an indication that, at 13 years old, Virginia was beginning to assert her independence, something she would want more of as she grew older.

Also, as well as her mother was apparently managing her career, there were occasional indications that finances were not being handled wisely. The reader may remember the incident recounted in Chapter 6 in which an agent claimed he had not been paid his commission for securing a Fox contract for Virginia. Now Virginia and her mother were dealing with legal troubles once again in 1924, troubles that actually began back to 1922 when a suit was filed in Los Angeles Superior Court by H.B. Martin against "Virginia Corbin" for $470. The suit alleged payment had not been completed for one light blue satin curtain, one sateen interior setting of three pieces with 30 pictures, two black curtains and one three-fold screen. These items were purchased and used by Virginia and her mother for her vaudeville performances. Interestingly, a tidbit in *The Los Angeles Times* from September mentioned Virginia's vaudeville career as being "one of the most decorative and elaborately staged," mentioning specifically "baby blue satin curtains and the like."[14]

It's not clear who H.B. Martin is because the complaint claimed that on December 9, 1921, the items were purchased from Eugene Cox of Chicago for $620. A down payment of $150 was paid at the time, but the balance was never satisfied. The bill was paid when the Sheriff sold a 1923 Jordan Sedan at auction for $1,400 in August 1924. However, the suit was not finalized until March 1925—apparently it was learned after the sale that the automobile belonged to Mrs. John Miehle. Mrs. Miehle was Virginia's sister, Ruth, who had married real estate agent John Miehle July 8, 1924. Ruth was 18, and Miehle was 22 years old. Ruth, however, did not challenge the sale of the automobile, and the matter finally came to an end after almost three years. Such a situation as this does not give the appearance that Virginia's earnings—which had been significant to this point—were being managed very well by her mother.

Even though a record of this complaint exists in the Los Angeles courthouse, the issue luckily dodged the press back in 1924. However, there was plenty of press coverage that year of what must have been the biggest disappointment of Virginia's entire career.

16. The Elusive Peter Pan

"'*Call for Peter Pan*.... Calling Peter Pan!' chant Paramount's page boys, seeking James Barrie's figment of the older Pan for the biggest picture role in years, crying up and down the streets of Hollywood. 'Not in, sir.... Doesn't answer,' they have thus far reported to Jesse Lasky, who for three years has held picture rights to the Barrie play and who is about to begin the much discussed production.... Who can play the role of Peter qualities—the spiritual elan, the droll whimsy, the elfin grace, the petite and all but sexless body, the magic to conjure fairies from the heart of grownups and children?"[1]

For months Hollywood—as well the rest of the country—had been abuzz concerning who would play one of the most coveted roles ever on the silver screen. Names of possible stars to fill the much-desired portrayal included Jackie Coogan, May McAvoy, Betty Compson, Bessie Love, Colleen Moore, Mary Philbin, Marilyn Miller, Viola Dana, Madge Bellamy, Gareth Hughes—and even Mary Pickford or Lillian Gish, among many others! Both men and women were possible candidates for the role. Although Peter Pan is a boy in the play, the name most associated with the character was Maude Adams who had portrayed the part on stage so successfully for years and who, just recently, had decided to retire from the production. It was she who had set the precedent for a female to portray the boy who refused to grow up.

More than one star aggressively campaigned for the role—some of them already at the top of stardom. And, of course, rumors persisted which not only gave the newspaper fodder for publication, but didn't hurt with advance publicity for the movie, either. For example, one article speculated, "Although Gloria Swanson recently went to London ostensibly for a vacation, the rumor persists that she went to see if she couldn't persuade Sir James [Barrie] to let her play Peter. That makes it rather hard for May McAvoy, Colleen Moore, Madge Bellamy and the others who have been favorably considered for the role, as they are too busy out in Hollywood to skip over and argue with Sir James. It wouldn't surprise me at all if some obscure young person would get the role—Virginia Lee Corbin, for instance."[2]

The July 20 article was very astute in its prediction of the choice for Peter, but then again, that would be easy since the announcement for the star who would play Peter had been made about three weeks earlier.

"Virginia Lee Corbin Selected From Long List for Role in *Peter Pan* of J.M. Barrie" the headline proclaimed. "At last it is decided. Virginia lee Corbin will have the title role in the movie version of J.M. Barrie's *Peter Pan*. The photoplay will be exhibited simultaneously in more than 50 cities Christmas week." It went on to say, "The announcement that Virginia, who is only 14 [she was actually 13] would have the part for which a score of stars including Mary Pickford and Jackie Coogan have been considered, was a surprise to movieland. 'Our Mary' refused to play it for business reasons, we hear. Jackie has his own company and isn't free to work for Famous Players who will produce the Barrie play with Herbert Brenon directing. Jacqueline Logan, May McAvoy, Gloria Swanson, Lila Lee, Viola Dana were all considered for the part. It was suggested from England that Charlie Chaplin do it. It is indicated that Barrie himself had a part in the selection of the miss who will create on the screen the part made world famous by Maude Adams and heretofore played only by mature women. An envoy of the producers went to England with photographs of prospective Peters."[3] At least twice the announcement was made in *The Los Angeles Times*, once on June 28 and again on July 6, with the same announcement appearing in newspapers around the country from late June through July.

One can only imagine the excitement felt by Virginia and her mother. This would certainly be the most important role of her career and ensure her elevation to the upper echelon of Hollywood stardom. As late as August 16, articles appeared in newspapers confirming Virginia's selection, even noting that she had "signed up the other day as leading lady."

However, barely a month after the announcement was made, doubts arose regarding the certainty of her selection. A July 29 article opined, "It was virtually settled that little Virginia Lee Corbin was to play the part of 'Peter Pan,' but we are all upset again. A 'Peter' has been chosen, we hear, but her name has not been divulged."[4]

What transpired that caused her to lose the role is not known. It is a fact that Barrie himself had a part in the selection, which could have very well been a stipulation of the rights given to Lasky for its filming. Barrie reportedly viewed tests of 100 candidates for the part. Then, what must have been devastating news for Virginia came at the end of August. The headline proclaimed, "It's Settled, Absolutely, Positively That She'll Be Movie Peter Pan." The article announced, "The most important movie part of the year has been given to a 17-year-old girl heretofore practically unknown in the movies. She is Betty Bronson who will create the beloved role of 'Peter Pan' for the films. It is settled positively and finally."[5] The year and a half search and speculation was over. Hollywood's most sought after role that was in Virginia's hands was snatched away. The only thing to do now was press on.

Of course, *Peter Pan* is available for viewing today, and Betty Bronson certainly makes a lovely Peter. The film was beautifully done, and did ensure her star status for the remainder of the silent era.

Working for Banner Productions wasn't the same as Paramount, but it was work, and Virginia did have a major role in her next picture—*The Three Keys* (sometimes *The 3 Keys*) with Edith Roberts, Jack Mulhall and Gaston Glass. *The Three Keys* was directed by Edward Le Saint. Although he had not directed Virginia before, he was working at Fox during the time Virginia was appearing with Tom Mix. Banner may have been a minor company—they had been around since 1915—but her three costars were established, respected thespians. She was in good company, and the melodramatic story would give her something different than the flapper roles she had been in recently.

Fortunately, a copy of *The Three Keys* survives in the Library of Congress and can be viewed today. The story, originally written in 1909, is a little muddled with all that is going on, but basically it's all about George Lathrop (Glass) who has squandered his inheritance. Just when George is about to commit suicide, his fiancée, Alice Trevor (Miss Du Pont), calls him and says her father needs to see him urgently. Trevor is about to go bankrupt and asks George to lend him $100,000, reminding him that he bailed his father out ten years ago. George says he'll get the money.

George goes to the club, distraught, not wanting to admit he's squandered his inheritance, and trying to figure out what to do. Friend Jack Millington (Mulhall) comes over and says he needs George's help. His father is out of the country, and there is a crisis concerning his father's

A portrait of a very pretty, and quickly maturing, Virginia that was taken around the time *The Three Keys* (1925) was being filmed. In the movie, she is Miss DuPont's younger sister and is in love with her sister's fiancé, George, played by Gaston Glass. However, her affections turn quickly to George's best friend, Jack, played by Jack Mulhall, who reciprocates with the same affection.

stocks. Jack must go to Chicago, so he gives George the keys to his father's safe deposit boxes and some instructions. Seeing a way to help his father's friend, George removes securities from the safe deposit box and gives them to Trevor as if they were his to begin with. It turns out, Jack's father is Trevor's Wall Street enemy, and their fight over stock control is exactly what has Trevor in financial trouble. These stocks will save the day for Trevor.

Jack overhears George and Trevor talking and realizes what his friend has done. However, rather than being angry, he sets out to save George from prison. He goes to Trevor and loans him the money he needs so he can get the stocks back. His timing is a bit off, though, because his father has returned, discovered the stocks missing, and has accused Trevor of theft. In the end, Jack has to create an elaborate scheme where he fakes serious injuries from a car crash to buy the time he needs to clear things up. In the end, he claims he had the stocks all the time, and no one is the wiser regarding George's misdeeds.

There are two side stories in the film. One involves Edith Roberts' role as Clarita, a Spanish girl. Her involvement with George is a mystery to the end, but it results in a broken engagement with Alice. At the end of the story, we find that Clarita is George's ward, and Trevor is actually her father. With Alice out of the way, George and Clarita are married.

The second side story is Virginia's part in the movie. She is Alice's younger sister and is in love with George. She has some charming parts in the film where she flirts with George, and appearing unannounced at his apartment one day discovers Clarita there. She is angry, but she does not give away his secret. Later, when George introduces her to Jack, she falls in love with him and he with her. Virginia does a superb job of being upset and distraught when she's at Jack's bedside as he's all bandaged up from head to toe as a result of the faked auto accident. A cute scene ends the movie when she is called back in the room to see Jack out of bed, fully dressed and smiling. She is at first angry and petulant, turning her back on him, but he comes up behind her, puts his arms around her, and that charming smile appears on her face. They embrace and kiss.

Gaston Glass is obviously the star of the film, but, other than Jack Mulhall, Virginia's part is equally as important as the other central figures and with essentially as much screen time. Some reviews refer to the "flapper" role, but, in the true sense of what a flapper was in the twenties, this is not the way Virginia's part was written. She's simply the younger sister who's in love with her big sister's fiancé—a role that would fit any decade, not just the twenties.

Even though Banner was not a major studio, and *The Three Keys* certainly wasn't a high budget film with major stars, *The Los Angeles Times* devoted a full page to it accompanied by large photos. The review was kind, but basically was on target when it said, "Action in the story at times is fast, and at others, drags." It said Glass and Mulhall "meet the requirements for such a play," and added that Charles Clary (Trevor), Miss Dupont and Virginia were "interesting."[6]

The Three Keys was released January 1, 1925. The filming was completed about the third week of November with the studio sending out enthusiastic reports that, after an unannounced preview at a neighborhood house in Los Angeles, the movie received a "veritable ovation." The studio reported that they expected *The Three Keys* to be "an exceptional attraction by reason of the unusually high calibre of the cast engaged and the intensive dramatic possibilities of the story."[7] The box office success of the film is not known, but the absence of reviews in such major publications as *Variety, Harrison's Reports* and *Photoplay* magazine lead one to believe it wasn't the success executives were predicting.

Virginia would make five more feature films in 1925, staying busy at various studios and, at 13 years old, playing leading lady roles—quite an accomplishment for the young star.

The next film to follow *The Three Keys* was *The Cloud Rider*, another action/stunt picture starring real life stunt pilot and flying ace Al Wilson. *The Cloud Rider*, released February 15, was the second and last film from Wilson's Van Pelt-Wilson Production Company. His partner, Ernest Van Pelt, was an actor, producer and director whose acting career began back in the mid-teens.

The film does survive today in the Cineteca Italiana Archive in Milano, Italy. The story is credited to Al Wilson and concerns an aviator, Bruce Torrence (Wilson), who is also a Secret Service agent. He must bring to justice Juan Lascelles (Harry Von Meter) who owns a fleet of planes that are used to smuggle drugs. The movie gave ample opportunity for airplane stunts. For example, his girlfriend, Zella (Helen Ferguson), is in a plane that has been tampered with by the villain, and a wheel comes off in mid-air. With a wheel strapped to his back, Wilson transfers from one plane to another in mid-air and replaces the wheel. In another stunt, he jumps from a low flying plane into the water where the villain's plane has crashed and captures him while at the same time saving the girl.

By the way, the story has somewhat of a twist to the romance. Torrence is actually in love with Zella Wingate, but later, finding her in the arms of the villain, he realizes he is in love with her younger sister, Blythe Wingate, played by Virginia.

Distributor F.B.O. promoted the picture telling exhibitors, "Talk about your society dramas and sex stories, and your hundred and one styles of features picture to get 'em

in—but not one of 'em will stack up alongside of *The Cloud Rider* for sheer power of thrills."[8] One theater owner commented, "Here is one that will make their eyes stick out. Thrills that are thrills…. Audience appeal ninety percent."[9] *Moving Picture World* noted that "it is filled with action and melodrama and holds the interest at all times," in spite of an "obvious and not altogether plausible story." The review did, at least, mention Virginia saying she "is attractive as the girl."[10]

One article said Virginia was in the air for two weeks and "learned more about aerial photography than a wartime correspondent." It added, "All of the love scenes in the picture were shot just under the roof of the sky, oftentimes above the clouds. Kisses were grabbed hit-and-miss fashion while traveling at a speed of 100 miles an hour."[11]

Up next was a little more serious drama, but still for a minor studio, Belban Productions. Nothing is known about this company except that *Lilies of the Streets* seems to have been their one and only production.

Virginia comforts Al Wilson after a crash in *The Cloud Rider* (1925). Wilson's pictures were basically a showcase for his aerial stunts, and *The Cloud Rider* received good reviews for the thrills it provided audiences. One article noted that during the filming, Virginia was in the air for two weeks and "learned more about aerial photography than a wartime correspondent."

Released May 3, it co-starred Wheeler Oakman, who had been a staple in films since 1912. For silent film fans today, his two most well-known appearances are probably as Dr. Jack Martin, the love interest for Jackie Coogan's sister in *Peck's Bad Boy* (1921), and as Dapper Bill Ballard, fellow crook with Priscilla Dean (his real life wife) in *Outside the Law* (1920) with Lon Chaney.

Johnnie Walker played a lawyer and Virginia's love interest in the film. He was 26 at the time to Virginia's 13 years of age. Although not a star of the first magnitude, Walker had been around since 1915, starred occasionally in a minor picture, but was in constant demand with nearly 100 film appearances between 1915 and 1939. He would once again work with Virginia three years later in the very enjoyable *Bare Knees* (1928).

Lilies of the Streets was a very heavy melodrama in which Virginia was cast as Judith Lee, a wild flapper who gets in an automobile accident. Delmore (Oakman) finds her, takes her to a dancehall where his accomplice and mistress, Margy (Irma Harrison), is located. He gets into a fight, is arrested, and both Judith and Margy end up in jail. Margy convinces the young girl to plead guilty to the charges, but what Judith doesn't

Lilies of the Streets was a heavy drama in which Judith (Virginia) unwittingly pleads guilty to prostitution and later claims she committed a murder that she didn't. Margy (Irma Harrison, left) is the bad girl responsible for most of Judith's problems. The story was based on the actual experiences of New York's first policewoman, Mary E. Hamilton, who also appeared in the film.

realize is that she is pleading guilty to prostitution. Once out of jail, Delmore uses Judith's record to blackmail her mother. Delmore is mysteriously killed, and Judith thinks her mother did it, so she confesses to the crime. Thanks to the work of a young lawyer, John Harding (Walker), and a police matron, Margy confesses to the crime, and Judith gives her heart to Harding.

Pre-publicity for the film said it was made with the cooperation of Mary E. Hamilton, New York's first policewoman, and based on actual experiences Hamilton had with a wayward young girl. It was written by Elizabeth J. Monroe, described as a young woman who had been prominently associated with Hamilton in police work.

Unfortunately, this is believed to be a lost film, so stills, reviews and synopses found in trade publications are all there is to tell present day audiences about this film. Making this seem a much greater loss is the fact that it received good reviews such as the one in *Harrison's Reports* that said, "There is fast action, good suspense, well handled direction, and satisfactory performances on the part of the featured players, especially Miss Corbin."[12] An advertisement issued to newspapers for the picture is a good example of the florid—and somewhat suggestive—language used by publicists. "A daring expose of the refinement of vice—beautiful sin painted in its lurid colors! A vivid light thrown on the purple shadows that lure young women to ruin—," and then, almost comically, adds, "let nothing prevent your enjoyment of this superb entertainment!"

This was a significant film for Virginia. *Harrison's Reports* was not the only publication heaping praise on the young actress' performance. One newspaper said, "We do not hesitate to prophecy [sic] that you are going to be more than delighted with the performances of Virginia Lee Corbin and Johnny [sic] Walker."[13] Although ads for the film named Walker, along with Virginia, as the co-stars, Virginia had the more significant and, essentially, lead role. The picture's success depended on her, and, apparently, she pulled it off beautifully.

It is fortunate that her next film, *Headlines*, survives in the Library of Congress. It has Dutch intertitles and is listed as missing one reel. However, upon viewing the film, it appears it may not be an entire reel that has been lost. The film was 5,600 feet in length. The LOC's print runs a bit fast, but, when slowed down to an appropriate speed, the time for the film is over 60 minutes. With a reel of film (1,000 feet) typically running anywhere from 11 to 15 minutes, this is very appropriate for 5,600 feet. And, the timing doesn't indicate an entire reel is missing. The missing portion is obvious and does leave one wondering what happened at that point, but it does not keep the viewer from making sense of the story and enjoying the film as a whole.

Virginia left Los Angeles for New York May 10 to begin filming there, and the movie was released July 16. Alice Joyce is the star of the film and portrays Phyllis Dale, a newspaper reporter. Virginia is her daughter, Bobby, who has been away at school. This has allowed Phyllis to keep her daughter a secret, not wanting to admit to boyfriend Larry (Malcolm McGregor) that she is old enough to have an older teenage daughter. When Bobby comes home, Phyllis passes her off as her sister. Larry comes to visit, Bobby flirts with him, and his attentions are misconstrued by Bobby as interest. Phyllis' coworker, Roger (Elliott Nugent) enters the picture too, and he is very interested in Bobby.

All of them go out to celebrate Phyllis' birthday at a nightclub, and Bobby exchanges glances with Donald Austin (Harry T. Morey), an older man. He comes over, asks her to dance, and then joins all of them at the table. Before leaving, he invites them to a tea party at his house the next day. Phyllis, knowing Austen's shady past from her newspaper work, doesn't like the man or her daughter having anything to do with him. Also in the nightclub is his wife, who is seeking grounds for a divorce. She is with her lawyer trying to "get something on" Austen.

Things get complicated when Bobby tells her mother that Larry is just the type of man she'd like to marry. This is actually a cute scene because Bobby is in her nightgown, curlers in her hair, and a mudpack all over her face. Suddenly Larry comes in and Bobby has to hide inside the curtain while Phyllis tries to keep Larry's back to Bobby. Bobby's anxiety, surreptitious signals and facial expressions to her mother are very comical.

As indicated by this one-sheet, Alice Joyce was the star of *Headlines* (1925), supported by Malcolm McGregor (shown here), Virginia, and Elliott Nugent. McGregor was the love interest for Joyce, while Virginia ended up with Nugent at the end of the film. It was a familiar story of a mother taking the rap for her daughter who was alone with a married man, ruining the mother's reputation but saving her daughter's.

After Bobby escapes, Phyllis admits to him that Bobby is her daughter, which does not matter to Larry. When Bobby returns, Larry tells her, "Listen, I know all about you! Your mother just told me everything." Bobby replies, "But you love me just the same, don't you, Larry?" which elicits a concerned look from her mother.

Bobby sneaks away to Austen's tea party, but there are other people there, and the "tea" is alcohol. As is typical in this case, everyone is apparently intoxicated acting crazy and silly, so when the alcohol is spilled on both Bobby and Austen, it is suggested they have to get a shower. Of course, the crowd of partygoers follows to watch. The suggestiveness of this to the viewer is a bit titillating, but we soon learn they are showering with all their clothes on.

Back at Phyllis' house, she and Larry learn from a comment made by the maid that Bobby must have gone to Austen's, and Larry arrives just as they are coming out of the shower. Realizing this is not good for Bobby's reputation, he gets her out of there. What he doesn't realize is that Bobby, as she is leaving, whispers to Austen that she'd like to come back the next day.

The next day, Roger comes over

and proposes to Bobby thinking the things she said while flirting with him the previous evening meant she was serious about marriage (Bobby's running line in the film with all of the men is "Why don't you marry me?") When she says he must have misunderstood her, he leaves angrily.

Larry comes over to invite Phyllis to go swimming at an indoor pool, but she said she is not feeling well, and suggests he take Bobby. This is the portion that is missing from the film. It shows Bobby and Larry in the pool tossing a ball around. The scene then switches back to Phyllis at a typewriter. The next scene shift shows Bobby leaving the pool fully clothed. Since we see Larry searching for her around the dressing rooms, it is obvious she sneaked out to go to Austen's. As noted, whatever is missing does not seem to be critical to the story and shouldn't constitute a full reel.

Austen calls Phyllis' house and thinks it's Bobby who has answered the phone. He tells her she is late for their tête-à-tête. Phyllis, pretending to be Bobby, says she'll be there momentarily.

Bobby and Austen are sitting on the sofa having a drink when Phyllis comes to his apartment. Bobby hides. Although Austen says he's alone, Phyllis sees two glasses and a smoldering cigarette on the table. Looking in the bedroom, Phyllis sees Bobby hiding in the shower but, hearing voices in the living room, returns without Bobby knowing she's been discovered. Austen's wife has arrived and tells Phyllis, "You'll pay in court for this!" Bobby goes to the bedroom door and hears the commotion, realizing her mother has given up her reputation to save her. Larry arrives, but Phyllis refuses to talk, so he assumes the worst—she has been there to see Austen.

Larry leaves, mother and daughter embrace crying, and all seems lost. Phyllis has resigned herself to having her reputation slurred and losing Larry, but Bobby has not given up hope and runs to Roger for help. Together they catch Larry as he is about to sail out of the country, Phyllis and Larry are reunited, marry, and leave on the cruise while Roger and Bobby return home to be married.

The highlight of the film truly is Virginia. She is animated—but not overly so—and portrays the perfect flapper who is charming and fun-loving, but not obnoxious. For example, when she comes home from school and lights up a cigarette in front of her mother, Phyllis asks rhetorically, "So you're smoking now?" and Bobby answers, "Certainly I smoke ... don't I have a modern education?" Phyllis, as the ever-patient mother, simply says, "You're growing up a little too fast. I think I'll have to make some changes."

And, as many of the flapper movies went in the twenties, when Bobby finally gets in over her head and actually causes her mother to be hurt, she realizes the error of her ways and settles down.

It's a fun movie, and all of the cast—Virginia, Alice Joyce, Malcolm McGregor, Elliott Nugent and Harry T. Morey as Austen—do a splendid job.

Harrison's Reports gave Virginia her best review since the Fox Kiddie pictures days and attributed the appeal of the picture to her. "The value of this picture lies chiefly in the characterization of Virginia Lee Corbin. Miss Corbin, as the little flapper, can certainly show cards and spades to other flapper-actresses. Her acting can be described by no other word than by 'wonderful.'"[14] *Moving Picture World* said, "Virginia Lee Corbin is excellent as the jazz baby daughter."[15]

In *Headlines* (1925), Virginia was once again cast as a flapper, Bobby, seen in this still with her mother, Phyllis (Alice Joyce). When Bobby returns home from boarding school, she smokes and boasts of the "modern education" she has received. Bobby's "modern" ways get her into trouble when she sneaks around to see a married man whose separated wife is trying to uncover a scandal that she can use in divorce court.

Interestingly, reports back in March noted that St. Regis was to begin filming *Headlines* soon, but the entire cast had not been selected. Virginia was named, but Anita Stewart was named for the part of Phyllis and Louis John Bartels for Austen. Two months later, Alice Joyce was being named as the lead without any explanation for the replacement of Stewart. Bartels' name was still in the pot at this time. Filming had actually begun before Morey replaced Bartels. Filming was taking place in March, a report noted that, for the newspaper room scenes, the cast was using the editorial rooms of the *New York World* located in the World Building on New York's famous newspaper street, Park Row. Filming took place one Sunday evening from midnight until 10 the next morning.

The ending has Virginia, Joyce, McGregor and Nugent on the ship—the scene actually being filmed on the *Leviathan* in New York harbor. By the time they finished, the ship had pulled away from the dock and headed out. However, the *Leviathan*'s Capt. Hartley helped out by hailing a tugboat that took the actors and actresses back to land.

A columnist for *Picture Play* magazine, referred to as "Fanny the Fan," said the pool scene for *Headlines* was filmed in the pool on the *Leviathan*. According to the columnist, Malcolm McGregor "got up a swimming party" since the setup for filming was going to take some time. A "crowd" consisting of Virginia, Alice Joyce and Alice's brother were present, but no one actually went swimming because the water was the color of coffee." The writer pointed out that Virginia had to go in the water "because she was in the scene—and it completely ruined a lovely pale-blue bathing suit. Virginia showed a lot of nerve doing those scenes. She can't swim at all, and yet she jumped right in, trusting to Providence or Malcolm McGregor to save her."[16]

As another side note, the band on the stage in the nightclub scene is reported to be the Club Kentucky Band, making it Duke Ellington's first appearance on the screen. The band is only seen from a distance in the existing print, so it's impossible to make a positive identification. At least one article notes that Johnny Hudgins and Miss Nobody From Nowhere were engaged for the film. Johnny Hudgins was an African-American vaudeville performer. It is not known who Miss Nobody From Nowhere was—and neither of them seems to appear in the film as it survives today.

The Handsome Brute is also assumed to be a lost film. Listed as a "police drama" and running only 4,779 feet, or approximately 52–60 minutes, it was released December 1 but did not seem to get wide distribution immediately. It was produced by Columbia Pictures, still considered to be a Poverty Row studio in the twenties—but it was destined to be the only Poverty Row production company to rise and become a major Hollywood studio in the sound era. It started in 1922 as. C.B.C. Film Sales Corporation—the initials representing the three founders: Harry Cohn, Joe Brandt and Jack Cohn. By the time *The Handsome Brute* was released, the name Columbia had only been around less than two years with Columbia Pictures being incorporated January 10, 1924.

So work for a major studio continued to elude Virginia in 1925, but, in the meantime, she was being noticed and getting good reviews for the films she was making—many with major stars. Unfortunately, *The Handsome Brute* wasn't one of those. The star of the film, William Fairbanks (no relation to Douglas Fairbanks), had been making action pictures and westerns since 1916 and continued to do so until 1928 with about 65 films to his credit. He never made a major motion picture, and *The Handsome Brute* was standard fare for him and what the public expected from the virile, energetic star.

The Handsome Brute is a police drama, or melodrama, in which Larry (Fairbanks) loses his job with the police department through "misadventure and bad luck." On his own, he goes after the Brady gang and soon exposes an international detective—who was actually called in to help with the case—as the mastermind. The love interest arises following a heist of a jewelry story owned by Nelly's (Virginia) father.

Advertisements called it "a thrilling melodrama—a wonderful love story—and a corking comedy—all in one!" As expected, the ads made it sound better than it probably was. *The Film Daily* called it an "average action picture. Not much in the story to brag about, but where they want action pictures, this will do nicely." For Virginia, it simply said her job in the film was "to believe in the hero," adding, "She hasn't much else to do."[17] Unfortunately, this picture did not give her the opportunity to shine as some of her most recent films had.

Looking at publications from the time, Columbia did not do a very good job of promoting this film. As a matter of fact, there is a dearth of information on it other than references to the film as one of several being released by Columbia. Major trade

William Fairbanks was a popular action star during the silent era, typically at his best in westerns. *The Handsome Brute* (1925) is a melodrama that casts him as a policeman who loses his job through no fault of his own but still ends up capturing a notorious gang of thieves. Virginia is his love interest, shown with Fairbanks in this one-sheet after he has captured a couple of the bad guys.

publications such as *Harrison's Reports*, *Variety*, and *Moving Picture World* did not review it. It also appears none of the major fan magazines gave it notice such as *Photoplay*, *Motion Picture Magazine* or *Picture Play Magazine*. Why? These publications certainly gave space to minor studios and films of equally low stature.

Newspapers usually ran short articles relating to a film's showing in their communities. Most attempted to garner interest in the film because of Virginia's presence—not Fairbanks—a credit to her drawing power at the box office. And, of course, virtually all reference how the former child star has grown up. For example, one said, "Do you remember that little blond girl who used to delight you a few years ago? Virginia Lee Corbin was her name, and whatever she wore off the screen, thousands of mothers all over the country duplicated for their daughters. She was a child star of enormous popularity then, she is fast becoming a star of international fame now. Virginia has graduated, and she appears on the screen today a young lady with all the childish, wistful charm and all the golden-haired beauty that first made her pack the theaters in which her pictures played." It goes on to say, "Directors say that Miss Corbin has that natural talent that is so rare, but that screen audiences understand and appreciate."[18]

Virginia had an entirely different co-star for her last picture of the year, *North*

The Canadian Northwest adventure *North Star* (1925) was a change for Virginia. This time she wasn't cast as a flapper, but, instead, the sister of a man who has been framed for a murder he didn't commit. She and leading man Ken Maynard, shown here in a non-western role, must save the day with the help of the star of the movie—Strongheart. Though he was not as popular as Rin Tin Tin, Strongheart's movies were good action films and well attended.

Star—none other than Strongheart, the Dog, one of Rin Tin Tin's biggest contenders for the crown of the screen's most popular animal star.

Again, this is presumed to be a lost film, but, newspaper accounts indicate the movie was played widely and received well, one account saying large advanced sale of tickets had required the theatre to run the movie continuously from 1 until 11 p.m. Of course, Rin Tin Tin was the king of them all, but there were other German shepherds on the screen such as Leader, Fearless, Wolfheart and Ranger. All were popular, particularly with young boys, and, although none would ever make anyone's Top Ten list, they, nonetheless, made for good box office. Unlike the other dog stars, Rin Tin Tin's popularity led him into a successful career in the sound era and on TV. However, Strongheart, who was found overseas just like Rin Tin Tin, beat the more popular dog star to the movie screens by one year.

Virginia's love interest in *North Star* is none other than cowboy star Ken Maynard, rather early in his career. Maynard arrived in films in 1923 in some uncredited roles and at least one short. By 1924, his horsemanship got him the role of Paul Revere in Marion Davies' *Janice Meredith*, and in some westerns, including *$50,000 Reward*, which has been available on home video for a number of years.

Another interesting tidbit is the appearance of Clark Gable as Archie West, only the third time Gable had appeared in a feature film. Unfortunately, since this is a lost film, it is unclear what part the character of Archie West had in the plot.

The main players were Virginia as Marcia Gale, and Harold Austin as her brother, Wilbur. Maynard was Noel Blake, a reporter, and one of the silent era's most unlikeable bad buys, Stuart Holmes was Robbins—and, of course, Strongheart as North Star.

The plot has Wilbur, who comes from a wealthy family, fighting a guy who had been annoying his sister. When the guy falls and hits his head against a marble column, Wilbur thinks he has killed him. Wilbur takes off for Canada not realizing North Star is hiding in the back seat of his car. To cover his tracks, Wilbur pushes his car over a cliff into a lake. Hurt but still alive, two tramps find North Star. However, when Blake comes across them abusing the dog, he tries to rescue the dog, but is laid low by a crowbar. However, North Star chases the tramps off and stays with Blake until he regains consciousness. In the meantime, Marcia enlists the aid of a "false friend," Robbins, to help her. Once in Canada, Robbins gets an Indian guide and goes to find Wilbur himself—seeing an opportunity for blackmail. Blake and Marcia meet at the doctor's office where Blake is being attended to, and he helps her find her brother. When they arrive, Wilbur and Robbins are fighting, but Robbins gets his just desserts when North Star drives him off a cliff. All is resolved when Wilbur learns that he did not kill the man.

The movie was based on a novel by Rufus King, the author being described as a "popular writer of animal stories." The novel had reportedly received "wide circulation." The story included most of the typical elements one would find in a Strongheart movie (or one of the other dog stars). As one newspaper said, "It's a usual Strongheart plot. The dog's master is 'framed' and becomes a fugitive. Through Strongheart, the truth comes out…. He assists at a romance between a young newspaper man and his master's pretty sister—Virginia Lee Corbin and how she's grown!—the villain is sent willy nilly to investigate the hereafter—and what will you?"[19]

Studio publicity promoted it as "a story of love and loyalty pitted against hate and avarice in the great North Woods." The exhibitors' publication *Harrison's Reports* said it was "a fairly good picture" and "should prove moderately entertaining to the bulk of picturegoers."[20]

With six pictures to her credit being released by the end of this year, 1925 had proved to be both busy and successful for Virginia on the screen. One writer observed, "This year has marked the curtain for Virginia as the 'girly-girly' ingénue. She is now playing grown-up leads and has become definitely established as a featured leading woman. Her ambition during 1926 is to become a grown-up star in her own right, just as she was a child star a few years ago."[21]

Curiously, it was reported initially in December that Virginia would be taking a brief vacation before starting to work on her next picture at the beginning of 1926. Then, at the end of the month, newspapers reported, "Virginia Lee Corbin, youthful motion picture actress, has suffered a nervous breakdown which will necessitate her absence from the films for several weeks, her mother announced here today."[22]

Nothing more was mentioned about the nervous breakdown. As noted before, Mrs. Corbin loved nothing more than to run to the press with anything that would garner publicity. The nervous breakdown, or at least a need for a rest from the busy year, was apparently the case. Virginia had one film released in January 1926 (filmed before the nervous breakdown announcement), but did not have another released until September, although it is certain she was back at work filming by late January. The last film she made in 1925 was Raymond Griffith's comedy *Hands Up!* which required a two-week stay in the Mojave Desert—so that could have possibly contributed to her condition. If the stress of work and, possibly, increasingly strained relationship with her mother were causing problems for her, it's certain that two lawsuits in 1925 must also have affected her health.

17. Court, WAMPAS and Good Reviews

The complaint said that "Virginia Corbin" (mother?) signed a promissory note June 7, 1920, for $459.59. The defendant (Virginia) paid $50 on the note twice later that month but never paid the balance. This case had been pending in the courts since 1924 when, in a sworn affidavit, the defense said that the debt had been paid. And, when trial was set for December 22, 1925, the defendant failed to appear. The complaint names "Virginia Corbin" as the defendant—and one would assume that would be Mrs. Corbin—but subsequent documents name "Virginia Lee Corbin"—making it difficult to believe that an adolescent could be held liable for the debt—or legally incurred it to begin with. At the December hearing, the attorney for Virginia noted that he was unable to get in touch with his client, and a letter he sent was returned undelivered. Another trial was set for February.

Once again, the Corbins failed to appear, so the judge ruled in favor of the plaintiff. This case dragged out at least until 1928 when an "affidavit for examination of judgment debtor" said the judgment was, at that time, "wholly unsatisfied." Interestingly, in 1927, even the Sheriff could not collect on the debt noting, "I have been unable to find any property belonging to the within named defendants or either of them not exempt from execution in Los Angeles County out of which to make the money judgment."[1]

The verbiage in the complaint notes that the plaintiff, Earl A. Maginnis, Inc., is "a corporation organized and existing under and by virtue of the laws of the State of California"—in actuality, he was a car dealer. The complaint also states that the promissory note included eight percent per annum in interest. When and if the debt was ever satisfied is not known.

In October 1925, the newspaper headline read, "Driving Ability Basis of Suit," and the lead continued, "Asserted criticism of his auto driving resulted yesterday in the filing of a suit for $38,900 by Ralph R. Magee against Virginia Lee Corbin, film actress, Mrs. Corbin, the Strongheart Production Company, and Howard Estabrook, its manager."[2]

Magee claimed he had been making $350 a week providing transportation services between studios and locations. August 14, during the filming of *North Star*, he was

116

engaged to take Virginia and her mother to Arrowhead Springs (or Arrowhead Lake), about 60–70 miles from the F.B.O. Studios where the movie was being filmed. The area would obviously double as the Canadian North Woods for *North Star*. Fifteen miles before arriving at Arrowhead, he said Mrs. Corbin and Virginia left the car at a place called Patton Station. Mrs. Corbin then sent a message to Estabrook asking for another car and driver asserting that Magee was either intoxicated or "on dope." Magee claimed the contents of the message were circulated in film circles damaging his reputation and his business.

Over 50 pages of documents still exist in the Los Angeles Courthouse detailing this case. According to the seven-page complaint for slander and damages, Magee said that during the trip "Mrs. Corbin conducted herself in a highly excitable and irritable way, and gave sundry directions and orders to plaintiff to drive his machine in such a way as to suit her and without regard to the wishes and discretion of Plaintiff [Magee] or the safety and comfort of the other occupants."[3] He said when Mrs. Corbin and Virginia left the car, he remained at the station for an hour to an hour and a half ready to take them on to the location and left only when their replacement transportation arrived.

November 12, Howard Estabrook and First Strongheart Unit, Inc., made a motion in court that "all of said complaint" be struck "upon ground that the same is sham." It further went into two pages of individual challenges to parts of the complaint on the grounds of either being "irrelevant" or "redundant." Later, a "demurer to complaint" was filed by Estabrook stating that Magee's complaint "does not state facts sufficient to constitute a cause for motion." Virginia and her mother also filed a "demurer to complaint."

Based on the amendments to the complaint, a second "demurer to complaint" was filed in December. The demurer was denied, and Estabrook's lawyers came back with a vengeance denying a variety of claims by Magee—that Mrs. Corbin was in any way (including agent) employed by the studio, that Magee was employed in any way by F.B.O., that he made $350 a week as claimed, that he had any kind of a "reputation" with studios, that Estabrook himself had engaged him to drive Virginia and her mother, that any such reputation damaging communication as he claimed was ever made or circulated, etc. This answer to charges admitted that Mrs. Corbin and Virginia requested a second vehicle because they were about to proceed up a steep, more dangerous road and were afraid to ride in the automobile with Magee driving as he had been—adding that the communication that was made was made in good faith and without malice on the part of the Corbins.

The attorneys went a step further and noted that on the journey, Magee had purchased a large quantity of "a certain compound, drug or substance" which contained acetanilide. Acetanilide was akin to aspirin in the 1920s and was used for fever, headaches, etc. The complaint said the drug, in large quantities, can serve as a "circulatory and nerve depressant interfering with the mental and physical efficiency of the user."[4]

This is the last of the case that appears in the courthouse records leaving one to believe that it was most likely settled out of court.

Stardom means that everything about Virginia's life was fodder for the press, so it's no surprise that even negative publicity about her sister, Ruth, would also make the papers. Just as the Magee court case was picking up speed in August, an article appeared noting that the investigation into the disappearance of "Mrs. Ruth Miehle, adopted sister of Virginia Lee Corbin, film actress, was closed yesterday after Detective Captain McMahon reported she evidently had gone to see her husband, from whom she has been separated."[5] Ruth, 18, and Miehle, 22, a real estate salesman, had married just the year before. Ruth was not employed. Once again, it was Mrs. Corbin who reported this to police—claiming a kidnapping. Mrs. Corbin's love affair with sensational publicity was continuing.

It is unfortunate that Virginia had found herself in court for the fourth time in her brief 14 years and had to deal with her mother's impetuous and irresponsible dealings with the police and press—but, fortunately, none of these incidents seem to have hurt her professional career—at least it appears so on the surface.

At the beginning of 1925, Virginia was announced as one of the 13 young starlets included in this year's selection of WAMPAS Baby Stars. The designation was so named because it was initiated by the Western Associated Motion Pictures Advertisers (WAMPAS), an organization founded in 1920 by professional publicists in the motion picture industry.

The organization hit upon the idea of identifying 13 young women who had star power, providing them with an enormous amount of publicity and sponsoring a huge and prestigious event for their coming out. The first was in 1922 and included such stars as Colleen Moore, Patsy Ruth Miller, Bessie Love, Lois Wilson and Lila Lee. Note that many who were selected had already been on the screen for several years, but in the eyes of the WAMPAS organizers, they had not yet achieved "major stardom." Of course, many were virtual unknowns at the time they were selected. Some went on to become stars and others faded into obscurity.

The designation was very prestigious and created excitement akin to being selected for an Academy Award in those pre–Academy Award days. As author Roy Liebman pointed out in his book on the WAMPAS Baby Stars, "Whether their designation as WAMPAS Baby Stars speeded the initial group of actresses toward fame, or their subsequent fame gave cachet to the designation, to be named a Baby Star soon became an extremely prestigious honor. It was to prove a major plum for the studios as well as for young women."[6]

As soon as January turned the corner, newspapers were publishing the names of the lucky 13, and Virginia was among them—along with Madeline Hurlock, Betty Arlen, Evelyn Pierce, Anne Cornwall, Olive Borden, Joan Meredith, Violet Avon, Dorothy Revier, Mary Brian, Natalie Joyce, Lola Todd and Duane Thompson. Then, approximately two weeks later, Ena Gregory's name was appearing on the list, and Virginia's name was absent. What happened? No publicity seems to address the change. Did she drop out? Did WAMPAS drop her for some reason? It is known that WAMPAS included two alternates in the event someone dropped out. Whatever the reason, this must have been a disappointing way for Virginia to start the new year.

Even though she missed out on some major publicity with her exit from the WAMPAS Baby Stars, movie magazines continued to keep her before the public. A very adult looking photo of Virginia with her hair pulled back and holding a bunch of flowers appears on the May 19, 1925, cover of *Moving Picture Stories*. The same magazine took note of her in its "Guess Who's in Town" column. "Virginia Lee Corbin is getting to be as bad as Alice Joyce—one day she's here—and the next day—she's back on the Coast,"[7] noting that she went East to film both *Lilies of the Streets* and then later for *Headlines*.

While in New York, she attended the opening of a new theater showing *The Sporting Venus* as their first film. Virginia was not the only star there. Others included Ronald Colman, Blanche Sweet, Barbara LaMarr, Dorothy Mackaill, and Mae Busch.

Motion Picture Magazine ran an article in July that dispelled that earth-shaking question of why blondes could not "vamp" as well as brunettes. At any rate, Virginia was quoted as saying, "I suppose I'm too young to really know anything about vamping—tho [sic] they call me the baby vamp—but I think I'm learning. Anyway, I'm not too young to have ideas on the subject." Considering the verbiage used in her comments, one must assume her responses were written for her. She continued, "A blonde is equally attractive in the glaring light of a summer sun, where she reflects its brightness, or in the chill of clouded winter where she creates a brightness and warmth in contrast to the day. But a brunette must have an established setting. She is suggestive of heavily shaded lights, Russian perfume and whispers."[8]

It was even publicized that Virginia had been made a very flattering offer by Florenz Ziegfeld to enact a leading role in the Follies of 1926. It went on to say that she hoped to accept the engagement after she concluded picture work for which she was contracted. Unfortunately, being a part of the Ziegfeld Follies never transpired.

By the end of the year, *Motion Picture Magazine*'s popularity poll had Virginia 16th on the list (Gloria Swanson was number one), an amazing feat for the teenage actress. To beat out stars such as Constance Talmadge, Marie Prevost, Lillian Gish, May McAvoy, Alice Terry and Barbara La Marr was certainly something to be proud of and an indication of her large fan base.

The loss of the WAMPAS Baby Star designation did not slow Virginia down, either. By the end of January she was attending the Theatre Owners Chamber of Commerce annual frolic in the ballroom of the Astor Hotel. The prestigious affair had 2,500 persons in attendance, and Thomas Meighan and Bebe Daniels were crowned the "king and queen" of the event. Virginia was among several celebrities who were introduced by the "overseer of entertainment" at the event.

Two weeks later, she attended the F.B.O. Thrift Club's first annual dance at the Hotel Martinique in Los Angeles. In September, she was judging a dance contest for the Order of DeMolay's Hollywood Chapter. Later that month, actress Dorothy DeVore hosted a dinner party at the Montmartre with guests Vera Reynolds, Harry Edwards, Syd Chaplin, Virginia Lee Corbin and Robert Ellis. It would seem unlikely that Mrs. Corbin would have attended such an event with her daughter, which leads one to question whether Virginia was on a date and with whom?

A lengthy article by writer Mona Gardner appeared in newspapers in September. Referring to her as a "girl of 16" (she actually would not turn 14 until December), the article noted that Virginia had returned to the screen "at first playing high school flappers for a few months and now passing as a perfectly proper leading lady of twenty-one or two." When questioned how it feels for such a young girl to "make love or to be made love to, or be married to some of the young Don Juans of the screen," she answered, "Yes, I love pictures. I'm only happy when I'm playing in them. Gosh, don't you love chocolate cake?" The reporter had to press her subject to focus and answer the question at hand. Virginia finally responded, "It's easy. You really don't have to think about it. Just as easy as pie. The director tells you what to do and you do it. Oh, it's easy. Doesn't that boy dance divinely?"[9]

As Virginia began to mature into her mid-teens, her interest in the typical things of a teenager was rising. She loved going out, attending parties, and dancing. This same article confirms that Virginia was a very good dancer too. "Incidentally, one of the most interesting things about Virginia is the way she can handle those feet of hers. Dance? Why, anything! Cartwheels, somersaults, and all the other acrobatic feats. She clogs! She soft-shoes! She does every variety of jazz steps, including a very mean Charleston."[10]

The article also gave insight into Virginia's desire for the types of roles she wants to play. "When I was playing the parts a long time ago, they used to all stand about and

Raymond Griffith's hilarious Civil War comedy *Hands Up!* (1926) predated Buster Keaton's *The General* (1927) by approximately one year, although Keaton's film is considered to be the superior comedy by historians and fans today. Griffith's dilemma at the end of the film is that he loves two girls—Virginia (shown on this lobby card with Griffith) and Marion Nixon. When he meets Brigham Young, he hits upon an idea, and the film closes with the three of them riding off in a stagecoach—a sign on the back announcing "To Salt Lake City."

try to make me cry. Gee, it was the hardest thing I ever did. I don't like to cry; it's no fun at all. No, I don't mean that, you know what I mean. What's the use of weeping all around? I want to do comedy. I just love it. Don't you adore Connie Talmadge, and, gee, aren't her plays a scream? That's what I want to do. But, of course, I'm not old enough to yet. But I will be soon. Everyone says I look 20 on the screen."[11]

Virginia's wish to play comedy came about with her next picture—*Hands Up!* starring Raymond Griffith. Filmed during the latter part of 1925, the production was released January 11, 1926, and was a big hit. Fortunately, this film does exist today and has been distributed widely on the home video market.

Back at a major studio, Famous Players-Lasky-Paramount, and under the direction of a top-notch director in Clarence Badger, Virginia was working with one of the silent era's finest comedians in Raymond Griffith. Pre-dating Buster Keaton's *The General* by a year, this comedy, set during the Civil War, opens with President Lincoln emphasizing the need for new finance in order to win the war. He sends a messenger out west to a mine owner who will supply the Union with gold. As a Confederate spy, Griffith must outwit Lincoln's messenger for the gold, and, in the process, free himself after being captured by Indians and escape from a hanging. During these shenanigans, he encounters the mine owner's (comically played by Mack Swain) two beautiful daughters—Marian Nixon and Virginia Lee Corbin. Both girls serve as the love interest and both fall in love with Griffith. The big joke at the end has Griffith's character about to be hung (for a second time in the movie) for bigamy as both girls claim to be his wife. The solution is seen when he encounters Mormon leader Brigham Young and he rides off in a stagecoach with the girls and a sign on the back stating, "To Salt Lake City."

One of Griffith's biggest fans was movie critic Walter Kerr. In his landmark 1975 book *The Silent Clowns*, he said *Hands Up!* "contains some work that is daring—for its period, certainly—and some that is masterfully delicate, the work of an inventive, unaggressive, amiably, iconoclastic intelligence."[12] *A-Z of Silent Film Comedy* author Glenn Mitchell said it "is regarded as one of the top handful of feature-length silent comedies."[13] Choosing to disagree, *American Film Criticism* authors/editors Stanley Kauffman and Bruce Hentsell said the film was "deservedly forgotten."[14]

What matters most, though, is the way it was received in 1926, and, from reviews, it must have been a hit for Paramount. *Harrison's Reports* called it "An excellent Civil War burlesque."[15] *Variety* went on to say that was "a succession of screams and laughter." More importantly, *Variety* gave a good review for Virginia favoring her over Nixon. "Marian Nixon and Virginia Lee Corbin play the leads opposite the star with the former girl featured in the program and billing, although Miss Corbin registered better as to appearance and work before the camera."[16]

While the film was making its rounds, the wisdom of the 14-year-old Virginia was shared with the press regarding screen lovers. "The first thing most women ask a screen actress who plays love scenes [is] whether it isn't dangerous to be too sincere in acting such a character lest one falls in love with such a man. It is hard to make them believe that screen love-making is not real ... in order to secure the best effects in love scenes on the screen, I prefer to be just good friends with the man who plays my lover. The love she feels for a man is a thing secret to her, and she will not—cannot—exhibit it to a gaping crowd. As a result, the love scenes are not convincing, the acting is wooden.

But, on the other hand, if the actress dislikes the actor, if she has had a little spat with him, it will be evident in the acting and the scenes ruined.... The best performance is given when they are just friends."[17] For Virginia, at least, this shouldn't have been difficult for her co-stars since the love interest in each of her films to this point had been 15 years or more her senior.

Her next film, thankfully, has survived the ravages of time. A print of *The Whole Town's Talking* is housed at the UCLA archive, a part of the David Packard Collection. Unfortunately, it has never been released to the home video market, and stipulations on the print held at UCLA state no copies may be made. The interested silent movie fan, though, may view the movie on a TV-size screen at the archive.

The sad part is this frantic comedy deserves to be seen on a big screen with an audience and with appropriate musical accompaniment. The story is by the husband-wife team of John Emerson and Anita Loos. In the 'teens, Loos by herself or in collaboration with Emerson, wrote several of Douglas Fairbanks' and Constance Talmadge's hit comedies. They also wrote at least one of Marion Davies' comedies. Loos is best

When Southern spy Raymond Griffith is assigned to get Mack Swain's gold mine before the Union can secure it, he meets and falls in love with the mine owner's two daughters— Marian Nixon (left) and Virginia. When one reviewer pointed out that Nixon and Virginia played the two female leads, he added, "Miss Corbin registered better as to appearance and work before the camera."

remembered for *Gentlemen Prefer Blondes,* her most famous hit. However, about the same time she wrote that classic comedy, Emerson had become disenchanted with the movie industry and decided he wanted make the move to theater. Their first play was *The Whole Town's Talking* and opened at the Bijou Theater in New York on August 29, 1923. It received good reviews and was a moderate success for the couple. Universal decided three years later that it would make a good screen comedy, and they were right.

A cast could not have been more appropriately selected for this delightful comedy, which deserves a more detailed synopsis since it is a "hostage" film in an archive. Otis Harlan is the rotund father, George Simmons, who has just come in at 3 a.m. from an evening with gold digger Sadie Wise, played by the beautiful, but not too well-known Margaret Quimby. Waiting for him is his wife, the even more rotund Trixie Friganza. When a purse is brought to the door by the taxi man, daughter Ethel (Virginia) rescues Dad by claiming it is hers—but only after Dad secretly promises her a fur coat.

Thanks to Otis Harlan's nervous wheedling, making up lies on the spur of the moment and obvious fear of his much larger wife, this sequence provides plenty of laughs early

The Whole Town's Talking **(1926) is one of those movies in which everyone is perfect for the part. In addition to Virginia, the cast includes Otis Harlan, Trixie Friganza and Dolores Del Rio, all shown here with Virginia. Edward Everett Horton was actually the star of the movie. Also in the cast were Malcolm Waite as Dolores Del Rio's jealous husband, Margaret Quimby as Harlan's gold digger acquaintance, and Hayden Stevenson as Horton's wartime buddy.**

on in the picture. It picks up speed even more when war veteran Chester Binney, played perfectly by Edward Everett Horton with his shyness and goofy, pursed-lip smile, returns. Chester thinks he can't have any excitement because the army doctor told him it was dangerous with the silver plate in his head. What Chester doesn't realize is that it was his buddy who has the silver plate. The doctor got the two men's hospital records mixed up.

Chester was Simmons' secretary before the war, and Simmons wants to make him a partner in the business—but more importantly, have he and Ethel married—mainly because Chester is due to inherit a lot of money. At Chester's welcome home party, Ethel is interested, but after a few minutes on the bench in the garden, she finds Chester lacking in the love-making department and very boring. When Father finds out, he decides to do something about it.

At the office the next day, he and Chester get a photo of a movie star, Rita Renault, played by the very beautiful Dolores Del Rio. On the back, Simmons inscribes a message reminiscing about a fictitious rendezvous in Hollywood and signing Rita's name to it. The plan is to have Ethel find it and think Chester is a real ladies' man.

The plan works, and all seems to be going along fine until Mrs. Simmons overhears Chester and Simmons talking about returning Sadie's purse. Simmons convinces her they were talking about a Mr. Shields by showing her the name and hotel in his address book. After she leaves, Simmons tells Chester he has no idea who Mr. Shields is—he just pulled the name off the register in the local hotel when he was there recently—but Mrs. Simmons wants to confirm there is such a person and calls the hotel. The clerk tells her that, yes, there is a Mr. Shields, but he is out at the moment. She leaves a message that her husband had a meeting with him but would be detained.

Rita Renault had arrived in town to appear at a local theater. She and her very jealous husband, played menacingly by the muscular Malcolm Waite, are staying at the local hotel. His name is Jack Shields. He gets the message and is puzzled. When he asks the clerk about the message and who George Simmons is, one of Ethel's admirers, Donald Montallen (Robert Ober) just happens to be there and overhears the conversation. Figuring something is awry, he mischievously offers to take Shields to the Simmons home.

From this point on, the movie could stand on its own along with the screwball comedies of the 1930s. When Chester is confronted by Shields, Chester denies that he knows his wife. However, Rita, wanting to teach her jealous husband a lesson, runs up to Chester and begins kissing him all over his face. Simmons is wide-eyed with disbelief, Mrs. Simmons is shocked, and Ethel is disgusted with Chester. Montallen is amused at the beating he thinks Chester is about to get from Rita's husband.

The climax of the movie is a lengthy and hilarious chase through the house with all of the characters converging on the Simmons home. Shields tries to get his hands on Chester, Rita and Mrs. Simmons have it out, Simmons tries to keep Sadie hidden from his wife, and a policeman is called in. The melee comes to an end when Shields, Chester and Montallen end up in a darkened room, and Montallen is mistakenly attacked by Shields with both ending up knocked out on the floor. The policeman finally comes into the room along with everyone else, and he turns out to be Chester's army buddy—the one who really has a silver plate in his head. When Chester learns he does not have to avoid excitement, he knocks Shields to the floor twice as he tries, groggily, to get up. The film fades with Chester telling Ethel, "and now I've got something to say to you, young lady!" and takes her out into the garden.

Most sources give a release date for *The Whole Town's Talking* as December 26, but the *American Film Institute Catalog* states that the release was August 14 or December 26. August 14 is the obvious date since the film was playing all over the country during the latter part of August, and on through September, October and November. Announcements about the cast selection appeared in early January 1926, and the film went into production in late January. Apparently filming did not wrap up until early April, a rather long production schedule compared to most of Virginia's other movies. However, it was a Universal-Jewel—the "Jewel" indicating a little higher level of production than the run-of-the-mill feature.

Publicity departments typically release tidbits while filming is taking place for a movie to generate interest and anticipation. One stated, "A few days ago, Virginia Lee Corbin stood quiet while a bee walked over her bare shoulder. A scene in *The Whole*

This lobby card shows a terrified Chester (Edward Everett Horton) trying to explain why he said he had a rendezvous with Jack Shield's (Malcolm Waite) movie star wife. The hilarious ending to the movie has the jealous husband chasing Chester through the house but also includes everyone else in the melee—the movie star, the daughter (Virginia), her mother, her father, a golddigger her father is trying to keep secret, a jealous suitor, and a policeman.

Town's Talking was being made. The bee kept on walking. It did not sit down or back up or push. But it gave a tense moment to the actress. There was only one retake. They do strange things in pictures!"[18] The scene was one in which Chester and Ethel are on a bench in the garden. He hands her a rose that unknowingly has a bee in it. When Ethel puts the rose against her neck, the bee crawls out and along her back. The bee eventually ends up stinging Chester on his rear.

Harrison's Reports said it was "a fairly good farce comedy" and added, "Virginia Lee Corbin is good as the heroine."[19] One newspaper writer noted that "Horton has never been more wistful nor Miss Corbin ever more delightful."[20] *Photoplay* magazine was kind noting that it was "An interesting version … of the stage play" and telling readers to "go see it if you want a good laugh."[21] *Film Daily* called it a "good comedy of a nonsensical order."[22]

And there were articles in publications that featured Virginia and promoted the movie at the same time. Writing in *Picture Play* magazine, Dorothy Manners expressed how "startled" she was to see Virginia drive up in a Cunningham limousine, pick her up and take her to the Athletic Club for lunch where Virginia was a member. (Note: Cunningham automobiles were produced until 1936 and designed for luxury, elegance and high style. It was not unusual for these huge vehicles to sell for $6,000 or more in the 1920s—more than ten times the cost of a Ford and seven or eight times the cost of a Chevrolet or Buick.) She said Virginia had braces on her teeth and apologized that she was having her teeth straightened. "Virginia's press agent assisted me to the soft cushions of the car, where I sank down perfectly speechless," she said.

Manners went on to report, "Virginia was quite 'hepped' over the idea that she was to be co-featured with Edward Everett Horton in his first picture under his new contract with Universal. She was looking forward to the engagement with high glee, although she wasn't yet acquainted with the details of her role. She hoped it wouldn't be another flapper part. Although she had played dozens of them, she felt that flappers weren't quite her sort of thing. Now, in Raymond Griffith's picture, *Hands Up!*, she had worn feminine, flouncy things and had acted the way one does act when one wears feminine, flouncy things. That had been much nicer. But no matter what you played, contracts were a thrill in themselves." Virginia then commented on how humorous she found it when "Mr. Z" said he didn't believe Virginia could sign her name while they were signing contracts for the picture at Universal. She noted that her mother still had to sign the contracts for her. "'I felt so silly signing my name like a little kid, on a separate piece of paper,' Virginia laughed."[23]

Filming *The Whole Town's Talking* at Universal apparently also brought back memories for some of the workers there. An article in *The Los Angeles Times* said, "All of the old-timers at the Universal studios 'remember when' Virginia played in her first picture…. Remembering Virginia Lee as a child of a few short years ago, the old-timers are amazed at seeing her as a grown-up leading woman. They know that she is still a youngster in years, but admit that she looks and acts as a 'young lady' years her senior."[24]

Moving from Universal to Warner Bros., Virginia's next film, *The Honeymoon Express*, another one that has not survived today, went into production in May and was released to theaters September 2. Based on a play entitled *The Door Mat*, the story con-

After the wild climactic chase in *The Whole Town's Talking* (1926), the normally shy Chester (Everett Edward Horton) very firmly tells Ethel (Virginia), "—and now I've got something to say to you, young lady!" and takes her out into the garden. Otis Harlan and Trixie Friganza are Ethel's parents, expressing shock at Chester's newfound confidence.

cerns a wealthy family that falls apart when the father (Willard Louis) gets entangled with a gold digger (Jane Winton). The self-sacrificing wife (Irene Rich) has "lost her beauty due to her devotion to her household" and a family who treat her as merely background to their own selfish pursuits. The son, Lance (Harold Goodwin) allows drinking to affect his work as an architect. Becky (Virginia) is a reckless flapper who gets involved with a "vitiated" millionaire. Daughter Jean (Helene Costello) is the only sensible one, repulsed by the lifestyle of father, brother and sister. It is Jean who goes with her mother when the mother finally decides there is no hope and must leave. She gets a job as an interior decorator and regains her youthful beauty. Son Lance comes to his senses and returns to his mother. Becky finds herself in trouble and runs to mother to save her, finally realizing the error of her ways. The father finally tries to reunite with his wife, but she refuses, and the story ends with the mother and children happily reunited minus Dad.

The mother is, of course, the door mat of the title. She is described as graying and wearing "frumpy" house dresses for her work around the home. Although this is a lost film, one scene that was recounted in the press gives an idea of the drama offered in this story. In a beauty parlor, a beautician asks the gold digger, "But what about his wife, dearie?" "Her?" responded the gold digger. "I should worry about her. She was hostess at the Boston Tea Party." And, the wife, who is in the next booth, overhears this.

In *The Honeymoon Express* (1926), Irene Rich (center) stars as a self-sacrificing wife with a husband who gets entangled with a gold digger, a reckless flapper daughter (Virginia), and a son (Harold Goodwin, right) whose drinking affects his job. In this scene from the movie, the mother and daughter unsuccessfully try to take the alcohol away from the son.

One sad note about the film was the passing of Willard Louis on July 22, about a month and a half before the film's release. He was only 44 years old, and his death was attributed to typhoid fever and pneumonia.

The Chicago Tribune's movie critic Mae Tinee said, "The picture is unusually well cast. Virginia Lee Corbin, who, not so long ago was just a little girl playing little girl roles in the movies, is seen here as a reckless, hard-as-nails jazz baby daughter who almost breaks her neck, as well as her mother's heart, before she comes to her senses. She does some magnificent acting."[25] *Harrison's Reports* said that Virginia was "very good" as the flapper. Overall, the movie received mixed reviews. *Harrison's Reports* called it a "very good domestic drama."[26] *Variety* said it was a "sweet, sentimental picture with special interest for the women,"[27] although the reviewer felt there were weaknesses. In a very brief review, *Photoplay* magazine said, "You may like this—it all depends on your viewpoint. We'll pass."[28]

Although Virginia stood out in her flapper role in this film, her career included more than just flapper parts (as in *The Whole Town's Talking*, for example), but, then again, her age was perfect for casting as a flapper, and she was so good at it! In the opinion of one reviewer in 1926, "There's one ex-juvenile player, now a young woman, who bids fair to make a name for herself. She is Virginia Lee Corbin, and as a player of flapper roles, she's not far behind the most outstanding exponents of that type of acting. It will be interesting to watch the race between her and Clara Bow for stellar honors. Her most successful picture thus far has been *The Honeymoon Express*."[29] Of course, the outcome to that "race" is well known, but it is interesting that, at one time, Virginia would have been considered competition for the effervescent Clara Bow.

Once again finding herself with a major studio, Virginia moved over to First National for *Ladies at Play*, a comedy originally written with the title *The Desperate Woman* and ending up on the stage as *Loose Ankles*. Filmed during the summer of 1926 and released November 15, *Ladies at Play* is not a direct retelling of the play. Producers took one idea from the play and expanded upon it. *New York Times* reviewer Mordaunt Hall said, "Anybody who has seen the play would never know that the picture had been inspired by it."[30]

It is particularly unfortunate for silent movie fans that this also is a lost film, especially when one looks at the positive reviews and the descriptions of this "hilarious" comedy—not to mention the very strong cast First National assembled for the film.

Virginia was described by one critic as a "hard-as-nails jazz baby daughter who almost breaks her neck, as well as her mother's heart, before she comes to her senses" in *The Honeymoon Express* (1926). Virginia was so good at the flapper roles, another critic observed, "It will be interesting to watch the race between her and Clara Bow for stellar honors." Seen here, the defiant daughter is being cautioned about her reckless ways by her mother (Irene Rich).

At the reading of a will, two spinster aunts (Ethel Wales and Louise Fazenda) are not happy that they have been left only a dollar each, along with some knick-knacks. However, their niece, Dotty (Virginia), has been bequeathed $10,000, and Dotty's older sister, Ann (Doris Kenyon), has been bequeathed $6 million, but only on the proviso that she is married in three days to a young man approved by the aunts. Setting her sights on Gil (Lloyd Hughes), the hotel clerk, she finds that the aunts will not approve him for a husband. So Ann and Dotty plot to get Ann into a compromising situation with Gil—an endeavor that fails. As an alternative, they decide to get the aunts into a compromising situation by hiring two youths to take them out and get them drunk. Reviews noted that Wales and Fazenda were "hilarious" and were particularly good in the scene where they are in a room with the youths, intoxicated, and Ann is hiding behind a screen trying to get a photo of them, very unsuccessfully.

Variety termed it "a very nice comedy" adding that "Virginia Lee Corbin did nicely

In the wacky comedy *Ladies at Play* (1926), Ann (Doris Kenyon) is bequeathed $6 million, but only if she marries a man in three days who is approved by her aunts (Ethel Wales and Louise Fazenda). It seems the only way to get the aunts to approve a husband is for Ann to put herself in a compromising situation—hopefully with the boy she loves (Lloyd Hughes). Sister Dotty (Virginia) helps with this scheme, but the plot is ruined when an extra man, Philo McCullough (shown here with Kenyon and Virginia), shows up in the room.

as a sweetly slangy girl."[31] *Harrison's Reports* said it was "an excellent comedy entertainment. In some of the situations the spectators should roar from laughter."[32] Mordaunt Hall recounted the previous day's screening in New York. "The Hippodrome was indeed a merry place yesterday afternoon, loud laughter blurting forth every few seconds at the action of a screen comedy bearing the title of *Ladies at Play,*" adding, that the movie "is hilarious." Hall also gave special notice to Virginia. "Virginia Lee Corbin is amusing as the round-eyed, vivacious flapper."[33] *The Los Angeles Times*, in a full-page spread on the movie, singled out Virginia for honors. "Miss Corbin is excellent. Personally, I know of no better definition of flapper, or whatever is the more recent term for such flippantly, insouciant youngsters. When she seriously searches the hotel for a candidate to compromise her sister, so that gentleman will marry her and therefore insure her fortune, she proves herself a true comedienne."[34]

Virginia's contract for this film, which is still retained in the Warner Bros. Archive at the University of Southern California, was dated July 10, 1926. It doesn't state how many weeks she worked on the film, but her salary was $750 per week with a proposed start date of July 12.

The films that Virginia had the opportunity to participate in during 1926 were, as a whole, probably her best since the Fox Kiddie days in terms of quality of productions, stars with whom she had the opportunity to work, and studios. Her popularity was at its peak, and she would continue to ride that wave for awhile—but, once again, lost opportunities and personal problems would continue to be a part of her life.

18. Lost Opportunities

*V*irginia finished filming three more movies before 1926 disappeared—all near the end of the year and indicating just how quickly movies could be turned out in those days. All three were released in January 1927 giving Virginia quite a bit of exposure in a very short time.

The first of these to be released was *The Perfect Sap*, another opportunity for Virginia to enjoy making a comedy. Working for the second time for First National, publications announced in September 1926 that she had been signed for the Ray Rockett production. The contract for the film was actually signed August 15, with Virginia to receive $750 per week for her work. It gave a start date of September 6 with Virginia being on salary from the time she left Los Angeles until she returned home. The studio also agreed to pay for "first class transportation and compartment" on the train for Virginia and her mother and pay $100 per week for living expenses while she was in New York for the filming.[1] Reports in trade publications indicate it was mid–September before she left for New York and that she returned in late October after completing her work there.

As a side note, a story circulated around this time noting that Virginia was the only actress who had ever held up a train for a photograph. "It happened last week when she arrived at the Grand Central from Hollywood. Photographers asked her to step into the doorway of a train standing at the platform. A half dozen shots were made, and then a polite trainsman stepped up and inquired if Miss Corbin would mind stepping off the train as she had already delayed its starting several minutes. Of course, she stepped. 'Aren't those New York Central people perfectly wonderful!' exclaimed Miss Corbin."[2] Photos of her stepping off the train at the Dearborn station in Chicago on her way to New York were also distributed.

But, she did arrive on time in New York to join co-star Ben Lyon and other cast members—Lloyd Whitlock, Diana Kane, Byron Douglas, Christine Compton, Charles Craig, Sam Hardy, Tammany Young, and Helen Rowland. During production, the filming title was *Not Herbert*, which is the title of Howard Irving Young's play on which it is based. When *The Perfect Sap*, aka *Not Herbert*, was hitting the screens, it had just enjoyed a successful Broadway run and was touring the country.

Lyon is the wealthy Herbert Alden who has been taking a correspondence course in detective work. He decides that the only way to really learn is by experience. So he enlists the aid of his valet—who, by the way, is a former inmate—to break into a house and rob a safe. He encounters two crooks, George (Tammany Young) and Polly (Pauline Starke). All are discovered, and following a chase, they end up at Herbert's apartment. Later, though, George arranges with another crook, Tony (Lloyd Whitlock), to rob the country home of Herbert's father during a ball. Things get complicated because Tony is really Tracy Sutton, a "social lion" who is engaged to Herbert's sister, Roberta (Diane Kane), and Tracy (or Tony) thinks Herbert is a famous criminal and seeks his advice about the country home robbery. Of course, Herbert masterminds a plan to catch Tracy in the act. In the story, Virginia plays Tracy's crook accomplice, Ruth. During the events at the ball, Ruth accuses Polly of being a crook. As it turns out, Polly is actually a reporter for the local newspaper, and she unmasks Ruth as a notorious crook.

This portrait of Virginia was one of many promotional photographs sent out in connection with *The Perfect Sap* (1927). She received some unexpected publicity when she posed for photographers at the train station in New York. The reluctance of the photographers to allow her to leave held up the train, and suddenly it was "big news" that she was the only actress to hold up a train for photographs.

The movie premiered in New York January 6, 1927, and went into national release January 16.

The story sounds like another wacky comedy that would be a lot of fun to see—but, as fate would have it, this is another supposedly lost film. It got good reviews too. *Moving Picture World* was very kind saying it "offers considerable merriment and no little excitement and is real entertainment."[3] *Variety* called it a "neat bit of nonsense with a dramatic climax." Other comments in the review whet one's appetite to see the film. "The production is elaborate and supremely well done…. Herbert has fitted up a trick apartment for himself to aid in his study of the detective profession and such devices as periscopes, sinking rooms and trap doors are introduced for good comic effect." It added that "the robbery at the masked ball is a good bit of staging, and the events leading up to it, chase and capture of the crook, are well managed."[4] And *The New York Times* said it "has its quota of interest and laughs."[5] One review gave kudos to both Virginia and Whitlock, noting, "Lloyd Whitlock, as the suave, handsome man-

When the Perfect Sap made a perfect arrest.

Virginia liked doing comedy best, and *The Perfect Sap* (1927) gave her another opportunity to shine, this time as a crook's accomplice. Ben Lyon, left, plays Herbert, a young man who is taking a correspondence course in detective work. Unfortunately, he gets mixed up with crooks who plan to rob his father's country home. Virginia is pictured next to him with Herbert's valet/former crook Fletcher, played by James Craig, to her left. Lloyd Whitlock (fourth from left) is the crook. With him is Diana Kane as Herbert's sister, his fiancée. Next is Herbert's father, played by Byron Douglas, and Pauline Starke portraying one of the crooks.

about-town and crook, and Virginia Lee Corbin as a devastating little blonde gold-digger, contribute much to the picture."[6]

Another tidbit that whets one's appetite for the movie is a photo showing Virginia laid back in Lyon's arms—without the glasses that were so prominent for his character in the film—both looking seriously and intently into each other's eyes. Obviously it looks as if he is about to kiss her. The caption called it "an interesting pose." What makes it particularly curious is Virginia was not Lyon's love interest in the film—Pauline Starke was. It would be interesting to know what this scene—if it is truly a scene from the finished product—was all about.

Virginia was finally at an age (or at least she appeared to be) where reporters and columnists would conjecture about her love life. After returning to Los Angeles from her filming in New York, she was, not surprisingly, questioned on the subject. "I'm not married, engaged or even in love. I didn't see an attractive 'butter and egg man' all the time that I was in New York," she said. The same article added, "She was emphatic in her denials of a reported engagement to Lyon, rumor of which reached the Hollywood film colony ahead of her. 'Ben is a lovely boy and wonderful to work with in a picture, but he is far too attentive to Marilyn Miller to have any off-stage time for anyone else,' said Miss Corbin."[7]

As an interesting side note, *The Perfect Sap* was filmed at the old Biograph studios, and it was the last film made by First National in the East.

Another of Virginia's films that is languishing in an archive is *Driven from Home*, the second of three film releases for her in January 1927. Copies exist in the holdings of Cinémathèque Royale (Bruxelles), Archives du Film du CNC (Bois d'Arcy) and Lobster Films (Paris).

The movie was made rather quickly by Chadwick Pictures, a Poverty Row studio that operated from 1924 to 1928. *Film Daily* announced that Chadwick had signed her for the picture November 30, 1926, and then announced January 5 that filming had been completed. The official release date was January 15.

The story was written by Hal Reid, actor Wallace Reid's father, and was a popular

Although Virginia did not play Ben Lyon's love interest in *The Perfect Sap* (1927), she was questioned in an interview about her off-screen relationship with Lyon. She told the reporter, "Ben is a lovely boy and wonderful to work with in pictures, but he is far too attentive to Marilyn Miller to have any offstage time for anyone else." This was three years before Lyon's marriage to silent film star Bebe Daniels.

melodramatic play that had been around for a while. It concerned a social climbing father (Melbourne MacDowell) who wants his daughter to marry a sleazy, titled foreigner (played by Eric Mayne). Finding the idea of marriage to this guy repulsive and being in love with her father's secretary (Ray Hallor), she leaves her wealth behind and runs off with the poor secretary.

As advertisements noted, complications were many with an undersea tunnel cave-in, a Chinese hop joint (which gave opportunity for the lovely Anna May Wong to appear in this film) with a threatening and sinister Oriental (played by Sheldon Lewis), a scheming housekeeper and more troubles before the couple finally win the approval of the girl's father and happiness comes to all.

Chadwick previewed the picture at a small theater near Los Angeles and noted that the preview was a success. The studio, of course, predicted this would be their most successful picture of all.

Reviewers did not agree. *Variety* called it a "fairly good programmer." The reviewer went on to say, "There are sympathetic characters, easy to understand plot, and a bit

A candid photograph of the cast from *Driven from Home* (1927) shows Ray Hallor who was Virginia's love interest in the movie, Margaret Seddon who plays the mother, Melbourne MacDowell as the father who wants Virginia to marry a sleazy titled foreigner, an unidentified child, and Virginia. The cast also included the lovely Anna May Wong, Eric Mayne and Sheldon Lewis.

of comedy, which, though badly handled, will probably please in the spots for which this one is destined. All in all, not so good, but a long ways from being bad."[8] Green Bay, Wisconsin, must have been one of those places that *Variety* was talking about when it said the film "will probably please in the spots for which this one is destined." One reviewer there said it "offers a thorough, good time to the most exacting film fan," adding, "we enthusiastically recommend [it]." The review also complimented Virginia. "Virginia Lee Corbin ... plays the leading role with simple forcefulness. In comedy and drama, she is equally at ease, and she had ample opportunity to show her versatility in this picture."[9] *Moving Picture World* said, "She more than proves her ability as a star" in this picture.[10]

Moving Picture World actually ran two full pages on the movie—one page of various photos and another featuring Virginia, director James Young, cameraman Ernie Miller, and elderly actor Alfred Fisher who played the kindly butler in the film and who helps the young couple out. The six paragraphs on Virginia offer some interesting comments on her financial status. "In the last eighteen months Miss Corbin's salary had been increased exactly 700 per cent ... if she has not already committed herself, [she] will probably be in the market for some lots around Will Rogers' home in Beverly Hills. Only that we would not want her fan mail to be 'mongrelized' by pamphlets from realtors, prevents us from breaking a confidence and actually telling how much one individual told us, she should now be adding to her checking account."[11]

As for homes, Virginia's confirmed residences were usually modest homes or apartments in and around Los Angeles. And, as will be seen later, her financial situation was not as "rosy" as this publication would lead one to believe.

Possibly the most familiar of all Virginia's films to audiences today is *Play Safe*, the third of her films to be released in January—January 30, to be exact. Actually, with only a few exceptions, today's film fans are only familiar with the last 20 minutes or so of the film—and only because of its inclusion in Paul Killiam's 1963 compilation feature *The Great Chase*. The sequence has been rereleased several times as *Chasing Choo Choos* and was also included on David Shepard's *Slapstick Encyclopedia* released in 1998.

Play Safe stars Monty Banks, an Italian born comedian who also wrote and directed. He was very popular from the late 'teens to the mid-twenties in comedy shorts, but in 1925, he moved to feature films. *Play Safe* was his third feature, but it did not receive great reviews due to its subdued plot development leading up to the final sequence— a rather lengthy sequence—that clipped along at breakneck speed with some of the best gags in silent comedy. As one review explained, "In contrast to the previous picture which depended solely on the hilarious mirth-provoking situations that followed each other in rapid succession, there are not nearly so many gags in *Play Safe*. In fact, the early part of the comedy is more of a human interest story building up the romance between the heiress who has run away to escape an irksome marriage and the boy who befriends her."[12]

As in her previous film, Virginia, who plays Virginia Craig, a wealthy heiress, is being pressured to marry someone she doesn't want to marry—this time her dishonest trustee's (Charles Mailes) son (Charles Gerrard). Monty, referred to only as "The Boy," rescues her from a ruffian's insult when she takes refuge from a storm. He also arranges for her to use his room while he seeks lodging elsewhere. The trustee succeeds in getting her

Many silent movie fans today are familiar with *Play Safe* (1927), but only in its two-reel version which featured the rousing train chase sequence at the end of the movie. This sequence was the highlight of Paul Killiam's 1963 theatrical compilation *The Great Chase* and was later issued as the two-reel *Chasing Choo Choos*. Virginia and star Monty Banks are shown trying to figure out how to escape the ruffians who are after them.

back to the mansion, and The Boy is fired from his job at Virginia's factory for helping her. To make matters worse, the trustee arranges to have The Boy appear as the leader of a gang trying to lead Virginia into a trap. In the end, The Boy helps Virginia elude the trap after they board a runaway train to escape from the villains. The daring antics atop the speeding train are worthy of a Harold Lloyd thrill picture—and Virginia is right in there with him giving a superb performance.

Variety essentially blasted the film noting that it was "a two-reeler done in five." The reviewer said, "Picture contains laughs, but not enough to justify its claims to being a straightaway comedy. The plot is a mere flimsy skeleton on which the gagmen worked. No heart interest because there is no reality or illusion to the characters. Virginia Lee Corbin, who has frequently shown to advantage in flaming youth roles, was blankly negative in this one."[13] *Photoplay* was particularly harsh. "If you want to play safe, stay away from this. A Monty Banks comedy that has a few funny moments. Pretty poor."[14] But not all were bad. *The Film Daily* felt that the "comedy thrill climax" made up for the slow pace of the first three quarters of the film, and *Moving Picture World* said, "Monty Banks distinguishes himself in the thrill comedy situations, and Virginia Lee Corbin is attractive as the girl."[15]

Virginia had not been under a studio contract since her Fox days (not counting the ill-fated five-year contract with Fisher Productions which was never realized)—instead moving from one studio to another on one-picture deals. However, in February 1927, John McCormick, general manager of West Coast production and Colleen Moore's husband, signed Virginia to a five-year contract with First National Pictures. Apparently the company was pleased with her two previous ventures for them—*Ladies at Play* and *The Perfect Sap*.

The long-term contract was included very generous terms for Virginia and was probably the biggest "coup" of her career. Although it didn't start out with a salary the level of what she received on her two previous First National films, it did provide for significant increases over the years. In her first year, she would receive $400 per week for 40 weeks. With the option to renew each year, her salary would increase to $600 per week in the second year, $900 in the third, $1,200 in the fourth, and $1,500 in the fifth. Signed March 31 and taking effect May 2, the contract stated the usual agreement that she would "act, pose and appear solely and exclusively for and as requested by the producer in such roles and in such photoplays as the producer may designate; that as and when requested to do so by the producer, she will make personal appearances on

This charming candid photograph shows Virginia trying to teach Monty Banks how to do the Charleston during a break in the filming of *Play Safe* (1927). Virginia loved to dance and was an accomplished dancer who incorporated that talent, as well as her singing ability, into her vaudeville act when she was touring a few years earlier.

the stage in connection with the exhibitions of photoplays produced by the producer." It goes on to state that she will "promptly and faithfully comply with all reasonable directions, requests, rules and regulations made by the producer." As expected, it said she would work for no one else without written consent, and that the studio owns rights to her image and name. And, not surprisingly, there is a standard morals clause in the contract.[16] A portion of the contract that would be used more than once was the studio's right to loan her out to other companies at any time they wished.

In spite of the good fortune of the First National contract, 1927 turned out to be a tumultuous year for Virginia. The three films that were released in January were all completed in 1926. Her activity in 1927 would be reduced dramatically—and include several lost opportunities which likely were the result of her personal problems—problems that will be discussed in the next chapter.

Even before the First National contract was announced, Virginia was reported to have the leading role in the Gotham Productions Lumas Film *Quarantined Rivals*. By the end of January, barely two weeks after the announcement of Virginia's selection, trade journals were reporting that Kathleen Collins would replace Virginia noting that she had withdrawn from the cast due to illness. Sadly, she seemed excited about the role in the comedy and the opportunity to co-star with Bobby Agnew (with whom she had an onscreen kiss in *Wine of Youth*). "The role of Elsie Peyson will give Miss Corbin one of the best opportunities she had enjoyed since she 'grew up,' and this beautiful girl asserts she will take full advantage of Mr. Sax's kindness in selecting her, in preference to a dozen other available stars."[17]

It is possible that a trade publication article in March gives a clue to the troubles looming ahead for Virginia at home, although it is intended to make Virginia appear as the dutiful daughter. "That Virginia Lee Corbin, one of Hollywood's most attractive seventeen-year-old leading ladies, and her mother, Mrs. Virginia Lee Corbin, are inseparable was brought to light this week when it became known that the recent illness of this blond actress was due also to the recent illness of her mother. Since Virginia was four-years old her mother has guided her in her theatre career. Last July, Mrs. Corbin was taken ill, and two months ago her condition was pronounced critical. Mrs. Corbin has just recovered, and little Virginia will be ready to don the grease paint again within the next two weeks."[18] There was no mention of what the illness may have been.

Things did not improve for Virginia after this, either. First National announced that *The American Beauty*, in support of star Billie Dove, would be her first assignment with the company. However, for whatever reason, she did not make the picture, and the role of Claire, a phone girl in New York's largest hotel, that she was to have went to Alice White.

Virginia was also cast for *The Private Life of Helen of Troy* in support of Maria Corda and Lewis Stone, but that never materialized either. Coincidentally, Alice White is also in this picture, which leads one to believe she enacted the role originally intended for Virginia.

Hard-Boiled Haggerty starring Milton Sills was another film in which Virginia was announced to appear. She wasn't chosen for the leading lady role—that went to Molly O'Day—but at least one source mentioned her among the intended cast. The final film, of course, did not include Virginia.

The Drop Kick with Richard Barthelmess is available for viewing today, and silent film fans familiar with the film will know that the lovely Barbara Kent is his love interest in the film. Kent's role, however, was originally given to Virginia. One writer proposed that Virginia was being considered for another Barthelmess vehicle that was released the next year, 1928—*The Little Shepherd of Kingdom Come*. That never happened either.

A letter in the Warner Bros. Archive seems to indicate that Virginia had already started work on the film before she was dropped from the cast. In a memo dated July 9, it says, "Virginia Lee Corbin has been taken out of the cast of *Drop Kick*. Please credit the picture *Drop Kick* with all the time on her which has been charged to this picture and charge her time to 408 idle in accordance with Mr. Al Rockett's instructions."[19] Unfortunately, whatever reason there was for her dismissal from the film has been lost to time.

A First National letter dated November 21 states that she was to be loaned to Duke Worne Productions for a film entitled *The Heart of Broadway*. The actual agreements are not included in the file, which is no surprise since she did not appear in the film.[20] When the film hit movie screens, the lead role of Roberta, that was originally intended for Virginia, was played by Pauline Garon. As will be seen in Chapter 20, events in Virginia's personal life at that time were very likely the reason she didn't appear in *The Heart of Broadway*.

The above films in which Virginia was definitely cast—at least initially—were all made by First National (with the exception of *The Heart of Broadway*) and hit the screens between September and December. For whatever reason, Virginia was only to have one First National release in 1927—*No Place to Go*, released October 30.

This type of film was well suited for Virginia—a romantic comedy that, although she did not have the lead, provided her with good company—stars such as Mary Astor and Lloyd Hughes and, most importantly, put her under the tutelage of the talented Mervyn LeRoy in his first director's role. LeRoy had been making a name for himself at First National

A lovely portrait of Virginia that was taken in 1927. Although she was not quite 16 years old when it was taken, photographs such as this show why it was very easy for her to play roles like Virginia Dare in *No Place to Go* (1927) in which she portrayed a character older than her actual age.

writing gags for Colleen Moore's pictures, and *No Place to Go*, although not a great film, was still the first in a prestigious and successful career in that chair that lasted until the early 1960s.

Astor plays Sally Montgomery who longs for a caveman-type lover to whisk her away to a South Sea island. Her boyfriend, Hayden (Hughes), is not exactly the type, but she lets him know she wants a man who will take her by force.

Her mother takes a party on a yacht trip to the South Seas, and Sally convinces Hayden to leave the ship one night and escape to a nearby island. Sally's dreams are not realized, though, as Hayden is more interested in food and golf than romance. Sally also did not realize there are cannibals on the island, and the two escape when Sally distracts the cannibals by dancing the Charleston.

They are rescued by her mother, but, since Sally has been "compromised," the two must marry. In their apartment, the still disillusioned Sally draws a line down the middle that neither must cross. However, one evening when she is frightened by the image of a savage in her mirror (actually reflected from an electric sign), she runs and falls into the arms of Hayden.

The film was based on a story by Richard Connell entitled *Isle of Romance*. Newspaper articles appeared for several weeks prior to the filming asking for a possible island location where the movie could be shot. In the end, the producers settled on a part of the Los Angeles River that bordered the First National property. "By installing a sandy beach backing the water up a hundred yards or so, and planting palms in the dense underbrush bordering the river, a coral island lagoon was created. In its edge, Mary Astor, Lloyd Hughes and Virginia Lee Corbin are working before the cameras in company with a band of cannibals carefully selected from the colored population of Los Angeles."[21]

The Los Angeles Times devoted a half page to the movie with several photos and comments that acknowledged *No Place to Go* wasn't a great film, but it would bring audiences in. "If more directors turned out pictures like Mervyn LeRoy's *No Place to Go*, the amusement world would be considerably lightened of care. True, there is nothing great in LeRoy's production—and obviously it has been made wholly for laughs, but that, in a nutshell, explains why the majority of people trek to theaters."[22] The article added that Virginia was good in her role as one of Astor's friends on the yachting trip, but she had little to do.

One interesting side note about the film. In her autobiography (*Mary Astor: A Life on Film*, Delacorte Press, New York, 1967), Astor said she was asked what she would change if she had her life to live over again. She said she had a "string of films" she would not have made. One of the titles she mentioned was *No Place to Go*. Another interesting tidbit about the film: Loretta Young has an uncredited part in it.

No Place to Go does survive today, but, unfortunately, it survives as an original 35mm nitrate print in the British Film Institute archives in need of restoration.

As noted, this was Virginia's only First National release in 1927, and why she missed at least five other roles for which she was announced may never be known. However, as noted, some of the events in her personal life are likely the reason for her disrupted film career.

19. Court, Crooks,
Cars and Cafes

*V*irginia once again found herself dealing with courts in a case that dragged through 1926 and 1927. A complaint was filed at the beginning of 1926 by Hugo D. Newhouse, a Los Angeles attorney. He claimed that within the previous four years, he had performed services as an attorney for Mrs. Corbin and Virginia Lee Corbin for which he had not been paid. These services included counseling and advising, "attending in and about the business of the defendants," preparing various documents and performing other professional services. He asked the court for a judgment of $500 with a seven percent per annum interest noting that the services were "reasonably worth" the amount he was asking.

Virginia, in answer to the complaint, denied that Newhouse ever performed any legal services for her, alleged that she knew nothing of the services claimed in the complaint, and added that by virtue of the fact that she was a minor, she could not have entered into a legal contract with an attorney. Therefore, she asked that judgment be set aside.

A court date was set in February, but Virginia and her mother failed to show up. Because the defendants failed to appear at the appointed time in court, on March 12, Virginia was ordered to pay a total of $536.63 to the plaintiff. Five days later, the court ordered the Sheriff to collect the debt, now $553.16 with court costs added. The Sheriff reported that after ten days, he was unable to collect the debt.

The next court record is a "Return of Garnishment" dated August 21, which "attached all moneys, goods, credits, effects, debts due or owing or any other personal property belonging to the defendants ... in the possession or under the control of First National Productions Incorporated."

In November, both Virginia and her mother entered sworn statements that they never were served with a summons. At that time, they were living in an apartment at 2028 Beachwood Drive in Hollywood. Another sworn statement by Mrs. Catherine A. Sutterfuss, the owner of the apartment, said she observed a man who walked into the hallway of the apartment, left a document on a desk there, but never did serve an individual with the document.

F.A. Fetheroff, "who has several years experience as a Deputy Sheriff and process server," filed an affidavit saying that he did hand the summons to "a young girl ... about five feet one inches in height, had golden hair and blue eyes, and was quite young." He went on to say that based on photos of Virginia that he has seen, he was quite sure he handed the summons to Virginia.

November 24, Virginia's attorneys requested that the judgment be set aside because "said judgment was entered prematurely and without authority of law," and because the summons was not personally served on the defendant. December 1, Judge John L. Fleming ordered that the default judgment be revoked.

But that was not the end. Less than two weeks later, there was a motion by Newhouse to move the case on the calendar. Going into 1927, the case was to be heard February 22, but Newhouse was planning to be out of the country for six months and asked that it be moved up. That didn't happen, and the case wasn't heard until November, at which time Virginia did appear and testified. Although a motion for non-suit was denied, the affidavit states, "On motion of attorney for plaintiff, case is dismissed."[1]

This and the other court records are a window into, not only the personal life of Virginia, but also the disarray of her financial affairs. In all cases, the amount owed was a few hundred dollars, yet payments were not being made, and attorneys were being employed to fight these complaints. With a case such as this that ran for nearly two years, wouldn't attorney fees to fight it cost more than the judgment called for? Unfortunately, these types of situations were contributing to a difficult and tension-filled relationship between Virginia and her mother.

In addition to the ongoing court case, the year started off on a sour note with Virginia's home at 262 North Plymouth Blvd. being broken into and over $4,000 worth of jewelry and clothing stolen (they had apparently just recently moved from the Beechwood Drive address). This was supposedly the second robbery at her home in less than a month with about $3,000 worth of jewelry and clothing stolen the first time. The burglary took place January 4, and the missing goods included 30 dresses, ten cloaks, two "costly" beaded bags, and a wristwatch of French make. Reports said the family had been annoyed for two months by burglars attempting to gain entrance into the home, and a night watchman had been employed. However, the recent burglary took place before the watchman came on duty. Virginia and her sister, Ruth, were away from the home taking their mother for an operation and then eating at a café.

Late in February, one woman and six men were arrested in connection with the Corbin burglary and other break-ins. Some were arrested on charges of receiving stolen goods, but police said all were associated with one another. Goods found in the woman's possession included much of Virginia's belongings. In early March, Virginia and her sister were in court to testify against the criminals. "Miss Corbin appeared, accompanied by her personal attorney, Nate Freedman, and her brunette sister, Miss Ruth Corbin, to testify in receiving stolen property charges against Alice Steinman and Jesse Carr, codefendants in the action. Miss Corbin identified personal property and clothing found in the possession of the pair."[2] The article went on to note that she would also be testifying against three men involved in the case on a future date. A later report said charges were dropped against Steinman.

A very unflattering press photo of Virginia shows her standing beside a chest of

The home where Virginia, her mother and her sister, Ruth, resided at 262 North Plymouth Blvd., Los Angeles, was broken into January 4, 1928. Virginia displays all that was left of more than $4,000 worth of jewelry and clothing stolen that evening.

drawers holding a pair of hose, drawers all pulled out and empty, and a make-up case and other items strewn about the floor—a disgusted expression on her face and her hat pushed back on her head. Although not necessarily bad publicity for Virginia, the story about the burglary, subsequent police work and the trial was covered in newspapers around the country.

Note also that in the newspaper coverage, Ruth was referred to as "Miss Ruth Corbin," not "Mrs. John Miehle," her married name. The report seems to indicate that all three—Mrs. Corbin, Virginia and Ruth—were living in the home. Most certainly Ruth was already separated from her husband whom she had married less than three years before. A few months later as divorce proceedings were taking place, Ruth was quoted as saying, "The honeymoon is over when the bride gives up her room to her mother-in-law and goes to sleep on a cot in the kitchen."[3]

Thieves weren't satisfied with just breaking into Virginia's home, either. Her car was stolen while she attended a party Saturday evening, June 25. The car was recovered the next day about a mile from where it was taken.

In April, Mrs. Corbin was involved in a traffic accident in Los Angeles. The report said she hurt her ankle, and she and four other people were treated at the local hospital and released. The address given by Mrs. Corbin was 919 3/4 North Serrano Street indicating another move within just a few months.

A more significant event was the passing of Virginia's father, Leon E. Corbin, at age 58 on April 29 in Los Angeles County. This is one event in Virginia's life that newspapers either passed over or were unaware of—more likely the latter. What sort of contact Leon Corbin had—or did not have—with his wife and two daughters is unknown. Virginia never mentioned him, and, considering the last time a visit from him was documented was in early 1922, it is unlikely Virginia had any kind of significant relationship with her father. In a 2001 interview by this author with a friend of Virginia's, the friend noted that she attended Ruth's 16th birthday party in 1921 at the Corbins' home in Azusa, and Leon Corbin was not present. If he wasn't present for an event such as this, it is unlikely he had any kind of role in the girls' lives. One fan magazine did carry a tidbit almost nine months after his death that said, "When Mr. Corbin died last spring, he carried with him to his grave the regret that his Virginia hadn't enjoyed the normal childhood of other little girls."[4]

More bad luck continued to haunt Virginia's movie career when she failed to get the role of Lorelei Lee in Anita Loos' *Gentleman Prefer Blondes*. Due to the popularity of Loos' story—which had already been adapted into a play—the announcement that a film version would be made had Hollywood and the entire country buzzing—not necessarily with excitement about the movie, but about who would play the lead role.

The story revolved around the search for a rich husband by dizzy blonde Lorelei and her brunette friend, Dorothy. Everyone had a different opinion about who would be the best Lorelei, and Virginia was mentioned quite often as being in the running. Of course, others included Lillian Gish, Constance Talmadge, Laura La Plante, Greta Nissen, Esther Ralston, Edna Murphy, Clara Bow and a host of others. *Photoplay* ran a full page with photos of 21 actresses entitled "The Pastime of Picking a Lorelei Lee." To be produced by Paramount, studio head Jesse Lasky said, "the success of *Gentlemen Prefer Blondes* as a screen play will depend to an unusual degree on the Lorelei.... Brunettes who possess 'the blonde personality' will be considered…. I mean the type of girl who is seemingly frivolous, artificial and simple, yet who is actually a more dangerous form of vamp than the flashing, dark type of beauty."[5]

One article noted, "According to gossip, none other than Virginia Lee Corbin is being considered for the role of Lorelei in *Gentlemen Prefer Blondes*, but as Famous Players cannot film it for a long while to come, Virginia may have outgrown the part at the rate she is increasing her height these days."[6] Pundits joked that the search for a Lorelei was taking so long, Baby Peggy may be in the running by the time the movie began filming. As for Virginia's growth, she was identified in one fan magazine from late 1927 as being five feet, four inches tall and weighing 105 pounds.

However, Loos had said earlier in the year that she favored Marion Davies for the role, and, although final selection supposedly rested with Loos, it was eventually announced that little-known 19-year-old Ruth Taylor was to be awarded the role. Once again, Virginia had lost a part that would have been a boon to her career.

Around this same time, an interesting letter was sent to First National dated March 25, 1927. The letter exists in the Warner Bros. Archives and is from "Welt-Detektiv" in Germany, or, translated into English, "World Detective." The letter is marked "strictly confidential." It states, "We received a confidential inquiry in regard to the cinema actress Virginia Lee Corbin…. We should be much obliged to you if you would kindly inform us where we might obtain detailed information about the young lady in question, where she stays at present, what is her family name, where is her permanent residence and what details might be known to you about the young lady. In what moving pictures did she act last and for which companies?"[7]

First National responded April 15. "Miss Corbin signed a five-year contract with our company March 31, 1927. Both of her parents are alive [although Leon Corbin would die before the end of the month]. Her father, L.E. Corbin, who was in the drug business here in the city of Los Angeles, has been ill, and due to his mental incapacity Miss Corbin's affairs are handled by her mother whose name is also Virginia Corbin. Virginia Lee Corbin has not yet attained the age of 18 years. She is therefore a minor until her 18th birthday, which falls on the 5th of December 1927 [she actually would not be 18 until 1929]. Her permanent residence is in the city of Los Angeles and she can be reached at any time at the First National Studios. She recently appeared in two of our First National Pictures—one entitled *Ladies at Play* and the other *The Perfect Sap*."[8]

It may be surprising that First National responded at all for such a personal inquiry, but the studio did only provide information that anyone could obtain easily and, to their credit, did not provide a home address. Instead, they suggested Virginia could be contacted at the studio at any time. It was interesting that they felt the need to emphasize that Virginia was a minor. The mysterious correspondence does have ominous overtones; however, thankfully, nothing more seems to have come of it.

But there were good things happening in 1927 for Virginia. First National was obviously promoting their new star with staged photos in various publications. For example, a series of photos were taken of her and another new First National acquisition, Yola d'Avril, on the beach in swimwear and wearing sailors' caps. Virginia also continued to appear in publications modeling clothes, except now she had graduated to more adult

Virginia signed a five-year contract with First National Pictures in 1927, and the studio promptly began to promote their new star. Photographs such as this with Virginia and another First National protégée, Yola d'Avril, on the beach at Santa Monica were sent out to magazines and newspapers around the country. Notice both starlets have a circular First National logo on the front of their bathing suits.

modeling. *The Washington Post* carried a page that was headlined "A New Kind of Underwear" and included a picture of a smiling Virginia, hands on hips, modeling a black number. She also continued product endorsement, and there is a very cute ad of her with a little toy dinosaur on her shoulders, Virginia's large, bright eyes looking up at the toy. The caption said, "'The eyes have it,' says the 'Twistum' dinosaur of Virginia Lee Corbin featured in First National Pictures."

The Café Montmartre opened in Hollywood in 1923 and was an upscale and popular place for celebrities to meet and enjoy the town's nightlife. One of *The Los Angeles Times'* social columns mentioned in January that Virginia and her sister, Ruth, were seen there entertaining a party of four. Whether that meant there were four others in addition to Virginia and Ruth or the two girls had dates is unclear.

Virginia was a guest at Alice White's new Beverly Hills home in March along with several other stars such as Blanche Mehaffey, Dorothy Revier, Natalie Kingston, Ruth Stonehouse, Ora Carew and others.

In June, Virginia hosted an afternoon tea party in the Cocoanut Grove at the Ambassador Hotel. The guest of honor was Lina Basquette who had just returned from New York. Other guests were Laura La Plante, Patsy Ruth Miller, Jane Winton, Joan Crawford, James Hall, Charles Farrell, Mervyn Le Roy and several others.

In August she appeared at Macloon's Music Box Theatre in Hollywood for "First National Night." Other First National stars on hand were Lewis Stone, Natalie Kingston, Jack Mulhall, Dorothy Mackaill, Harry Langdon, Johnny Hines, Doris Kenyon, Billie Dove, Ben Lyon, Alice White and others.

Later that month was the motion picture make-up artists' "Mardi Gras" at the Hollywood Roof ballroom. Various make-up and costume contests were held throughout the evening with such luminaries as Lon Chaney (appropriately), Aileen Pringle, Lew Cody, Owen Moore, Richardo Cortez, Karl Dane, Ramon Novarro, Conrad Nagel and others presenting the awards and prizes. Virginia served as one of the judges for the contests along with Hope Dare, Alice White, Mervyn LeRoy, J. Farrell MacDonald and Wesley Barry.

A couple of weeks later, she was entertaining at another Montmartre Café luncheon, this time with guests Mrs. Sam Warner, Phyllis Haver, Janet Gaynor, Louise Brooks, Lois Moran, Marceline Day and sister Ruth.

In October, Virginia was one of a large number of celebrities who attended the performance of *Meet the Wife* with stage star Lynn Starling at the Hollywood Playhouse. Virginia and other stars such as Olive Borden, Edmund Lowe, Lilyan Tashman, Estelle Taylor, Jack Dempsey, Belle Bennett, John Barrymore, John Gilbert, Marguerite De La Motte, and a host of other would see the play and greet the public.

In early November, she attended a birthday party actor Jack Donovan gave for his mother at his "sumptuous" beach residence. Again, a large number of stars assembled including Richard Arlen, Jobyna Ralston, Molly O'Day, Ruth Roland, Joan Crawford, Barbara Kent, Mervyn LeRoy, Grant Withers, Alice and Marceline Day, and many others.

A cute exchange at one of the dinners Virginia attended was related in a fan magazine. "The two next best lines, pulled at the same dinner, belong to Virginia Lee Corbin. A boy from

Virginia's popularity had been used for promotional purposes since her Fox Kiddie days for everything from automobile tires to children's clothing. In the late 1920s, her image was still being used to promote sales of items that included underwear, toys such as the Twistum Dinosaur shown here, and other goods.

Maryland began showering the pastel Virginia with soulful sighs and glances. Virginia gazed at him coldly. 'Take off the mask and play yourself,' she said scornfully. The boy continued to protest his love, his affection, his all. 'Aw, count yourself,' wisecracked Miss Corbin. 'You're not so numerous.'"[9]

Back at the Montmartre later that month, a brief mention noted, "Raymond Keane was host to Virginia Lee Corbin and others."[10] Could this have been a date with Keane? He was a young (only five years older than Virginia), good-looking, up-and-coming actor, so this could have been possible.

Who or how often Virginia dated is lost to time. However, a 2001 interview with a former neighbor of hers, Esther Linn, noted that she encountered Virginia and her mother on the elevator in their apartment building at St. Andrews and 6th Streets, the Corbins' residence in late 1927. Ms. Linn said Virginia was dressed to go out, and Mrs. Corbin was crying. When she asked the reason for the tears, Mrs. Corbin replied, "Virginia's going out on her first date, and I can't stand it!"[11] It is difficult to tell from this encounter if this is simply motherly concern or Mrs. Corbin's desire to control every aspect of Virginia's life. Whatever the reason, this incident apparently was only a spark in the explosion that was about to happen in the Corbin household.

20. Insanity

"Mrs. L.E. Corbin, 45 years of age, ... made an asserted attempt to commit suicide earlier in the evening by taking poison ... [she] was moved to the psychopathic ward.... Mrs. Corbin was rushed to the police receiving hospital after an ambulance was summoned by Mrs. Bettina Aronson, 651 South St. Andrews Place, a neighbor of the Corbins. According to Mrs. Aronson's story told to Detective Lieutenant Clark of the Wilshire division, the former received a hysterical telephone call from Mrs. Corbin, her neighbor, which said, 'I have just swallowed enough poison to kill ten men!'"[1]

Newspapers ran amuck with the story for days in early November—not just because of the suicide attempt, but because Virginia apparently had grown up and had enough. Fan magazines, since they are not as timely as daily newspapers, were running the story well into 1928. "Charging social and financial tyranny, Virginia Lee Corbin, film actress, last night told police she will file an insanity complaint against her mother.... While police surgeons at the George Street Receiving Hospital last night were waging a battle to save Mrs. Corbin's life, Miss Corbin... sat in the detective bureau, a few doors removed from the hospital ward, and told Detective Lieutenant Luke she was ready to sign the complaint which would place her mother under observation in the General Hospital for insanity."[2] A large photo of Virginia with a scowl on her face as she was leaving the detective bureau accompanied the article.

It went on to note that Mrs. Aronson rushed to the apartment and found Mrs. Corbin on the floor writhing in agony. The police surgeon said, due to the quantity of poison Mrs. Corbin took, her recovery was "doubtful."

Virginia told detectives, "Mother and I did not quarrel. Everything is all right. Mother just grew hysterical over some little matter of business we had been discussing. I can't understand why she did this. We didn't argue or quarrel. It is not true that I left home in anger as mother has said. She is inclined to be highly hysterical at times." She added, "All right. I am ready to sign the complaint and get it over with. I am big enough to take care of myself now. Mother wanted more money tonight, and I wouldn't give it to her. Besides, she wouldn't let me go out. I guess that's the reason for all this. Let's get it over with. If she acted this way before, she'll do it again."[3]

The "little matter of business," no doubt, concerned Virginia's earnings. She also

151

told police that she was "'on the verge of being made a pauper' through the dissipation by her mother of thousands of dollars the actress has earned in motion picture work."[4]

As reporters delved deeper into the story, more of Virginia's criticisms of her mother came to light. She told detectives that her mother had "spoiled" her parties and "gambled" away her earnings. One report contradicted Virginia's previous statement that she had not left the house in anger. "Miss Corbin calmly told detectives she had walked out of the house slamming the door in her mother's face when the mother demanded that she be her age and stay at home as she should. 'Mother was continually complaining of the boys and girls who came to see me, and she never would let me go to their homes,' the daughter declared resentfully. 'If I did go to a party, my evening was sure to be spoiled by having to answer the telephone every few minutes. It was always mother telling me to come home.' They quarreled, the daughter said, after every party, and continually wrangled over money matters."

She also told police that her mother had made suicide attempts twice before following dramatic scenes with her daughter. "Mother had full control of my earnings.... I've always turned my pay envelope over to her. I earned thousands of dollars, and mother spent it all. I have nothing to show for my work. Mother hasn't it either. She does not know how to handle money. She just gambled it away."[5]

The years of being taken to court over unpaid bills and moving as many as three or four times a year indicate a trend of financial mismanagement considering Virginia's employment and earnings. Certainly she was not earning at the level of major stars of the day such as Mary Pickford, Greta Garbo, Lillian Gish, Colleen Moore and a host of others, but after being in pictures for over 11 years, she and her mother should have been living comfortably.

The incident also gives some insight into a mother who obviously had personal demons to deal with. Her life for over a decade had been solely devoted to Virginia and her career—and Mrs. Corbin must be credited with guiding her daughter's career successfully. However, she did not have the ability to manage Virginia's earnings with an eye to the future, and the revelation of her gambling activities by Virginia would certainly account for their constant money problems.

However, Virginia, at nearly 16 years old (the newspapers claimed she was 17), was old enough to want a social life and old enough to realize their financial state was out of hand. The earlier referenced story told by a neighbor that Mrs. Corbin cried because Virginia was going out on a date, and Virginia's claims that she could not enjoy a party for her mother's constant telephoning, give some insight into the inability of Mrs. Corbin to accept her daughter's natural maturation. It is easy to understand the conflict between mother and daughter when a teenager wants a certain level of independence and a social life.

While Virginia was being interviewed by police, the question arose regarding whether she, being underage, could sign an insanity complaint against her mother. This brought up the first mention of appointing a guardian for her. Virginia discussed with the detective the possibility of having a court appointed guardian to save some of the money she had made as an actress and "insure a future on the screen."

Two days later, a report said Virginia and her sister, Ruth, appeared before Superior Court Judge Gould requesting the withdrawal of the insanity complaint. Ruth apparently stepped in following the incident to try and smooth over the issue and downplay the dramatics for the press. "She didn't know what she was signing when she signed that complaint," she told the judge.[6] Virginia confirmed this, and the judge dismissed the complaint. The article said Virginia disappeared after appearing before the judge, and the work of transferring Mrs. Corbin from the General Hospital to Rosemeade Sanitarium was handled by Ruth. Ruth told reporters her sister had to leave to go to work at the studio, but the article said inquiries at the studio failed to locate Virginia—with the studio publicity chief exclaiming that he'd like to know of her whereabouts as well.

Continuing to downplay the drama, Ruth told reporters, "There is absolutely nothing to the statements that Virginia is angry at mother over money matters. Mother has

Virginia was certainly maturing as First National publicity photographs such as this indicate, even though she was barely 16 years old at the time. The caption on the back of the photograph says, "This is not a hosiery or underwear advertisement. It is just a delightfully informal pose of Virginia Lee Corbin, First National featured player, wearing the latest black georgette undies style."

been ill—she had a serious major operation last January—and that, coupled with father's death, has made her very nervous and bordering on the verge of hysteria."[7] As for the comments that Mrs. Corbin had taken all of Virginia's money, Ruth said that was a misstatement by the police.

Regarding Mrs. Corbin's condition, "Dr. Victor Parkin, under whose care Mrs. Corbin has been placed, yesterday declared that undoubtedly she will recover. He said that it will be at least twenty-four hours before the effects of the sleeping potion she swallowed wears off, and then an accurate verdict on her physical and mental state can be obtained."[8] The sleeping potion she took was 25 grains of luminal, another name for phenobarbital. The doctor added that it would be several months before she would be fully recovered.

In a later article, Virginia backed away from claiming her mother was insane. "I know mother took that stuff just to scare me. She's done it before. Mother has been acting strangely ever since father died several months ago. She needs rest."[9]

November 9, a photo appeared in newspapers showing Mrs. Corbin in a wheelchair, smiling, with Virginia sitting on the arm of the chair on one side and Ruth on the other, both daughters also smiling, hands under their mother's chin. The picture was captioned, "Corbin Family Harmonious."

Nevertheless, the article below the photo was headlined, "Actress Seeks Guardian." Virginia felt the need to proceed with having a court-appointed guardian and putting her personal affairs in the hands of a business manager. It also stated that, along with Ruth and her attorney, Virginia was at her mother's bedside the previous day. She and her mother came to a complete understanding that Mrs. Corbin needed to remain in the sanitarium and rest while Virginia continued her film career and put her financial affairs in the hands of a business manager.

The next report said, "Tomorrow, it is learned, Miss Corbin will establish a trust fund in a Hollywood bank as her first step toward recuperating asserted financial losses brought about by what are described as maternal extravagances. It is understood the trust fund will be placed in the charge of George E. Dodge, cashier of the bank. This action ... will be followed by an application for appointment of a guardian for the 17-year-old actress. [Her attorney] said the guardian to be proposed is an employee of the Board of Education and a close friend of both Miss Corbin and her mother.... The guardianship is expected to be without opposition on the part of the mother. It is also expected the actress will be under supervision of Ruth Miehle, her adopted sister. The two girls have established a new home together, leaving the apartment at 620 South St. Andrews Place."[10]

Two weeks after Mrs. Corbin's suicide attempt, newspapers reported that papers were in the process of being drawn up to appoint Miss Mildred B. Campbell, supervisor of professional children's interests with the City Board of Education, as legal guardian for Virginia. "Word was received yesterday by Nathan O. Freedman, attorney for the girl, that the Board of Education has no opposition to the appointment of Miss Campbell as guardian of Miss Corbin. The letter, signed by Raymond B. Dunlap, director, expressed gratification that Miss Corbin has voluntarily sought such guardianship."[11] Mrs. Corbin, it was reported, was still recuperating in the sanitarium and gave no opposition to the appointment.

Although all seemed to be settled at the moment, the subject of guardianship would arise again as late as 1929.

21. Moving On

$\mathcal{M}$rs. Corbin's stay in the sanitarium was over by the beginning of 1928. And, as the year opened, it was not surprising that Virginia and her mother were back in a courtroom again. This time was, thankfully, not a suit, but Virginia answering for a speeding ticket. She had been caught speeding at midnight December 22—a full 33 miles per hour on Vine Street near Melrose Avenue. She was also charged with having illegal headlights and not having a license. Virginia explained to the judge that she had not had time to take the examination. She was fined only $15 on the condition that she have her headlights "regulated" and take the driver's exam.

The article was accompanied by a smiling Virginia seated on the arm of a chair in which her mother sat, both dressed very stylishly. Referencing the previous year's debacle with her mother, the headline over the photo proclaimed, "Encore of Latest Role Unwanted." It was also stated that she was living with her mother at 357 South Wilton Place, their fifth confirmed address in less than 18 months.

Court was in the picture again just two months later for Mrs. Corbin. Apparently, Leon Corbin died the previous year in debt, so creditors sought relief from his wife. However, the issue was settled out of court, and an order for her to appear in court and account to the creditors was dismissed.

Virginia's most recent studio contract, which had been signed with First National almost a year previously, was now at an end. The official announcement was that Virginia terminated the contract. Quoting both Virginia and her mother, who was quickly back in the picture, newspapers said the reason for the termination was due to the fact that First National had not been able to find any suitable roles for her resulting in an absence from the screen. The Corbins emphasized, however, that relations between Virginia and the studio had been pleasant. "Virginia has splendid training and experience both on the stage and screen. She is 17 now, and we feel that she should have some good opportunities to exercise her talents," Mrs. Corbin said.[1]

A two-page termination agreement in the Warner Bros. archive doesn't give any reasons for the termination. Although signed January 9, it does state that she still had 16⅓ weeks left on the initial year of her contract, which would expire May 1, 1928. Her compensation for those remaining weeks would be $6,533.33.[2]

The January 24 announcement came suspiciously close to the events surrounding

Mrs. Corbin's suicide attempt just two months earlier. True, Virginia had been off the screen for much of the previous year, but she did have a First National release in both January and October, and one has to question why she was announced to star and then did not in at least five First National Pictures the previous year. Was Virginia unable to perform in the pictures in which First National had originally cast her? Could the contract termination have been at First National's request? The comment by Mrs. Corbin that First National had not been able to find any suitable roles for Virginia may have some basis in fact. A June 7, 1927, memo stated that she had not worked during the first month of her contract. As will be seen later in this chapter, she was loaned out to other studios for at least two pictures during the first eight months of her contract, a possible indication First National did not have anything for her. And, although the contract provided for 12 weeks of idle time, that same June 7 memo stated she had been advanced four weeks' salary. Another June 16 memo noted she had been advanced an additional week's salary.[3]

The contract termination announcement was coupled with another announcement that Virginia had signed a four-picture deal with Harry Millarde (sometimes mistakenly listed as S.S. Millarde and sometimes spelled without the "e") Productions. Harry Millarde had been a frequent actor from 1913–16 and had numerous directing credits between 1915 and 1927, but only one production credit—and that was in 1922. He did nothing after 1927 (including the previously mentioned *The Woman He Feared* in which Virginia appeared), and no further mention is made of Virginia's reported contract other than the initial announcement of the signing. Millarde died in 1931.

Virginia's first release for 1928 was the delightful film, *Bare Knees*, which has been available for home viewing for several years. The low budget film was a Gotham production, distributed by Lumas Film Corporation. Gotham was back to small time for Virginia, but it was no fly-by-night company, having been around since 1915. The movie was filmed in December, so it was completed after Mrs. Corbin's suicide attempt and when Virginia's life was still in so much disarray. Virginia was on loan-out from First National for this film with Gotham paying First National $750 a week for her services.[4]

The picture was released February 1, and Virginia was *the* star. She was supported by Donald Keith, Jane Winton, Johnnie Walker, and Forrest Stanley. Virginia is Billie Drury who has returned home to live with her sister, Jane (Winton) and her stuffed shirt husband, John (Forrest Stanley). Constantly hanging around the house is friend Paul (Walker). The opening title sets the scene with "It all began in Hanford City ... where there are still long skirts, long hair, and long marriages." Jane's birthday party that evening continues to set the tone for the type of community this is—everyone dressed very properly, a fat lady playing piano and a nerdy guy playing saxophone for slow dancing, and a group of young girls sitting together looking extremely bored. The party is shook up, though, when Billie arrives, the quintessential flapper, with silky flowing dress well above the knees, stockings with little designs in them, short haircut and snappy lines. The music stops, and everyone looks on wide-eyed and jaws dropped, while Billie comments, hands on hips, "Well, I could roll over and butter myself with sorrow! Is this a party ... or a wake?" Later she tells sister Jane, "Introduce me to the mourners."

At the party, Billie especially attracts the attention of young Larry (Keith), John's assistant in the county attorney's office. While everyone is dancing slowly, Billie asks

In the delightful *Bare Knees* (1928), John (Forrest Stanley, left) thinks gifts such as a wool shawl and a hot water bottle are great birthday gifts for his wife, Jane (Jane Winton, right), while Billie, Jane's sister (Virginia), looks at him as if to say, "Really?" John's ignorance of such things and neglect of his wife leads to an affair between her and friend Paul (Johnnie Walker). Of course, it's up to Billie to save their marriage.

Larry, "Can you shiver and shake, Sheik?"—and they begin to dance as if the music was "hepped up" jazz. Of course, John is appalled. When Billie sees his expression, she breaks out into a solo dance—obviously improvising, but likely some combination of the Charleston and Black Bottom. The sequence is a treat for Virginia Lee Corbin fans because she was a good dancer, loved to go out dancing, and also used her dancing skills when performing onstage. Here, fans get to see her talent, albeit briefly.

All of this is to set up the conflict between Billie's idea of having fun against Jane and John's (as well as their community's) staid, old-fashioned ways. What transpires is not surprising in the film—Jane is tired of John's neglect. He works late, taking her for granted, and gives her a wool shawl for a birthday present, whereas Paul gave her flowers and perfume. One of her gifts is even a fancy hot water bottle that John thinks is just fine! It's difficult to understand John's blindness to this, but, as one would expect, Jane is having an affair (non-sexual?) with Paul.

Of course Jane has preached to Billie about her ways. "Young lady, your bare knees and bare back are going to get you into trouble. Men find it difficult enough to be moral even when women dress decently." Billie sighs and retorts, "It isn't what you wear on your body, it's what you wear in your head."

The climax comes when Jane and Paul meet in a private dining room of the night-club, supposedly a rendezvous before running off together. Coincidentally, John and Larry are investigating the nightclub due to numerous complaints John's received in his law office. Billie has suspected something was going on between her sister and Paul, but when she finds a note Jane left telling John she's leaving him, Billie goes to confront her sister at the nightclub. As this confrontation is taking place, John and Larry are looking around the private dining rooms and walk in on this scene. Billie pretends she and Paul were eloping to save her sister. Larry, who wants to marry Billie, is obviously hurt and disappointed.

But the story doesn't stop there. Before all can leave, the pier where the nightclub is located has caught on fire. Everyone must flee. All make it except Paul and Billie who are blocked from leaving the pier when burning timbers fall and block their exit. Seeing no way to escape, they decide to go out in style by riding the roller coaster. The fire has weakened the supports of the roller coaster, though, and the cars Billie and Paul are in fly off the track and into the ocean. Larry swims out to rescue them.

When all is said and done, John discovers the note, but instead of confronting his wife, he burns the letter and does not mention it. He has seen the error of his ways toward his wife, hugs her and suggests she may consider short skirts and bobbing her hair. Billie and Larry are also reunited.

Although it's a low budget film, *Bare Knees* really does have a little bit of everything going for it. It has plenty of comedy. The intertitles are very well written. In addition to those already mentioned, Billie loves to take jabs at John's stuffiness with lines like "Dear old John! Do you still blush when you see a car with stripped gears?" Looking over at the group of bored, long-faced group of girls gathered to the side at the party, Billie asks Larry, "Did someone tell them there ain't no Santa Claus?"

There is also a dash of sexiness in the movie. For example, in addition to the wool shawl Jane got for her birthday, she finds that someone gave her sister a hot water bottle. So Billie pulls out her gift—a black sheer nightie, "guaranteed to keep husbands home at night!" she says, winking at her sister. One of the most charming sequences in the film has Billie revitalizing the girls' softball team—the same group of girls who were so bored at the party. Looking at a photo of the team, Billie sees the girls dressed in big balloon pants and voluminous shirts with a sailor collar and tie. They are to play the men's team the next day, and Billie has an idea. At the game, the girls make a planned late entrance wearing tight shorts that are mid-thigh high and tight, sleeveless shirts. The men lose the game because they are so distracted by the girls' outfits.

Deftly worked into this comedy is the drama of Jane and John's weakened marriage and the intruder, Paul, who, in the end, admits to Jane he doesn't want to run away with her. "What would I do with you?" he asks hurtfully. The fire at the pier provides a rousing climax to the film, and, of course, everyone likes a happy ending.

Maude Fulton must be mentioned for adding humor to the story as the maid who walks with toes pointed out as if she constantly has sore feet. Her expressions are price-less, and she likes Billie—eventually putting on a tight French maid's outfit that Billie recommended—an outfit that appalls John.

When Jane (Jane Winton, beside Virginia) is caught in a rendezvous with her husband's friend, Paul (Johnnie Walker, left), Billie (Virginia) takes the rap for her sister saying she was the one about to run away with Paul. Forrest Stanley (third from right) is the suspicious husband, John. Next to him is Donald Keith as a very discouraged Larry, John's associate, who is in love with Billie. The unidentified man in the doorway is an employee of the nightclub where this scene from *Bare Knees* (1928) takes place.

In addition to being a pretty neatly packaged story, written by Adele Bufffington, it is put over the top by Virginia's performance—sassy, sexy, perky, and vivacious with Virginia looking most attractive.

This one also gave Virginia good reviews. *Film Daily* said, "*Bare Knees* is a story with a moral, and one that manages to be convincing and effective without preaching. It gives the modern flapper a fine break and exposes her as a bit of a gem in spite of her gaudy setting.... Offers good entertainment for the majority," adding that Virginia's performance was "very good."[5] "*Bare Knees* is interesting, well directed and has the goods— a sharp moral smartly delivered. Virginia Corbin does herself proud as the show 'em lassie," said *Chicago Daily Tribune* reviewer Mae Tinee.[6] An Arkansas theater owner in *Exhibitors' Herald and Moving Picture World* said, "Good picture. An excellent comedy drama with a well-balanced cast. Miss Corbin got over fine and made many friends. Here is a picture that will stand advertising and will deliver the goods. It's a box office sure thing."[7]

Gotham also ensured that the movie was promoted well, including a personal appearance tour for Virginia. It doesn't appear the "tour" was very extensive, though, since the only newspaper accounts that can be found in relation to the movie have her appearing in Akron and Mansfield, OH. Her appearance at the Strand Theatre in Akron, OH, the first week of June—with three performances a day—garnered several days of newspaper articles and publicity for her. One article noted that in her appearance, she "trips out on stage … to talk a song about 'We aren't as bad in Hollywood as you would think we are,' then sings 'Is He My Boy Friend' and a few similar selections and finally goes into her dance,"[8] all a testament to Virginia's talent not only as an actress, but also a singer and dancer. Virginia had been quoted as saying that she would be making a Movietone version of her present act for distribution by William Fox, but, unfortunately, there is no trace of the existence of such a film or a record confirming that it ever happened.

One of her personal appearances was at Akron University's Annual Senior Prom at the Portage Country Club where she was special guest. Austin Wylie's orchestra provided the music.

While in Akron, she was interviewed about the movie and other subjects. She told the reporter that riding "the dips in the scenic railway," had supplanted horseback riding as her favorite pastime. When asked if she was planning to find any scenic railways while in Akron, she responded, "Yer dern tootin'!" noted to be her favorite expression now. She also admitted that the experience on the roller coaster for *Bare Knees* was her first time on this type of amusement park ride. As a matter of fact, she liked it so much, she remained at the park all afternoon and evening to continue riding it.

She said she played tennis but had never taken up golf. Another favorite pastime is watching movies—with *The Man Who Laughs* (a Conrad Veidt film, 1928) and *Glorious Betsy* (with Dolores Costello, 1928) the two most recent films she had enjoyed. The report added that she neither drinks nor smokes, but she did enjoy talking Pig Latin.

Referring to her canceled First National contract, the article said she recently called off a contract so she could leave Hollywood for a time and avoid being permanently cast as a flapper. She went on to say that there would be no flapper parts in any contract that she signed from then on. These types of statements are either publicity hype or Virginia trying to elevate her "stature" in the film world. Continuing this attempt to gain a higher regard for her talents, she also said she was going to spend several years in New York in study and voice culture. With the coming of sound—gaining ground rapidly in 1928—Virginia was apparently very concerned about her voice and elocution. This concern would come up again when she went away to England for a year not too far in the future.

As for Virginia's desire to elevate her status, there were several announcements that she was leaving films forever and going to New York to appear in a Broadway revue. One even mentioned that she was to be "glorified by Flo Ziegfeld." Another noted that among those already appearing on the New York stage or booked to do so were Harry Carey, Virginia Lee Corbin, Priscilla Dean, Buck Jones and Larry Semon. No evidence, though, could be located to confirm she ever appeared on the Broadway stage.

Considering her role in *Bare Knees* and its popularity, it was only appropriate that

Virginia should be asked her views on the "modern day" flapper. "I myself might well come under the classification of 'flapper,'" she said, "and when I read Miss Buffington's story of 'Bare Knees,' I at once realized that here was one person who really knew what it was all about. The idiosyncrasies of costume of the modern girl are based on two things—comfort and attractiveness." And quoting from her movie, she said, "Besides, it's not what you wear on your body that counts. It's what you wear in your head. A girl can be just as moral in a one-piece bathing suit as in a Mother Hubbard wrapper."[9]

Released just ten days after *Bare Knees* was the Warner Bros. production *The Little Snob*, a starring vehicle for May McAvoy with Virginia in a supporting role. The film also starred Alec B. Francis, Robert Frazer, John Miljan and Frances Lee. Virginia was on loan-out from First National for this film as well, with the same terms as *Bare Knees*. Her start date was indicated to be October 20.

McAvoy is Maizie Banks whose father, Colonel Banks (Francis), runs a Coney Island concession called "The Kentucky Derby." Maizie dresses as a jockey to help her father lure the crowds in. Jim (Frazer), who runs a concession across from her dad, is her "pal." However, dad wants something better than carnival life for his daughter, so he has saved up to send her to boarding school. Unfortunately, boarding school has made a little snob of her, and, of course, to keep up appearances, she has kept her father's occupation a secret from her friends at school.

This is a publicity photograph of Virginia distributed in connection with *The Little Snob* (1928). She and Frances Lee, an attractive blonde who is best known for her Christie Brothers comedies, were cast as snobbish college friends of the picture's star, May McAvoy. Virginia received good notices for the film with one reviewer saying, "Miss Corbin and Miss Lee ... are the last word in flapperism."

The climax comes when some of these friends (Lee and Virginia) and the fortune hunting Walt Keene (Miljan)—who, by the way, thinks she an heiress—come to Coney Island, discover her secret, and begin to make game of her dad, even accusing him of being dishonest and crooked. Of course, this brings out the real, feisty Maizie, and Jim joins in when he gives Keene a good thrashing.

The film generally got good reviews. *Variety* said, "Light, airy film padded here and there. However, it has a moral. Some corking photography and splendid direction where the school parties are on. Work of Miss McAvoy stands out."[10] One newspaper called it "one of the most amusing, as well as most humanly gripping, comedies of the season."[11] And, although it wasn't a lead role, Virginia did get noticed. "Miss Corbin and Miss Lee as leaders among the college girls are the last word in flapperism."[12]

Frances Lee, by the way, was a very beautiful blonde who is best remembered for her many appearances in Christie Brothers comedies. She did make a few features, though, and continued acting until 1935. Supposedly, she was considered for the lead in *King Kong* (1933), a role that finally went to Fay Wray.

Although *The Little Snob* sounds as if it would be a very entertaining film, it, alas, is considered to be another lost film in Virginia's filmography.

Both *Bare Knees* and *The Little Snob* were made in late 1927—and, as discussed earlier, her world was turned upside down with the suicide attempt of her mother in early November. How she completed these two pictures is truly amazing. However, it is possible her mother's situation was the reason for her reduced activity in 1928. For whatever reason, she did not film a movie until September. Trying to determine what was taking place in her life during much of 1928 is difficult because what media coverage does exist is sketchy.

As mentioned, she was in court in January for her speeding ticket. In February, she was to judge a dancing contest at the Montmartre Café. The event was a "fashion promenade" presented by the May Company. A dancing contest was also a part of the event, and, as guest of honor, Virginia was to select the best couple in the competition.

A few days later, she was involved in an "elaborate" program of entertainment and a "huge" fashion show at the Roosevelt Hotel in Hollywood presented by members of the Junior Hadassah. It was noted that the fashion revue would be led by Miss Virginia Lee Corbin.

A March photograph shows her at the Chicago train station with "Gothamites" Jack Sampson and Jerry Abrams—unidentified otherwise. Apparently they were Gotham employees, but why was Virginia in Chicago? It could be speculated that she had been to New York to pursue the Broadway revue she had announced, and it didn't materialize. One tidbit published about her in May said she was among the new acts soon to be seen in the local (New York) Keith-Albee houses, but no information could be found regarding any New York appearance. Jumping to October, a photo of her in a new DeSoto roadster mentions that she purchased it while making a personal appearance in Topeka, Kansas, and then drove it on to Salt Lake City, Utah. However, there don't seem to be any newspaper accounts of her making a personal appearance in either of these cities in 1928—all rather puzzling.

There is a reference later in the year to her appearance in one or more "Fashion Features," a series of color films presenting the latest fashions. Other stars in this series of films were Loretta Young, Alberta Vaughn and Mae Busch. The most likely location for filming such a series would have been New York, so possibly the Chicago photo was on her way back to Hollywood from these sessions.

In September, she began filming for her second Gotham feature, *The Head of the Family*.

The movie was a starring vehicle for William Russell, a husky actor who had been appearing in movies since 1910 playing in a variety of roles. *The Head of the Family*, though, was a comedy, not the type of picture he typically made. He seemed best suited for westerns in which he was believable and performed well. *The Head of the Family* also starred the 13-year-old Mickey Bennett, Richard Walling, William Welsh, Aggie Herring and Alma Bennett among others.

Based on a *Saturday Evening Post* story, Welsh is a henpecked husband who goes away for a health cure but leaves Eddie (Russell) the plumber in charge of a nagging wife (Herring), a flapper daughter (Virginia), and a reckless son (Walling). By the time the husband returns, Eddie has brought the household in order including taming Alice and rescuing the son from the machinations of a vamp. Of course, Eddie and Alice fall in love—which really was a stretch since Russell was 43 years old at the time, and Virginia was several weeks away from her 17th birthday.

The movie was released December 14, and apparently Gotham had scored once again with the adaption of a *Saturday Evening Post* story. *The Film Daily* was unusually enthusiastic about it. "Recommended heartily. A laugh number that delivers chuckles right through the footage. Also has strong human interest angle.... It has laughs aplenty ... a corking original story.... It was only planned as a good program number, but can easily hold its place as a first run anywhere because it furnishes spontaneous laughs from a brand new angle.... Virginia Lee Corbin furnishes the blonde atmosphere."[13] Even *Variety* praised it: "A pretty good comedy-drama. It is full of laughable situations and no little heart interest, as well as a love story."[14]

Fortunately, 1928 held no great surprises, court battles (other than the speeding ticket in January) or dramas at home for Virginia. Sister Ruth entered into what would be the second of four marriages in her lifetime in June. She married Los Angeles insurance agent Richard Scott Thornton on June 27.

In November her "homecoming" and her mother's birthday were celebrated at the home of Harry Kiener with several other guests in attendance such as Lina Basquette, Sally Blane, Mr. and Mrs. William Russell (Helen Ferguson), Mary Brian and her mother, and others. There was a program of songs, bridge, dancing and a buffet supper. The reason for a "homecoming" is open to question unless it refers to her completion of *The Head of the Family*.

In December, a social column noted that she and handsome actor Grant Withers were "tripping the light jazz-o" at the Ambassador Cocoanut Grove. Withers was only six years older than Virginia and beginning to come into his own in movies in the late twenties. The reference in the column does sound as if the two were out for an evening together.

Throughout the year, Virginia continued to appear in newspapers and magazines modeling clothes or other frivolous things such as the automobile purchase. One newspaper had her modeling a velvet frock for which a pattern could be ordered from the newspaper's fashion department. *Picture Play* magazine ran a page of photos of her, Alice White, Jeanette Loff, Corinne Griffith and Esther Ralston modeling teddies. In another, she was modeling a swimsuit. Still another, she had on an elegant outfit of "French broadcloth of the new beige rose shade with broadtail caracul trimming in the new tier effect."

The Los Angeles Times pictured her behind a large "1928" to introduce the new year in their January 1 issue. The newspaper also pictured her in a spread entitled, "Gals Are So Gorgeous!" along with Olive Borden, Laura La Plante, Dorothy Sebastian, Phyllis

Haver, Ruth Taylor and Joan Crawford. A full page close up photo in *Photoplay* magazine showed how lovely the "grown up" Virginia was. Color artwork of her even graced the cover of the June issue of *True Detective* magazine.

Virginia continued to endorse products. Her photo was used for a Winx liquid lash dressing ad, one of 24 movies stars pictured in Lux Toilet Soap ads, and she modeled a swimsuit for Bradley Knitwear.

With somewhat of a return to normalcy for Virginia in 1928, it seemed her life and career were getting back on track in spite of the reduced film output for the year. Her concerns about her voice were typical of all movie stars at that time as 1928 made the coming of sound pictures a certainty. However life-changing she may have anticipated the advent of talkies would be for her, it was nothing compared to an event in 1929 that would impact her for the rest of her life.

22. Talkies and Troubles

lthough Virginia's third film for Gotham, *Jazzland*, was officially released December 1, 1928, it didn't begin a nationwide distribution until January. Gotham had announced in October that filming would begin on the movie, which was being serialized in newspapers in 1928 under the title *Restless Love* by Samuel Merwin. Jacqueline Logan was announced to star, but she was replaced for unknown reasons by Vera Reynolds.

The story of *Jazzland* is not the most original, and reviewers were quick to criticize that. The small New England town of Ackland is very reserved, and when a new nightclub, Jazzland, opens up, it is cause for concern. The gang running the club is headed by a very prominent citizen in town, Joe Bitner (Carl Stockdale). However, his involvement in the sin palace is a secret, and newspaper editor Hamilton Pew (Forrest Stanley) determines that he will find out. His investigation, though, results in his murder. His brother, Homer (Carroll Nye) takes over the paper. Hometown girl Stella Baggott (Reynolds) returns from college and a writing career in the city and assists Homer in finding out his brother's killer. The duo finally expose Bitner, avenge Hamilton Pew's death, and the two fall in love. Bryant Washburn's part in the film is secondary, a friend from the city that Stella has called to come and help. Virginia is Martha Baggott, Stella's younger sister. She complicates matters when she goes to the club and gets involved with the nightclub ruffians.

One of the taglines for the film called it "a story of modern youth and modern sin," hopefully to tantalize patrons to come see it. However, *Film Daily* wasn't impressed calling it an "inane film, poorly directed and acted, rates poor, little to recommend it … just another adaptation of a magazine story that proves a washout in picture form."[1] *The Chicago Tribune* reviewer wrote, "STORY: Blah."[2] Interestingly, *Variety* took a totally opposite viewpoint. "*Jazzland* is a gem in the indie feature class. It's excellent handling, cast and smoothly moving, convincing and actionful continuity stand it on its own. The picture is a safe bet for the better second runs. It is a sure wow for the usuals," adding that "sophisticated fans will find themselves thoroughly entertained and unable to hand out at its close a single piece of justifiable adverse criticism."[3] Apparently the *Film Daily* and *Chicago Tribune* reviewers weren't "sophisticated."

Unfortunately, fans today are not able to judge the merits of the movie for themselves since this is another lost film.

Vera Reynolds was the star of *Jazzland* (1928); however, this one-sheet poster features Virginia apparently causing angst for her mother, played by Florence Turner. The film was about the trouble a nightclub named Jazzland causes in a small New England town, including Virginia's character when she gets involved with ruffians at the "sin palace" (image courtesy Hershenson/Allen Archive).

A few months into the year, brief announcements could be seen in exhibitors' publications that Virginia's next movie for Gotham would be called *Knee High*. Gotham described it as "a worthy sequel to the first run success, *Bare Knees*. A hilarious comedy woven around a girl with the most beautiful legs in the state." The premise sounds very intriguing—especially since it was designed as a follow-up to *Bare Knees*. The only problem is that the movie was never made. There are online sources that list it among Virginia's filmography, which, obviously, are in error.

Instead, Virginia was able to claim the distinction of starring in Mack Sennett's first "all-talking, all-singing, all-dancing, all-color" comedy short. It was entitled *Jazz Mammas* and co-starred Sennett stalwart Vernon Dent. Made in the spring of 1929, this was Virginia's first acting job of the year. It is curious that she made just this one two-reeler and didn't make any other films for Sennett.

It is also likely that Virginia was chosen for the "all-singing, all-dancing" comedy because of her talents in those two areas—not to mention how adept she was at comedy. Assuming she is singing and dancing in this short, it makes it all the more tragic that *Jazz Mammas* is a lost film.

Although her film production may have slowed, her social life continued on its usual course. In February, she attended a performance of *Weak Sisters* at the Majestic Theatre with Franklin Pangborn, Priscilla Dean and Maurice Costello in the cast. Following the performance, several "charmingly gowned young women" promenaded down the aisle and onto the stage. Among them were Virginia, Sally Blane, Pauline Garon, Jane Winton, Mae Busch, Jackie Saunders, Belle Bennett and others.

Back to her favorite café, the Montmartre, a few days later, Virginia entertained "a charming affair" in honor of Mrs. Charles Caplan of New York and Miss Madeline Sheldon. There is no identification of these two ladies or their connection with Virginia.

In April, she was the weekend guest of Mrs. Marcel Grand and was her honored guest at the Rendezvous Ball Room in Newport Beach.

That same month she was back at the Montmartre hosting a luncheon in honor of her sister, Ruth. Among the several guests was Lina Basquette with whom Virginia was a friend.

Once again she was pictured in a newspaper's fashion page wearing "an exquisite afternoon ensemble of green chiffon, the ruffles and scarf on dress and coat giving it an individual touch," designed by Jean Swartz, a popular designer on Hollywood Boulevard.

Virginia was arrested once again in March—she still had not gotten her driver's license. She did not go to court, and, thankfully, this didn't receive the coverage her speeding ticket got in December.

The last time the subject of a guardian for Virginia came up was in late 1927 when papers were being drawn up for Miss Mildred B. Campbell of the City Board of Education to be her guardian. Throughout 1928, the subject never came up again. Considering the involvement of her mother in Virginia's life during the past year, it is likely mother and daughter had made up and were on good terms once again.

But in April of 1929, Virginia was again seeking to free herself from her mother. As before, she cited her mother's dissipation of her earnings and added that her mother was frightening her once again with "threats." The "threats," no doubt, were to attempt suicide again.

For once, her age was listed correctly—which it likely had to be for court purposes—as 17 years old. She had just celebrated that birthday the previous December. On April 12, a court placed Virginia in temporary custody of Mrs. Helen Keyser, a friend of the family. Miss Campbell had apparently exited the picture. The whole affair took on an air of mystery in early May when Virginia was reported as missing—likely by Mrs. Corbin since she was fond of contacting the media on the slightest provocation regarding her daughter. Although the previous petition for a guardian had been withdrawn when mother and daughter reached an agreement, only one day later, Virginia and her mother were once again having trouble, according to her attorney. There was no cause for concern, the attorney assured everyone, because Virginia was not missing. "Miss Corbin said she'd go crazy if she stayed with her mother another day and that she was going away. I know where she is and know that she's all right," he said.[4]

Then, less than two weeks later, Virginia appeared in Superior Court to have a different guardian appointed. This time it would be Mark C. Gilchrist, an "elderly, retired businessman" who had known the actress from her childhood. The arrangement was said to have been agreed upon by Mrs. Corbin, but once in court, Virginia changed her mind and told the judge she'd rather have a female for a guardian. Her reason was that she may want to live with her guardian. The case was to continue the next day, and, if Virginia and her attorney could not agree on a guardian, an ad would be placed in newspapers asking for prospective guardians to apply. This was apparently Virginia's idea—not the judge's.

Her next trip to the courtroom was no more successful. With no guardian to offer the court, a one-week delay took place before the next hearing. What transpired after that is not known. It is likely, though, that her big break to make her first sound film put personal problems on hold—and bad publicity which no one wanted while the film was being made.

Ever since *The Jazz Singer* hit the screens in 1927, Hollywood had been abuzz with both excitement and worries about sound—a revolution that some

At 17 years old, Virginia had become a very beautiful young lady, as photographs such as this attest. This publicity photograph was titled "The Charm of Youth," adding, "was never better exemplified than in this picture of Virginia Lee Corbin, former child star, now grown up..."

predicted would never catch on but others embraced and forged ahead. In 1928, the number of sound films being produced was growing by leaps and bounds, and in 1929, the number of silent films was very small. Virginia certainly had no worries about sound films with her stage experience, although many stars were concerned that their voices would not be suitable for the microphone.

However, Virginia's first foray into sound pictures turned out to be a good experience for her. Not only was she received well, she had the opportunity to make her sound debut in a well-produced film, with a major studio (First National again), and alongside a major star—Colleen Moore.

The two male leads in *Footlights and Fools* were up and coming young actors. Raymond Hackett had made films sporadically since he was a kid in the 'teens. Fredric March, on the other hand, was just starting out in 1929 on a stellar screen career that would continue into the 1970s.

Moore played Fifi D'Auray, supposedly an exotic French actress who is the talk of the town in "The Sins of 1930." In reality, she is Betty Murphy who had gone to France at the urging of her producer to gain a more sophisticated, international persona. She has been in love with Jimmy Willet (Raymond Hackett) since her chorus girl days. Although she doesn't know he's a gambler and a crook, she still won't give in to his pleas for marriage until he gets a real job. In the meantime, the wealthy Gregory Pyne (March) shows up and takes an interest in Fifi. He bribes Fifi's friend, Claire (Virginia), to take Fifi to a cabaret after the theatre where he will meet her. Pyne arrives, and, not recognizing Fifi out of costume, identifies himself. Before Claire can introduce Fifi, she pretends to be someone else and says derogatory things about her alter ego, Fifi. Pyne leaves in disgust after defending Fifi. To make up for the quarrel, Pyne offers Jimmy a job as treasurer of the theater.

So Betty/Fifi agrees to secretly marry Jimmy since he now has a good job, but when there is a robbery at the theater, Jimmy is arrested and Fifi claims Pyne framed him. It comes to light that Jimmy and Betty/Fifi are married, and, of course, Pyne is disillusioned. Betty/Fifi learns that Jimmy has used her all along. The story ends with Betty/Fifi planning to divorce Jimmy and turning down Pyne as well—neither of the men winning the girl in the end.

Virginia signed a contract to do the film May 27. She was contracted for $350 a week with only a one-week minimum, much less than the $750 per week she received from First National for *Ladies at Play* and *The Perfect Sap* two years earlier.[5] Her start date was given as June 3, although filming on the movie began in May and concluded July 12. Exactly how much of that time Virginia was involved in the filming is unknown, but her part was significant, secondary only to the three leads. The movie was all-talking with lots of singing and dancing, at least by Moore—and Technicolor sequences. There is no mention of Virginia's part requiring either of these talents, but, if it did, once again, her expertise in these areas may have accounted for her selection to appear in the film. *Footlights and Fools* is a lost film with only Vitaphone sound discs surviving in the UCLA archive.

Obviously, reviews focused on Colleen Moore, but *The Los Angeles Times* reviewer gave Virginia special notice, proclaiming, "One of the biggest hits is made by Virginia Lee Corbin as a friend of the heroine. It is she who joins Colleen in providing the comedy."[6] In another issue, the same reviewer said, "A real Lorelei is presented by Virginia Lee Corbin who is manifestly clever."[7] *Variety* thought Virginia did her part well, noting,

Virginia's talkie debut was in Colleen Moore's starring vehicle *Footlights and Fools* (1929). Both played chorus girls; Virginia was Moore's best friend. The film was also an early role for Fredric March who plays one of two men in love with Moore's character. Moore was given ample opportunity for singing and dancing in her sound debut, but, since it is a lost film, it is not known if Virginia may have had the opportunity to display her singing and dancing talents or not.

"Virginia Lee Corbin is adept as a dumb chorine."[8] *New York Times* reviewer Mordaunt Hall didn't mention Virginia, but he slammed Colleen Moore's dancing—"And also many of the dancing scenes in which Miss Moore makes a sad mess of the terpsichorean bits"—but did compliment one of her songs—"There is one song sequence, however, 'If I Can't Have You,' in which Miss Moore does some good singing."[9] Interestingly, in her autobiography, Moore barely mentions this movie (and no mention of Virginia)— only pointing out that Fredric March was her costar, and that director William Seiter, so accustomed to silent film, would burst out laughing in the middle of recording a comedy scene.

Although the film was not Colleen Moore's biggest hit, Virginia was given a great start to a career in the talkies. With First National again, she wasn't working for a second-class studio. She was in a well-budgeted production with a major star, and she got good notices. Unfortunately, by the time it was released on November 8, Virginia's life was once again splattered all over the newspapers, and not for good reasons.

23. Enter Teddy

*A*s soon as *Virginia finished* her work on *Footlights and Fools*, she "disappeared." Her guardian, who ended up being Helen Keyser, reported this to missing persons saying that Virginia disappeared after receiving a $2,400 paycheck (equal to about $33,000 in 2018) from First National. She had also failed to attend a meeting with her attorney, David A. Hill, relative to the legal affairs between her and her mother. Both Hill and Keyser suggested that she was abducted since she had last been seen in the company of a "dark and foreign-looking man." Keyser said the last time she saw her was the previous Sunday (July 14) and had reprimanded her about staying out late. One newspaper report said she was on her way to New York to join the cast of a Florenz Ziegfeld-Sam Goldwyn production.

Before the day was out, authorities were able to determine that she was aboard the Santa Fe train en route to Chicago. Then, the next day, word spread that she was on her way to New York to meet up with "Teddy" Krol (misspelled Kroll), a broker, in New York. This was confirmed by Krol, himself, who said he hoped they would be able to name a wedding date soon. Keyser downplayed the whole issue saying that Virginia was old enough to make the trip if she wished, and that Virginia had written a letter to her while traveling on the train, which she had received. Keyser assumed she was going to New York to join a stage show there. Of course, Mrs. Corbin could not stay away from the media. She told reporters that Virginia had hinted at elopement with a "Hollywood man." She added, "It would not surprise me to hear that she has been secretly married."[1]

Suddenly, the story went away and didn't reappear until the third week in October, at which time Mrs. Corbin told the press that Virginia and Theodore Krol (this time referred to as "Crow") had married eight weeks previously in Greenwich, Connecticut. Virginia returned home in early October to complete some contractual commitments, although it is unclear what these may have been since she was not making a movie at this time. Krol was still in New York but planned to come to Hollywood in order to take his new wife abroad.

One columnist noted a change in Virginia's hair color. "Mrs. Corbin's famous blonde daughter, by the way, no longer is Virginia Lee Corbin, and she no longer is blonde.... Her hair, golden since babyhood, now is its natural, and, it must be confessed, less becoming shade of medium brown."[2]

There is one event confirmed that Virginia attended while she was back in Hollywood. In early November she was back at the Montmartre, this time to attend a birthday party for Alberta Vaughn's son. Mrs. Corbin was also there.

But, after a brief two weeks back home, she and Krol left in mid–November for New York and then on to Europe. The report said Virginia and her new husband would make Hollywood their home, and that Virginia planned to continue her screen career.

Marriage records confirm that Virginia and Krol married December 18 in New York. This may have been to ensure everything was legal since Virginia would have been 17 years old when they married in Greenwich, and she would have been 18 years old for the second wedding, having turned 18 on December 5. Therefore, the departure for Europe would have taken place sometime after December 18.

It was obvious Virginia's ordeals with her mother impacted her decision to get married at 17 years old. The relationship with her mother also easily explains the secretiveness behind her elopement with this man who suddenly appeared from nowhere. One report said she was going to New York to marry an "admirer," and Krol may have been an admirer who sought her out and charmed her. Considering the events of Virginia's life at this time, she would be very easily charmed, particularly if it were someone who could support her and get her away from the hell she had been experiencing with her mother—a hell that only got worse as Virginia grew older. It wasn't just the fights. Virginia's constant reference to her mother's dissipation of her earnings shows she was both angry and hurt that she had worked all those years, was at an age now to begin taking on some responsibility for her earnings, and there were no earnings left. Krol, no doubt, was her savior, coming along at the exact time she needed someone to rescue her from her mother.

And the newspaper reports that mentioned a "dark, foreign looking man" were pretty much on target—whatever "foreign-looking" means. Krol was the son of Russian immigrants, and he was dark and handsome. Sometimes referred to as a New York broker and, at other times, a Chicago broker, Virginia would find out one day that the term "broker" was a bit broad, at least for her "Teddy," and didn't really pinpoint a nine-to-five type of job. Their trip abroad was predicted to be about six months—not an unexpected stay in those days before flights and when travel took longer. The stay would prove to be much longer, though—and detrimental to Virginia's career. Esther Linn, Virginia's neighbor mentioned in Chapter 19, suggested the couple stayed out of the country for so long so that Krol could avoid an indictment. However, this could not be confirmed.

The Krols sailed to England, and stayed at the upscale Savoy Hotel on the Strand in London. Obviously, Krol was going first class for their honeymoon. In February 1930, reports back in the States said Virginia had signed to do two pictures with British International Films. Once these two films are completed, the Krols said they would be traveling to Rome, Paris and Berlin. Word reached the States in July that she would be playing the lead opposite Percy Marmont in a British International movie. It seemed that the honeymoon would not be putting her career on hold. The only problem was, she never made any movies for anyone in 1930.

The British fan magazine *Picturegoer* ran a full page interview with her in its April 1930 issue. Although she was quoted about marriage, her plans to continue acting and so on, there was no mention of a contract with British International. "This is my first trip," she said. And, in spite of having a cold, she excitedly told the reporter, "Teddy and I are just going to run around now and enjoy ourselves for a bit…. While I'm in London, I want to go to all the interesting places and to some theatres, too." Regarding her marriage, she said she hated "fussy" weddings, so she and Krol eloped. Then, altering the way things actually transpired a bit, she told the reporter, "We were in New York at the time—I was in a show there—then we went back to California and broke the news to mother." She continued, "I think I like film work best of all, and I love talkies. They

This photograph was taken somewhere in England during Virginia's year-long honeymoon with husband Theodore Krol. They were married in December 1929 and sailed shortly after to England where they stayed for most of 1930. Virginia claimed that while in England she studied elocution to further her career in sound pictures. Unfortunately, she would find the absence hurt her career rather than helped it.

make pictures so much more real." When the reporter asked her if marriage would make any difference in her screen career, she replied, "I hope not.... I think film people make a mistake when they marry a member of the same profession. They're apt to get jealous of one another. But Teddy and I have different professions, and we're interested in each other's work. I'm sure we'll always be happy."[3]

American fan magazines hadn't forgotten her either. *Motion Picture Magazine* ran a story on her entitled "Little Bread-Winner." Since Virginia was out of the country, Mrs. Corbin is quoted throughout the article. Commenting on how different her two daughters are, she said Ruth was very reserved and thoughtful while Virginia "is lively and reckless. She's always singing and dancing and clowning. But she's a wonderful little girl, and a good girl. She has supported her mother and her sister and herself all her life, and still supports me."

Surprisingly, she was very candid in the article about her separation from her husband. "I broke with my husband because of it [Virginia's career]. He objected to his baby's being exploited, and things were never the same between us after I left him in Long Beach, and took Virginia to Hollywood. I put my elder girl in the convent and left her there till she was seventeen so I could devote all my time to Virginia."

"I kept her out of school," she continued, "kept her away from children, and made her study music, dancing, singing, and painting. I did it, as I thought, for her own sake, but I see now that it deprived her of her childhood. You can't hold a child to her studies, make her work all the time between the ages of four and twelve, and expect her to develop naturally."[4]

Pointing out that Mrs. Corbin's own dreams of being on the stage were squelched, the article gives some further insight into the obsession Mrs. Corbin had with Virginia's career—living her dream vicariously through her daughter—to the point that it was her whole life. No wonder there was conflict when Virginia began to grow up and exercise her independence.

Mrs. Corbin continued regular contact with the newspapers informing them in July that Virginia and Krol planned to return to Hollywood in September. *The Los Angeles Times* reported November 19 that Mrs. Corbin had telephoned them the day before to let them know Virginia had sailed from Southampton on the 17th. She also informed the newspaper that "a certain picture company" was negotiating with her daughter, adding that Virginia had been studying French, dancing and voice culture while abroad. It is likely the only truth to any of this is the fact that she had left England.

The Krols arrived in New York aboard the *Leviathan* on November 24, a little less than a year after leaving on their honeymoon. "Virginia Lee Corbin ... came home from London today with a nice new English accent. 'When talkies began to displace the silent films, I decided an English accent would be a great help.' So she spent most of the year studying elocution and voice culture in England."[5]

One columnist poked fun at Virginia's announcement. "Virginia Lee Corbin, one of the squawky queens, has returned to Hollywood with the startling announcement that when the pictures began to talk, she knew she must do something about it; so she went and lived in England for a year and now has a perfectly lovely English accent. We've known lots of American gals who went across the pond to get an English accent, but when they came back, they still talked right through their cunning little snooties, and all the English accent they had was: 'I say,' 'my word,' 'how perfectly ripping,' and 'well, rawthah,' which is our notion of zero in English accents."[6]

By all appearances, Virginia was happy in her new marriage and had thoroughly enjoyed their year in Europe. She had determined that there was benefit in going to England for a year, that it would help her with her elocution, and that she would return to the United States and continue her film career as if nothing had changed, but things had changed, much more than she realized.

The Krols' lives were apparently untouched by the stock market crash of 1929. The market had crumbled just as they were leaving on their honeymoon, so obviously Krol's money, wherever his money came from, was not tied up in stocks. As for their year in England, it is curious how he was paying for this lavish, 12-month long excursion. Looking at their life together, it does not appear Krol was independently wealthy, so how would he generate income while overseas?

Virginia also underestimated the changes that had taken place in Hollywood since she left. A whole new wave of movie stars had risen to the top of the heap, and the majority of those who had successful careers in the silents either left the business entirely, faded quickly after a few attempts at sound, or were relegated to secondary, or even uncredited, roles. The continental speech that Hollywood was clamoring for at the beginning of sound wasn't much in demand anymore. Edward F. Gloss said it well in his newspaper column about Virginia's return from Europe. "Broad accents, cultured on distant shores were the 'thing' Hollywood wanted when the celluloid first learned to babble. Now Virginia is back with an English accent, which she hopes will pave the way to immediate success. Back with an accent that the movies wanted when she ran away—and don't particularly care for at this moment. An actor or an actress who has a good, strongly entrenched penchant for pronouncing his 'r's' as hard as rock and unable to find a 'w' in 'can't,' 'bath,' or 'laugh' is just as popular around the studios today as the best linguist Oxford ever graduated."[7]

Given her background on the stage, Virginia was confident she could make the transition easily. After all, hadn't she done well in *Footlights and Fools*? But Virginia's stage experience was vaudeville, not the "legitimate" stage. Also, Hollywood quickly forgets, and she had been gone for over a year. Whatever reason there was for her upcoming struggles to re-establish herself in movies, it is obvious the year in England did not help her career as she had hoped—more likely, the time away injured it.

24. But It's Work

*A*fter *Virginia had been* home for a few months, she was telling reporters in April 1931 that she had several offers for film roles but had not decided which one to accept. The reality of the movie industry in the 1930s, though, was that studio heads saw former silent stars as passé. One columnist in June of 1931 referred to "those hoary-headed old-timers Jackie Coogan, Ben Alexander and Virginia Lee Corbin" although Virginia was only 19 at the time.

By June, though, she was definitely cast for at least a couple of pictures. The first, *Morals for Women*, was a starring vehicle for Bessie Love. Virginia was in a supporting role and has barely more than three minutes of screen time altogether, as a dizzy blonde talking in a babyish voice. Along with Love, she is one of four characters who play "kept women" in the movie, her friend Lina Basquette and Natalie Moorhead playing the others, Flora and Claudia. Helen (Love) is met by Flora and Claudia, two wise-cracking friends, in the hallway outside her apartment—an apartment paid for by the rich Van Dyne. Virginia shows up with the baby doll voice wearing satin pajamas. A silly scene takes place inside Helen's apartment where Maybelle (Virginia) tells the other two girls about her benefactor, the Rolls Royce he has given her, and how she allowed a friend to sell it so he could invest money in the stock market—keep in mind this is the beginning of the Depression. The other two girls laugh at her, but Maybelle says she has tripled her money. Claudia and Flora pull a knife and tease Maybelle about cutting her up into two rabbit's feet. Maybelle is terrified by their "craziness," and leaves. Although the rest of the movie does have a passable, mediocre story, this sequence falls flat and does nothing to help Virginia. By the way, Virginia's bio from the early thirties lists her at five foot five. The movie confirms at least that since she seems to tower three or four inches above the other girls.

Small-town girl Helen goes to the city and does well, but only by being the mistress of the wealthy Van Dyne (Conway Tearle) who provides her with a job as his secretary and a lavish apartment. When a childhood friend, Paul (John Holland), who has since become wealthy, arrives and wants to marry her, she decides to go home and give up her life in the city. However, her brother (David Rollins) gets in a fight at a local nightclub defending Helen's honor and puts the other guy in the hospital. It will take $1,000 to prevent the offended family from pressing charges. Helen, in order to get the money, returns to the city and her former life. Her mother, father and Paul arrive in the city one night when she is hosting a party for Van Dyne. At the party, Paul learns of her affair with Van Dyne and walks out. Helen decides once and for all to go home and give up her life in the city. In the end, Paul returns to her, and they are married.

Morals for Women, re-released sometime later as *Big City Interlude*, was released October 25 by Tiffany Productions. Tiffany was a minor company that began in 1921 and turned out an occasional quality production. However, by the early 1930s, it was in financial trouble and ceased operations in 1932. Obviously, the several offers Virginia was contemplating earlier in the year did not include any of the major studios.

As one would expect, no one got excited about the film. *Film Daily* called it a "weak modern story," adding that the ending "falls flat."[1] *Harrison's Reports* told its readers that it was "ordinary and at times boresome. It's a sex play without any subtlety. There is little sympathy for any of the characters."[2] *Photoplay* offered a kind word or two, though. "You'll find a few entertaining twists in this ... if for no other reason, it deserves a hand for bringing back that good trouper, Bessie Love."[3] To Tiffany's credit, the movie was somewhat of a gathering of former silent stars. In addition to Love and Virginia, former names in the film that were popular in the silent days were Conway Tearle, Lina Basquette, David Rollins and Edmund Breese.

Morals for Women began production in late June, and even before Virginia had finished with this picture, announcements were being made about her selection to co-star with cowboy star Tim McCoy in his next picture, *Shotgun Pass* for Columbia Pictures.

A typical "B" western, the story has Tim Walker (McCoy) in charge of delivering 1,200 horses, in partnership with the Seagrue ranch, to the military. Bad guy Jake Mitchell (Monte Vandergrift) and his gang intend to prevent him, claiming Tim is gathering horses on "their range." The Seagrues are Sally (Virginia) and her brother, Lon (Dick Stewart). Tim frustrates an attempt by Jake to get the intoxicated Lon to sign a partnership agreement with him to round up horses. At Shotgun Pass, Spider Mitchell (Joe Marba) accidentally shoots Lon mistaking him for Tim. Tim's investigation finds a belt buckle impression at the site of the crime and is able to pin the shooting on Spider. Nevertheless, the Mitchell gang intends to stop Tim from delivering horses to the military by putting a fence across Shotgun Pass. When Tim arrives with the horses, after words with Jake Mitchell and his gang who are defending the pass, he blows up the fence. Jake is accidentally blown up with it, and the sheriff arrives to arrest Spider. In the end, Tim delivers the horses, and the movie ends with the obligatory embrace, kiss and fadeout.

After a synopsis of the plot, *Film Daily* said, "The film shapes up better than it sounds. Plenty of fast action, fighting and suspense nicely built up."[4] Grading it only a notch down from their highest "Very Good" rating, *Motion Picture Herald* did give the movie a "Good" rating. "This is a typical old-fashioned melodrama and is reminiscent of the stories used in the early days of the movies. But it is a tale of cowboys; the exciting riding of horses would appeal to boys."[5] Although minor in the grand scheme of things, at least one reviewer took notice of Virginia's part in the movie. "Virginia Lee Corbin as his sweetheart gives a most appealing characterization. Her acting at all times is convincing—and she makes an attractive cowgirl."[6] However, the role of Sally gave Virginia

After returning from England, Virginia was fortunate to get bit roles in films or a supporting role in a "B" western, such as *Shot Gun Pass* (1931) with cowboy star Tim McCoy. She did well as McCoy's love interest, but, unfortunately, when former stars appeared in "B" westerns, it was typically a sign of a career that had waned.

nothing to do but stay at the ranch, give a very unemotional reaction to her brother's shooting, and participate in a couple of love scenes with McCoy. The only time she is involved in the action is at the very end. McCoy and Sagebrush have lit the fuse for the dynamite to blow up the fence in Shotgun Pass, then ride away at a distance with the other men and herd of horses. Along comes Sally to ride through the pass, not realizing the situation. When Tim sees her get down off her horse to open the gate on the fence, he rushes in on horseback, sweeps her up onto his horse and gallops off before the explosion occurs.

Almost always when actresses who had enjoyed a level of stardom in the movies ended up in "B" westerns, it meant their day had come and gone. Unfortunately, it was no different for Virginia. The next two movies were her last credited roles, and both were low budget films for Poverty Row studios.

Morals for Women and *Shotgun Pass* were released within a week of each other, and Virginia's next film was released less than a month after *Shotgun Pass*. Virginia had begun filming on the first of her 1931 releases back in the summer, but these low budget films were turned out quickly which accounts for her having four films released in the span of six weeks at the end of 1931.

Back at Tiffany studios, *X Marks the Spot*, released November 29, was a crime drama that starred Lew Cody, with a long career in silent film behind him, and Wallace Ford. Cody is Ford's newspaper editor friend, and he does a very impressive, very natural job of acting. Sadly, his time in sound films would be short. Cody passed away just two years later at age 50.

Ford acted in over 200 films between 1932 and 1965. In his early films, he was a quick-talking, wavy-haired lead in many B pictures. By the 1950s, he was playing a grizzled old-timer in most of his roles. He actually has the lead role in this film—only his second full-length feature at the beginning of a long career.

X Marks the Spot tells of a reporter, Ted (Ford), whose young sister is hit by a car and paralyzed from the waist down. He needs $5,000 for an operation for her, and the only person he can get to give it to him is the gangster Riggs (Fred Kohler). Riggs gives him the money, and Ted tells him he'll never forget. Eight years later, a chorus girl is murdered, and Ted is the suspect. Ted sets out to clear himself and finds out that Riggs was the murderer. Because of the favor Riggs did for him eight years earlier, he can't turn Riggs in, and he also provides the crook with money that he needs. Unfortunately, Ted is followed by his friend and newspaper editor, George (Cody), to Riggs' apartment, along with the police. The movie ends with a courtroom scene where Riggs pulls a gun that a fellow crook hid under a table for him, takes a hostage and holds off the police. Thinking Ted turned him in, he threatens to kill his hostage unless they send Ted into the room. Ted goes in with a gun and has a shootout with Riggs.

The New York Times said the movie presented "the excitements which go into ... tabloid journalism ... with success," adding that "in the final scenes, with a condemned murderer loose in a court house, it rises to a breathtaking climax."[7] Lew Cody, Wallace Ford and Fred Kohler were singled out for praise. *Harrison's Reports* called it "A very good picture.... It succeeds in holding the interest well."[8] It is interesting, considering Virginia's small part, that this review mentioned her among the cast.

Of the four films in which Virginia appeared in 1931, this would, by far, be the best story. However, after a three-minute segment near the beginning, Virginia doesn't appear again. About 16 minutes into the movie, we see her as one of several chorus girls who run into their dressing room from the stage. Hortense (Virginia) has a short conversation with Vivyan (Mary Nolan) as they are dressing about Vivyan's good fortune with her new "benefactor." Then the girls walk out of the stage door where Ted is waiting. Trying to get something for a story, he attempts a conversation with Vivyan, but she won't give him the time of day, gets in a Rolls Royce and is driven off. Hortense comes out, and Virginia is given the opportunity for some typical 1930s wordplay filled with innuendo.

"Hello, Hortense!"

"Oh, hello."

"Say, a little ritzy there, isn't she?" says Ted referring to the aloof Vivyan as she leaves.

"I'll say."

"Nice car."

"Yea, if that wouldn't make an honest girl want to rub mud in her powder puff!"

"Rolls!" says Ted commenting on the expensive car.

"...and chauffeur!" adds Hortense.

X Marks the Spot (1931) was a crime drama that gave Virginia only about three minutes of screen time. She plays Hortense, a gold digging chorus girl, who has a few minutes of snappy dialogue with reporter Wallace Ford. This lobby card shows Virginia, seated in her underclothes on the left side of the dressing table after a show and getting ready for an evening with her rich "sugar daddy" (courtesy Kirby McDaniel MovieArt, Austin, Texas).

"She's come up in the world."

"I'll say! Last season she was lucky to have rolls and coffee."

"That one's in." Ted writes what Hortense said on his notepad. "Rolls and chauffeur. Rolls and coffee."

"...and an apartment on Park Avenue and a maid. And the good ol' salary is still $75 dollars a week."

"One might reasonably ask how does she do it?" Ted asks.

"Well, $75 goes a long ways on Broadway." Hortense says with innuendo.

"That one's in, too." Writes in his notepad. "Thanks, Hortense. I'm gonna do something very, very nice for you."

"What?"

"I'm gonna run a picture of you in the paper."

Hortense, laughs. "Oh, they always run my pictures."

"But I'm gonna run one with your clothes on."

Ted looks out at a large, expensive limousine waiting for someone.

"Whose car is that?"

"That old thing?" Hortense says. "Mine."

As she gets in the car, Ted shouts, "I got it! Broadway arithmetic!"

For the first time ever, Virginia was seen onscreen with brown hair—her natural color. Newspapers ran a story on how this came about. When she went to casting, the response was, "Too bad. You would be perfect if you were a brunette—or a redhead. Blondes are out." Virginia dashed out to make-up artist Perc Westmore and returned in a brown wig. "Do I get the job?" she asked. She did.

The last credited role of Virginia's career was in *Forgotten Women*, released December 1 by Monogram and starring Marion Shilling. Shilling, just one year older than Virginia, started out in films in 1929. She had some good roles in early sound films opposite stars like William Powell and Constance Bennett, but, with films like *Forgotten Women*, her career began to fade, and she also ended up being a western queen with several popular cowboy stars of the thirties. She finally retired at age 25 in 1936. *Forgotten Women* also co-starred Clara Bow's future husband Rex Bell.

Interestingly the story was written by Adele Buffington, the same author who wrote *Bare Knees*. Pat (Shilling), an aspiring actress, loves Jimmy (Bell), a reporter. Pat rooms with an elderly lady, Fern (Beryl Mercer), who also works as an extra in the movies. When Fern accidentally learns of Sleek Moran's (Edward Earle) secret involvement in a movie studio, she tells Jimmy, and he runs a story that gets him a promotion to city editor. Jimmy gets involved with the newspaper owner's rich daughter (Carmelita Geraghty). Pat doesn't realize this is the reason for his reluctance to marry her. Despondent over Jimmy's rejection, Pat takes Sissy's (Virginia) advice and allows Sissy and her "sugar daddy," Tony, to introduce her to Moran. At Moran's apartment, Pat agrees to go on a South Seas cruise with him. While at the apartment, one of Moran's men comes in to tell him they've had a gun battle and killed four police. Moran and his men must flee. Pat agrees to go with him. Fern goes to the newspaper office and tells Jimmy what happened, and a car chase along the Pacific Coast Highway ensues. Jimmy runs the gang off a cliff and captures Moran just as police arrive. Jimmy and Pat then agree to get married.

Film Daily didn't care for the movie. "They threw a lot of the good old hoke elements into this one, and came out with a film that has its entertaining moments for uncritical audiences. The story is too far fetched and illogical to make much impression on the more critical audiences."[9] *Photoplay* wasn't impressed, either. "Marion Shilling, Carmelita Geraghty, Virginia Lee Corbin and Edna Murphy are all attractive to the eye, which is about as much as you can say for this story of a cub reporter on a big daily. Rex Bell is the pencil and notebook boy."[10]

Virginia has a significant role in the film and plays it well. As Sissy, she's the wisecracking friend of the down-to-earth and hard-working Pat. However, Sissy is a mistress to bootlegger Tony. As the story opens, she is doing a bit part in a movie, and when the director chides her, she tells him off and gets fired. Typical of the 1930s movies, she also has a heart of gold. As they are leaving the studio, Sissy goes to Tony, who is waiting in his car, gets some money, then gives it to Pat telling her to pay this month's rent with it.

Later she drives Pat home to her rooming house. Pat talks to Jimmy in the hallway—he has suddenly decided to leave the rooming house for a nice apartment. Inside

Pat's room, it's Sissy who tells Fern about Jimmy's involvement with the newspaper owner's daughter, but at Fern's insistence, she agrees not to tell Pat.

Virginia returns for her third appearance about three-quarters of the way into the movie. Pat has just returned from spending the night at Jimmy's apartment and comes home dejected because she realizes Jimmy isn't going to marry her. Pat tells Fern her ordeal and cries. Sissy comes into the room and shows Pat a newspaper story announcing Jimmy's engagement to the newspaper owner's daughter. "Men are either brutes or suckers, and the best way to get even with the brutes is to forget about 'em and take it out on the suckers," Sissy tells her. "You gotta start livin' and get a lot of fun out of life." They go to Sleek Moran's apartment. Virginia is also good in this scene, swaggering in, sitting down at the piano, and saying to Tony, "Gimme a cigarette." Speaking to Moran, she says, "I'm beginning to feel at home in this dump." Her acting is relaxed and natural, and she meets the requirements of the role very well.

The part was an improvement on the roles in her previous three sound films. Unfortunately, the movie wasn't of the quality that was going to help anyone's career who appeared in it. Virginia remained hopeful to the end of her life that she would make a "comeback," possibly with the same popularity she enjoyed in the silent era. Not only would she be disappointed that her dream would never be realized, she also didn't know that her dream marriage would soon turn into a nightmare.

25. Children, Divorce and Renewed Hopes

Although most of 1931 went well for Virginia, particularly in these happy, early days of her marriage, but, unfortunately, it was inevitable that legal troubles would have to raise their ugly head again.

In July, a complaint was filed by H. Lichtig and Ben K. Englander, motion picture booking agents, claiming they procured Virginia her role in *Footlights and Fools* back in 1929 and were not properly compensated for their work. They claimed Virginia earned $1,920 for her work from May 27 to July 6, 1929. They were, therefore, entitled to 10 percent, or $192. Virginia had only paid them $122, and they asked the court to award them the balance.

In November another complaint was filed by Dr. E.W. Trice claiming that she incurred a bill of $300 for medical care nearly four years earlier that she had not paid. No resolution to either of these complaints was subsequently published.

In spite of these problems, Virginia continued her social life in 1931 as her work schedule would allow. September 8, she made a personal appearance at the Los Angeles Theatre along with the Universal feature *Graft* starring Regis Toomey and Sue Carol.

September 12, she attended a dance contest a the Roosevelt Roof Garden Tea "Dansant." Stars did not compete in the contest, but several were in attendance such as Ginger Rogers, Mary Brian, Alice Day, Neil Hamilton, Ernst Lubitsch, Jack Holt and others.

In early October, society columns said Virginia had just returned from several days' vacation in San Francisco. She also enjoyed horse races, one column noting that when she goes to Agua Caliente, she carries a lucky rabbit's foot with her.

As 1932 rounded the corner, Virginia was still on movie screens with all four of her 1931 sound films playing throughout the year somewhere in the country. However, she did disappear from view on a personal level, but that was easy to explain when it was reported in March that she was expecting. Her first son, Harold Phillip Krol, was born August 16, and within a month, photos of her with the new baby were circulating in newspapers around the country. Several of the reports said she had retired from the screen. Some even said she had retired in 1929 after marrying Krol. Obviously, her last four sound films had slipped by those newspaper writers.

Once again in November 1932, though, someone was filing suit against Virginia—this time naming Krol as well. Charles A. Stevens & Co. of Chicago claimed the Krols had an unpaid clothing bill of $152.60, a debt that had been due since September 15, 1931. Whether this was paid or not isn't known. What is known is that the Krols left for Europe in November and wouldn't return until the summer of 1934. Their address before leaving for Europe was given as 4865 Magnolia Avenue in Chicago. While in Europe, they stayed at the Hotel Palma Etoile Maillot near the Arc de Triomphe, known today at the Hotel Villa Brunel.

Again, how Krol was making a living overseas is unknown, and what the Krols' itinerary may have been during 1933 is a mystery. It was during this trip that the most serious marital problems to date came to the fore. In the fall of 1933, Virginia took Phillip and left Krol. They were still in Paris, and Virginia was not to return home until the following summer.

Virginia's mother was back with the media again in June 1934 when almost every newspaper in the country was running headlines such as "Ex-Star Feared Lost in Europe," "Actress Reported Stranded," and "Virginia Lee Corbin, Baby, Feared Stranded in Europe," information being provided to them by Mrs. Corbin. If Virginia left Krol in the fall of 1933, then Mrs. Corbin's claim that she received a letter from Virginia dated November 25 that she would return home by Christmas is logical, but by June 1934, she said she had not heard from her daughter for "several months." She went on to say, "Six weeks ago I heard from a friend that an English newspaper had said Virginia and her baby were stranded in Brussels." She added that she was attempting to contact her daughter either by cable or through consular channels. Such a story could not fail to dig up the past differences between Virginia and her mother. Mrs. Corbin assured, "But all that is over and forgotten now. Virginia and I are the best of friends, now."[1]

Only a day after this story circulated in newspapers around the country, the headline read, "Virginia Corbin Is Safe at Home; 'Forgot to Write.'" Saying it was "just a matter of a daughter forgetting to write her mother over a period of seven months," Virginia was reported to be "cozy" in her New York home. She arrived via ship on June 4 in New York. No mention was made of any troubles with her husband.

In October, Mrs. Corbin told the media Virginia would be returning to Hollywood soon to re-enter films, but also announced that Virginia was expecting her second child in February. Obviously, the problems she and Krol were having in the fall of 1933 were resolved—at least for the time being.

The year 1935 proved to be a calm year for Virginia. She and Krol had a second son, Robert Lee, born January 29. A very lovely, dark-haired Virginia was pictured in numerous newspapers holding her new son. Krol was never pictured with her in the media, but one photo caption did mention that the New York broker was in Chicago for the event. In later years, Robert (known as "Bob" in his adult years) said he learned from relatives that his father was not present at his birth.

The apparent reconciliation of Krol and Virginia didn't last. In August 1936, all hell broke loose as acrimonious accusations were tossed around in the media after it was learned Krol had filed for divorce. He charged "habitual drunkenness" noting that

Virginia in 1935 with sons Phil and a newborn Robert. Unfortunately, what appears to be a happy domestic scene turned ugly later in the year as Virginia and her husband, Theodore, entered into acrimonious divorce proceedings. Two years later, Theodore won the battle for custody of the boys, and Virginia never saw her children again.

his wife began to drink shortly after their marriage in 1929. He claimed that for the past two years, she had been "almost continually" intoxicated. Krol's hardest blow, however, was to ask for custody of the two boys. He also asked the court, and received, an injunction preventing Virginia from taking the boys out of the jurisdiction of the Cook County Circuit Court. He claimed that he had found tickets to transport the children to Hollywood in his wife's purse when they separated the previous Friday. As an interesting side note, Krol was no longer being referred to as a broker but a "salesman" instead.

Virginia came back fighting two days later. In "a bundle of injunctions and writs" to answer her husband's suit, she filed a bill for separate maintenance of the children. She charged him with being "unethical" in his practices as a broker and said he left her "destitute" in Europe three times to escape arrest. Further, she said he was associated with Jake (the Barber) Factor's British financial deals. Factor was the brother of famed cosmetics king Max Factor and was at one time sentenced to 24 years in prison in England. He escaped to the United States and employed the assistance of Al Capone to fake a kidnapping. He was reported to be involved with mob interests in California, Las Vegas and Chicago.

Virginia also denied the drunkenness charges saying she never drank liquor excessively at any time and contended she was a "good wife and mother." In her bill for separate maintenance, Virginia claimed desertion and non-support. She said that he had entered the apartment at 420 Surf Street (apparently they were living separately) with "four husky men" the previous Friday while she was away, took $300 in cash, a $1,000 fur coat of hers, and left with the children. She was successful in obtaining a "writ of no exeat" which had Krol taken into custody. He was forced to post $3,000 bond and guarantee he would not leave the state. Another report said Krol and the "husky men" ejected her and her mother from the apartment. While in court, she also told the judge Krol was involved in "questionable stock dealings" in Europe and had been questioned by Scotland Yard on more than one occasion.

"What hurts," Virginia told reporters, "is to have the memory of me, still living in the hearts of thousands who saw my pictures as children, sullied by Mr. Krol's charges."[2]

A few days later, Krol was successful in getting the judge to "quash" Virginia's writ of no exeat, his attorney stating that the petition had not been properly endorsed.

As the newspaper coverage entered into its second week of the divorce proceedings, Virginia told the judge that bridge brought her and her husband into the divorce court. She said her husband was a professional bridge player who often stayed up all night playing for stakes of five or ten cents a point. She added, "He seldom comes home and hardly notices the children. He sleeps all day so he can play cards all night." Virginia continued to complain that he used slang that was objectionable to her such as "I'm building up for a big mooch." Continuing to press the point that his business dealings were questionable, she told the court that the British government was "prejudiced" against him due to his business activities, and he was once asked by the "home office" to leave England. She said he has been questioned several times by police in Europe.

The judge then took Krol and Virginia into his chambers for about an hour, following which the two went to lunch together "in an effort to patch up their difficulties."[3]

They appeared in court together the next day, and the judge announced that Mr. and Mrs. Krol had agreed to dismiss all proceedings. Outside the court, the judge told reporters, "This does not necessarily mean a reconciliation. But there doesn't seem to be a desire here for a permanent separation or a divorce.... It has been indicated that relatives have interfered beyond a point of usefulness in the couple's affairs. They have indicated they will work out a solution by themselves, and there is no dispute between them."[4] The judge's statement that "relatives have interfered beyond a point of usefulness" leads one to conjecture about Mrs. Corbin's involvement in all this. Interestingly, the decision out of the courtroom that day gave Krol custody of the children and Virginia visitation rights until the details of the reconciliation were worked out.

Court was not in the picture for the rest of 1936, and most of 1937 was free of bad publicity for Virginia. She would appear in the newspaper now and then in articles about child stars who had been forgotten. She was given credit for surviving longer than most, but they usually noted that she was trying to make a comeback. Her picture would also appear sporting the newest hairstyle or in a Lux Soap ad. She hadn't been forgotten as attested to by the myriad of coverage she got for her divorce proceedings.

But this was the calm before the storm. Krol was back in court in November 1937 suing for divorce again. Virginia was now serving as a coach for models, making her own living without support from Krol. The surprise this time, though, was the announcement by Krol's attorney there would be no contest to the complaint and declared that Mrs. Krol would waive alimony and the custody of the two children—Phil who was five years old and Robert who was two and a half. Krol was charging cruelty saying that on May 10 Virginia struck him on the head with a coffee pot and on May 15 scratched his face. He brought two witnesses with him to the courtroom to testify to these "attacks." Virginia and Krol had been living together until the May incident, but separated after the second incident. Krol further claimed that Virginia had not "come near" the children since the separation. Two weeks after filing, the divorce was granted on grounds of cruelty, but Virginia was given the right to visit the children "at all reasonable times."[5] Virginia apparently could not get out of Chicago fast enough, declining to appear for the December 8 divorce hearing—which ensured a quick decision in favor of the plaintiff—and making it clear she was on her way to Hollywood to fulfill a picture contract.

So why the sudden decision by Virginia to let the divorce go through uncontested, ask for no alimony and, without challenge, give up custody of the children? Virginia's son, Bob, said in conversations between 1998 and 2002 that he suspected his father "had something on" his mother and, more likely, the man she would marry—Charles Jacobson. According to Bob, the reference by the judge in 1936 to interference from relatives was more than a reference to Mrs. Corbin. Bob said the whole divorce was "engineered" by his Uncle Henry, his father's brother, "who had all the clout and didn't mind using it."

Although adultery was never mentioned in the courtroom, family members are confident Virginia was seeing Jacobson long before the divorce.

In a 1998 telephone conversation, one of Krol's nieces, Patsy Karp, remembered her uncle being gone for a full year to the Philippines. "Here's a young girl in her mid-twenties left alone for a year at a time. What would you expect her to do?" Karp could not remember the exact year, but she and Bob both felt this would most likely have been the time when Virginia met Jacobson.

Jacobson was described as a Chicago broker, but he also was a co-owner of the Latin Quarter Theatre Restaurant and Nightclub at 23 West Randolph Street. Bob said he always felt that his mother's accusations regarding Krol's ties with underworld types had basis in fact. He also theorized that his mother's decision to give up custody of him and his brother was, in some regard, to protect Jacobson and their marriage. Phil said in later years, "I suspect she was pressured into giving us up."[6]

Virginia and Jacobson were married in 1938 in Miami. They would spend time in Chicago and the Miami area during the next four years of their marriage, by all accounts, a happy marriage.

As for Bob and Phil, Phil remembers moving to California in 1938 right after his father married Jean Sawyer, a sometimes actress. Bob was three years old, and Phil was six years old. "I remember the airplane ride, waving to Uncle Henry from the window of the C47 at Midway airport. I got airsick. We landed in Arizona to refuel. I remember the car ride to Coldwater Canyon, and the room we slept in. Jean had a bookshelf in there loaded with toys. I remember I was scared."[7]

Virginia wanted more than anything to get back to movies—the place that had always been her safe haven. Although stating that she had a "contract" may have been a little overambitious, she did find herself in March 1938 playing what was probably the smallest bit of her career.

26. Once They Were Great

*H*edda Hopper reported in her April 7, 1938, column that she had visited the set of *Letter of Introduction* the previous day. The John Stahl directed comedy-drama for Universal boasted several big names—Adolphe Menjou, George Murphy, Edgar Bergen and Charlie McCarthy, Ann Sheridan, Eve Arden and Andrea Leeds who took the lead role in the film. In the midst of several paragraphs about the filming that day, she threw in a paragraph, "Virginia Lee Corbin, who made quite a name as a child actress, was there doing a bit." The "bit" was actually appearing as one of the many people in the background during an early scene. Kay (Leeds) has been burned out of her apartment on New Year's Eve. She ends up in Barry's (Murphy) apartment where a New Year's Eve party is taking place. Virginia is one of about 15 or so people crammed into the small room. She can be seen dancing in the background briefly. Except for a few seconds where she and her partner are looking on as Barry introduces Kay to the crowd, she has her back to the camera talking with other people there. The whole sequence is about five minutes, and Virginia is visible only for a small portion of that. That, unfortunately, is the extent of her involvement in the production.

Released July 29 by Universal, *Letter of Introduction* was a much more prestigious movie than her previous sound film endeavors, as evidenced by the cast. It was the story of John Mannering, an aging, but prestigious, actor (Menjou), about to marry for the fourth time, who is surprised when the daughter (Leeds) he didn't know he had appears with a letter of introduction. She is an actress and is trying to make it on Broadway. She hopes the famous John Mannering will be able to help her. He tries to establish a relationship with her but finds it difficult to tell the world he has a daughter.

Virginia was absent from movies and the media for over a year—until the fall of 1939. Hedda Hopper's column September 30 announced that she was playing the nurse to Baby Sandy in the upcoming Universal release *Little Accident* starring Hugh Herbert, Florence Rice and Richard Carlson. In this one, Herbert, the editor of a "better baby" column, is left with an abandoned baby, and forces his daughter and her fiancé to care for the child. The announcement that Virginia would be playing the part of Baby Sandy's nurse in the film ran in the newspapers for weeks, even after the film was released. Some even ran a photo of a very beautiful, dark-haired Virginia in a nurse's cap, holding Baby Sandy. The caption read, "'I had almost given up the idea of playing in pictures

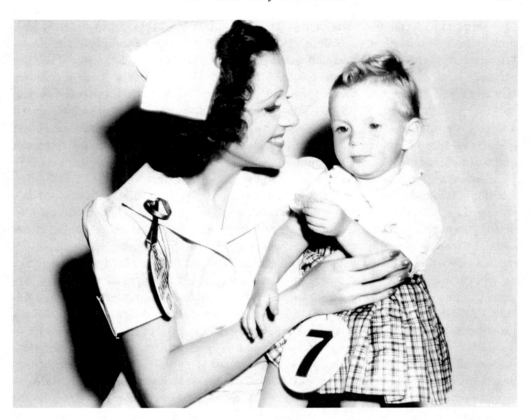

Little Accident (1939) starring Baby Sandy is the last time Virginia would be seen on the screen other than in a background crowd. It wasn't a speaking part, but as the nurse who holds Baby Sandy during a "Perfect Baby Contest," Virginia is onscreen for a few minutes and even has one close-up with Baby Sandy, clearly showing that with her natural brown hair she was still very lovely.

again.' Miss Corbin told director Charles Lamont and Hugh Herbert. 'But the opportunity to work with Sandy was too attractive to resist."[1]

The film was released October 27, and there is some confusion regarding Virginia's appearance in it because there is another nurse's role that was played by Virginia Sales—a speaking part and credited role. Nevertheless, Virginia is indeed in the film. She appears in a sequence in which a "Perfect Baby Contest" takes place. This segment runs for about two and a half minutes. Seven nurses in uniform walk up on the stage, each carrying a baby who is competing for the honor. Virginia, no longer a blonde but now an attractive brunette, is carrying Baby Sandy. Of course, Sandy wins the contest, so Virginia is on stage for the entire sequence. There is one close-up of her holding Baby Sandy, but, unfortunately, her role in the film was not a speaking part.

Enough time had passed since Virginia's silent days that articles were now getting their information confused or just plain wrong. For example, some said she was a former Our Gang "heroine." Several named *Knee High* as one of her movies. The reference to the movie that was never made is probably understandable since newspapers back in 1929 carried quite a few stories announcing it as an upcoming film for her.

Virginia was quoted in one saying she was single now. "I thought I wanted to be a housewife, so I quit films in 1930 to get married.... But, I guess acting is in my blood. I'm single now and am going to make every effort to win a new place for myself on the screen."[2] In addition to being married, stating that she quit films in 1930 is another obvious error, having been in four sound films in 1931. Other articles focused on the fact that she had "made $1,000,000" and had nothing to show for it. "I've got to earn a living," she told reporters, adding that she planned to keep her next million. When she was asked what happened to her fortune, she said, "Poor investments, the depression and bad judgment in critical moments."[3]

Adventures in Diamonds was released by Paramount April 4 and starred George Brent and Isa Miranda. It's a neat story about a glamorous jewel thief, Felice (Miranda), and her lover/accomplice (John Loder) conning Captain Stephen Dennett (Brent) into getting them into a diamond mine in South Africa. The duo are caught stealing. However, she is offered parole in return for working with the Captain in capturing a murderous jewel ring. It turns out her former lover/accomplice is the leader of the ring.

In early 1940, it was announced that director George Fitzmaurice was giving Virginia a chance to make a comeback in this film. "It's not a big part, certainly," she said, "but I do get to speak a few lines and get my face in front of the camera. It's really a great break for me."[4] Unfortunately, Virginia does not appear in the print reviewed.

She did make at least one personal appearance in 1940—at the Golden Gate International Exposition at San Francisco's Treasure Island. The Exposition was held two years—in 1939 and 1940. It was essentially a World's Fair that was held to celebrate the city's two newly built bridges—the San Francisco-Oakland Bay Bridge (opened in 1936) and the Golden Gate Bridge (opened in 1937). Virginia appeared in the "Golden Days of Forty," a production that premiered May 25. A photo of a beautiful, dark-haired Virginia with a model of the "gigantic" stage that was to be used for the production was circulated to newspapers around the country. Another photo of her surrounded in flowers and looking off to one side and toward the sky was also sent to newspapers.

Virginia was the subject of numerous brief references or entire articles about former stars who were now down on their luck. For example, "These were the faces of Virginia Lee Corbin and Charlotte Henry—Virginia who was the second greatest of all child stars in her time, and Charlotte, who once starred in two memorable pictures— *Babes in Toyland* and *Alice in Wonderland*. Once they were great; once tons of photographers' flash bulbs lighted their faces at premieres, and fans stormed them for autographs—but that was some years ago when they rode the crest of this ephemeral thing called popularity. Today, they are extras at $10 for the day. Two girls just now in the twilight of their careers and still in their very early twenties."

Then Virginia was quoted as saying, "I've had my chance, and something happened to make me lose out. What that something was no one can tell me. There was a sudden lack of interest in me; maybe the public wanted me to stay a kid—just like Jackie Coogan—and resented my growing up. All I know is that I am an extra—that I am doing everything possible to get back into favor. I may make it; I may not. I don't think anybody knows. That is Hollywood."[5] Virginia was definitely being very philosophical about her present status in Hollywood, and this was the second time she was given a chance to bring up her mother's dissolution of her earnings—and she didn't. Maybe Virginia had

Virginia made a personal appearance in 1940 at the Golden Gate International Exposition at San Francisco's Treasure Island, which was essentially a World's Fair of sorts. She appeared in a production entitled "The Golden Days of Forty." Here she is seen in a promotional photograph for the production with a model of the gigantic stage that was used in the opening day show.

had enough animosity, enough bitterness—and just wanted to move on with the thing she loved most—the movies.

Also at this time, Virginia was reported to be working at Columbia on *The Howards of Virginia*, released September 19. Cary Grant and Martha Scott had the leads in the Revolutionary War drama about an aristocratic Virginian (Scott) who marries an unsophisticated, rustic surveyor (Grant) prior to his going off to war.

Virginia and Charlotte Henry were among 50 extras in a dance scene. "The warm stage air was filled with the strains of a minuet and such intermingled noises as any happy group might make. But in that throng of dancers were two pretty faces—somber faces that kept turning away from the camera as though there was shame in recognition.... And so Charlotte Henry and Virginia Lee Corbin, with their minds closed against the past, danced gracefully to the strains of a minuet—a smile on their faces."

Director Frank Lloyd said, "But these faces were always turned from the cameras, whereas the other girls were always certain to hog the lens, sometimes to the point where they obscured the dancing of Grant and Miss Scott. There is an element of sadness in that shyness. You'll find it on every set utilizing extras. A matter of pride being unwilling to acknowledge defeat."[6]

One of the dancers nearer to the forefront of the frame does seem to be Virginia. She is not turning from the camera, but focused entirely on her partner with a lovely smile. Unfortunately, these dancers are visible for barely ten seconds of the movie.

Maudlin articles such as the one above were common. Another one about Virginia said, "A dark, slender young woman with a pretty, piquant face and a pointed chin sits near a telephone all day. She knits or reads or straightens the apartment, but always she remains within earshot of that telephone. Every hour or so she goes to it and dials Garfield 3711. She gives her name, asks one question, and gets one answer—usually negative. She is an extra. In this case, she is Virginia Lee Corbin, once a juvenile star."

It goes on to say, "The telephone seldom rings, and only once a month or so does it ring with the news she wants to hear—'This is Central Casting—you are wanted in a picture.' So, impatient at the silent telephone, Miss Corbin and 7,000 other extras dial GA 3711—Central Casting—many times a day to give their name ... 'If you happen to call in at the right moment,' Virginia says, 'you have a good chance. And if you aren't at your telephone when Casting calls, there are a dozen others waiting.'"[7]

By fall, Virginia was serving as a stand-in for Frances Dee on *Flotsam*, renamed *So Ends Our Night* for release by Paramount February 14, 1941. Starring Fredric March (with whom Virginia worked on *Footlights and Fools* in 1929) and Margaret Sullavan, it was the story of three refugees hiding and avoiding deportation during World War II.

By this time, it's likely Virginia's health was deteriorating. Krol's niece, Patsy Karp (mentioned in Chapter 25) was a teenager in the thirties. One of the memories that stood out in her mind when she used to visit her uncle's and Virginia's home was that Virginia had a bad cough. Because Virginia was called on to smoke in movies, even as a young teenager, it's likely she did smoke, but time would prove that smoking alone was not the cause of her cough.

She and Jacobson lived part-time in West Palm Beach, Florida, which, because of the warm weather, would have been a healthier climate for her. Did they know she had tuberculosis at this time? How far advanced was it? Tuberculosis typically affects only the lungs, although it can affect other parts of the body, and coughing is generally a symptom, but other symptoms could include spitting up blood, night sweats, fever and weight loss. It is contagious, and in the 1940s, it carried somewhat of a stigma—no one wanted to admit to getting treatment for it, and it was not unusual for the cause of death to be listed as something else. Medicine at that time wasn't very successful at treating the disease, either. It wasn't until 1946 when the antibiotic streptomycin was discovered that tuberculosis could be treated effectively and cured.

Virginia's condition was bad enough by the spring of 1942 that she and Jacobson returned to Chicago so she could receive treatment. Then, in June, the sad news was announced around the country. Former child star Virginia Lee Corbin had passed away in DuPage Hospital in Winfield, Illinois, outside Chicago, the evening of Thursday, June 4, 1942. She was 31 years old. No one apparently knew about her sickness—a very well-kept secret, and newspaper reports gave the cause of death as heart disease, misinformation that has been repeated constantly over the years. How sad that a possible cure for her condition was only four years away.

When Virginia and Theodore Krol separated in May 1937, it was the last time she ever saw her two sons. According to Bob and Phil, their father did not want them to see their mother or associate with anyone in the Corbin family. Virginia had a photo of the two boys at her bedside in the sanitarium when she died, and Krol's wife, Jean, was trying to arrange for the boys to see their mother before she passed away. One source said Virginia declined, feeling it wasn't good for the boys. Bob and Phil were told their mother passed away before the meeting could be effected. Either way, both boys were too young the last time they saw their mother to have retained any memory of her. They never saw their grandmother or their Aunt Ruth again after the divorce, either.

Funeral services were held for Virginia at a chapel at 5145 Broadway in Chicago at 10:30 Monday morning, June 7. She was buried in Westlawn Cemetery, located in Norridge, IL, just outside Chicago. Her unpretentious, ground-level tombstone simply says, "Beloved Virginia Lee Jacobson 1914–1942." One again, her birth year was given inaccurately.

Charles Jacobson died in 1976 at the age of 68. Theodore Krol received five years probation in a stock swindling case in 1961. He died in New York in 1969 at age 74. Ruth Corbin was married four times—to John Miehle (divorced in 1927), Richard Scott Thornton (divorced ?), Viscount Jacques de Vries of France (divorced in 1935), and finally to John Lipari to whom she remained married until her death. She died in San Mateo, CA, in 1986. Mrs. Corbin stayed in California either living with Ruth or close by until her death in 1966 at age 84. At the time of her death, she was residing in the Hillsdale Manor Convalescent Hospital in San Mateo. Robert "Bob" Krol passed away in 2002. Phil Krol turned 85 in 2017.

Filmography

Intolerance—released 9/5/16. Three hours, 37 minutes. Fine Arts Film Co. Dir. D.W. Griffith. Cast: Robert Harron, Mae Marsh, Lillian Gish, Sam De Grasse, Miriam Cooper, Walter Long, Ralph Lewis, Vera Lewis, Mary Alden, Eleanor Washington, Pearl Elmore, Lucille Browne, Julia Mackley, Tom Wilson, F.A. Turner, Margery Wilson, Bessie Love, Howard Gaye, Monte Blue, Spottiswoode Aitken, Eugene Pallette, Francis Carpenter. Survival status: Print exists. (Author's Note: Although the children at the end of the film appear to be Francis Carpenter and Virginia Lee Corbin, no documentation could be found to confirm her appearance.)

By Conscience's Eye—released 8/11/16. Rex Motion Picture Company. Two reels. Dir. George Cochrane. Cast: Rex De Rosselli, Marjorie Ellison, Maxfield Stanley, Virginia Lee Corbin. Survival status: Unknown.

The Castle of Despair—released 8/22/16. Universal Pictures. Three reels. Dir. Ben Wilson. Cast: Malcolm Blevins, Percy Challenger, Neva Gerber, Virginia Lee Corbin. Survival status: Unknown.

Behind Life's Stage—released 10/12/16. Universal Pictures. Two reels. Dir. Allen J. Holubar. Cast: Flora Parker De Haven, Charles Cummings, Virginia Lee Corbin. Survival status: Unknown.

The Chorus Girl and the Kid—released 10/27/16. Knickerbocker Star Features (through Balboa Amusement Producing Company). Two reels. Dir. ? Cast: Marie Empress, Virginia Lee Corbin. Survival status: Unknown.

The Woman He Feared—released 11/14/16. Universal Pictures. Three reels. Dir. Harry F. Millarde. Cast: Franklyn Farnum, Vola Vale, William Canfield, Clarissa Selwynne, Adele Farrington, Virginia Lee Corbin. Survival status: Unknown.

Pidgin Island—released 12/25/16. Yorke Film Corporation. Five reels. Dir. Fred J. Balshofer. Cast: Harold Lockwood, May Allison, Lester Cuneo, Lillian Hayward, Philip Gastrock, Steve Barton, Elizah Zerr, Yon Foune, Virginia Lee Corbin. Survival status: Print exists in the Library of Congress.

Heart Strings—released 1/22/17. Universal Pictures. Five reels. Dir. Allan J. Holubar. Cast: Allen J. Holubar, Francelia Billington, Paul Bryan, Maude George, Irene Hunt, Charles Cummings, Virginia Lee Corbin. Survival status: Unknown.

The Old Toymaker—released 1/28/17. Universal Pictures. Two reels. Dir. Allan J. Holubar. Cast: Allen J. Holubar, Leah Baird, George C. Pearce, Virginia Lee Corbin. Survival status: Unknown.

Vengeance of the Dead—released 4/4/17. Balboa Amusement Producing Company. Four reels. Dir. Henry King. Cast: Henry King, Lillian West, Philo McCullough, Virginia Lee Corbin. Survival status. Incomplete print exists in the Library of Congress.

The Light of Love—released 5/26/17. Universal Pictures. One reel. Dir. Ben Horning. Cast: Jessie Arnold, T.J. Crittendon, Marjorie Ellison, Virginia Lee Corbin. Survival status: Unknown.

Jack and the Beanstalk—released 7/30/17. Fox Film Corp. 10 reels. Dir. Chester and Sidney Franklin. Cast: Francis Carpenter, Virginia Lee Corbin, Violet Radcliffe, Carmen De Rue, J.G. Traver, Vera Lewis, Ralph Lewis, Eleanor Washington, Ione Glennon. Survival status: Incomplete print exists (approximately 48 minutes).

Aladdin and the Wonderful Lamp—released 10/14/17. Fox Film Corp. Eight reels. Dir. Chester and Sidney Franklin. Cast: Francis Carpenter, Virginia Lee Corbin, Violet Radcliffe, Carmen De Rue, Violet Radcliffe, Buddy Messinger, Alfred Paget. Survival status: Incomplete print exists (approximately 40 minutes).

The Babes in the Woods—released 12/2/17. Fox

Film Corp. Five-eight reels (source vary). Dir. Sidney Franklin. Cast: Francis Carpenter, Virginia Lee Corbin, Violet Radcliffe, Carmen de Rue, Herschel Mayall, Rosita Marstini, Robert Lawler, Ted Billings, Buddy Messinger. Survival status: Incomplete print exists (approximately 36 minutes).

Treasure Island—released 1/25/18. Fox Film Corp. Six reels. Dir. Chester Franklin. Cast: Francis Carpenter, Virginia Lee Corbin, Eleanor Washington, Mershel Mayall, Elmo Lincoln, Charles Gorman, Ed Harley, Violet Radcliffe, Lloyd Perl, Lewis Sargent, Buddy Messinger. Survival status: Presumed lost.

Six Shooter Andy—released 3/3/18. Fox Film Corp. Five reels. Dir. Sidney Franklin. Cast: Tom Mix, Bert Woodruff, Sam De Grasse, Charles Stevens, Pat Crisman, Bob Fleming, Enid Markey, Jack Plant, Ben Hammer, George Stone, Lewis Sargent, Buddy Messinger, Virginia Lee Corbin, Violet Radcliffe, Beulah Burns, Ray Lee, Vivian Plank. Survival status: Presumed lost.

Ace High—released 6/9/18. Fox Film Corp. Five reels. Dir. Lynn Reynolds. Cast: Tom Mix, Kathleen Connors, Virginia Lee Corbin, Lloyd Perl, Lewis Sargent, Lawrence Payton, Colin Chase, Jay Morley, Pat Crisman. Survival status: Fragment survives at Lobster Films (Paris).

Fan Fan—released 11/17/17. Fox Film Corp. Five reels. Dir. Chester and Sidney Franklin. Cast: Francis Carpenter, Virginia Lee Corbin, Carmen de Rue, Violet Radcliffe, Buddy Messinger, Joe Singleton, Gertrude Messinger, Lewis Sargent. Survival status: Presumed lost.

The Forbidden Room—released 3/2/19. Fox Film Corp. Five Reels. Dir. Lynn Reynolds. Cast: Gladys Brockwell, William Scott, J. Barney Sherry, Harry Dunkinson, Al Fremont, William Burress, T.S. Guise, Louis King, Robert Dunbar, Lillian West, Virginia Lee Corbin, Francis Carpenter. Survival status: Presumed lost.

The White Dove—released 3/28/20. Jesse D. Hampton Productions. Five reels. Dir. Henry King. Cast: H.B. Warner, James O. Barrows, Claire Adams, Herbert Greenwood, Donald MacDonald, Virginia Lee Corbin, Ruth Renick. Survival status: Presumed lost.

Enemies of Children—released 12/13/23. Fisher Productions. Six reels. Dir. Lillian Ducey and John M. Voshell. Cast: Anna Q. Nilsson, George Siegmann, Claire McDowell, Lucy Beaumont, Joseph Dowling, Raymond Hatton, Ward Crane, Charles Wellesley, Virginia Lee Corbin, Kate Price. Survival status: Presumed lost.

Fight and Win—first installment released 6/21/24. Universal Pictures. 10 two-reel installments. Dir. Erle Kenton. Cast: Jack Dempsey, Esther Ralston, Carmelita Geraghty, Charles "Chuck" Reisner, Virginia Lee Corbin, Hayden Stevenson. Survival status: Presumed lost.

Sinners in Silk—released 9/1/24. Metro-Goldwyn-Mayer. Six reels. Dir. Hobart Henley. Cast: Adolphe Menjou, Eleanor Boardman, Conrad Nagel, Jean Hersholt, Edward Connelly, Jerome Patrick, John Patrick, Hedda Hopper, Miss Du Pont, Virginia Lee Corbin. Survival status: Presumed lost.

Wine of Youth—released 9/15/24. Metro-Goldwyn-Mayer. Seven reels. Dir. King Vidor. Cast: Eleanor Boardman, James Morrison, Johnnie Walker, Niles Welch, Creighton Hale, Ben Lyon, William Haines, William Collier, Jr., Bobby Agnew, Virginia Lee Corbin Pauline Garon, E.J. Ratcliffe, Gertrude Claire, Eulalie Jensen. Survival status: Print exists in Turner Archives.

The City That Never Sleeps—released 9/28/24. Paramount Pictures. Six reels. Dir. James Cruze. Cast: Louise Dresser, Ricardo Cortez, Kathlyn Williams, Virginia Lee Corbin, Pierre Gendron, James Farley, Ben Hendricks. Vondell Darr. Survival status: Presumed lost.

Broken Laws—released 11/9/24. Thomas H. Ince, Corp. Seven reels. Dir. R. William Neill. Cast: Mrs. Wallace Reid (Dorothy Davenport), Percy Marmont, Ramsey Wallace, Jacqueline Saunders, Arthur Rankin, Virginia Lee Corbin, Pat Moore, Jane Wray. Survival status: Print exists in Cinémathèque Royale (Brussels).

The Chorus Lady—released 11/23/24. Regal Pictures. Seven reels. Dir. Ralph Ince. Cast: Margaret Livingston, Virginia Lee Corbin, Alan Roscoe, Philo McCullough. Survival status: Presumed lost.

The Three Keys—released 1/1/25. Banner Productions. Six reels. Dir. Edward Le Saint. Cast: Gaston Glass, Edith Roberts, Jack Mulhall, Virginia Lee Corbin, Miss Du Pont, Charles Clary, Stuart Holmes, Joseph Girard. Survival status: Prints exits in the Library of Congress.

The Cloud Rider—released 2/15/25. Van Pelt-Wilson Productions. Five reels. Dir. Bruce Mitchell. Cast: Al Wilson, Virginia Lee Corbin, Harry Von Meter, Helen Ferguson, Frank Rice, Melbourne McDowell, Brinsley Shaw, Frank Tomick, Boyd Monteith, Frank Clark. Survival status: Prints exists in Cineteca Italiana (Milano).

Lilies of the Streets—released 5/3/25. Belban Productions. Seven reels. Dir. Joseph Levering. Cast: Virginia Lee Corbin, Wheeler Oakman, Peggy Kelly, Johnnie Walker, Irma Harrison, Mary E. Hamilton, Elizabeth J. Monroe. Survival status: Presumed lost.

Headlines—released 7/16/25. St. Regis Productions. Six reels. Dir. Edward H. Griffith. Cast: Alice Joyce, Malcolm McGregor, Virginia Lee Corbin, Harry T. Morey, Ruby Blaine, Elliott Nugent. Survival status: Print with Dutch intertitles exists in the Library of Congress.

The Handsome Brute—released 12/1/25. Perfection Pictures. Five reels. Dir. Robert Eddy.

Cast: William Fairbanks, Virginia Lee Corbin, Lee Shumway, Robert Bolder, J.J. Bryson, Daniel Belmont. Survival status: Presumed lost.

North Star—released 12/27/25. Howard Estabrook Productions. Five reels. Dir. Paul Powell. Cast: Virginia Lee Corbin, Ken Maynard, Stuart Holmes, Harold Austin, Clark Gable, William Riley, Syd Crossley, Jerry Mandy, Marty Faust, Jack Fowler. Survival status: Presumed lost.

Hands Up!—released 1/11/26. Paramount Pictures. Six reels. Dir. Clarence Badger. Cast: Raymond Griffith, Marian Nixon, Virginia Lee Corbin, Mack Swain, Montagu Love, George Billings, Noble Johnson, Charles K. French. Survival status: Prints exist.

The Whole Town's Talking—released 8/14/26. Universal Pictures. Seven reels. Dir. Edward Laemmle. Cast: Edward Everett Horton, Virginia Lee Corbin, Trixie Friganza, Otis Harlan, Dolores Del Rio, Malcolm Waite, Margaret Quimby, Hayden Stevenson, Aileen Manning, Robert Ober. Survival status: Print exists in the UCLA Archive.

The Honeymoon Express—released 9/2/26. Warner Bros. Seven reels. Dir. James Flood. Cast: Willard Louis, Irene Rich, Holmes Herbert, Helene Costello, John Patrick, Jane Winton, Virginia Lee Corbin, Harold Goodwin, Robert Brower. Survival status: Presumed lost.

Ladies at Play—released 11/15/26. First National Pictures. Seven reels. Dir. Alfred E. Green. Cast: Doris Kenyon, Lloyd Hughes, Louise Fazenda, Ethel Wales, Hallam Cooley, John Patrick, Virginia Lee Corbin, Philo McCullough, Tom Ricketts. Survival status: Presumed lost.

Driven from Home—released 1/15/27—Chadwick Pictures Corp. Seven reels. Dir. James Young. Cast: Ray Hallor, Virginia Lee Corbin, Pauline Garon, Sojin, Anna May Wong, Melbourne MacDowell, Margaret Seddon, Sheldon Lewis, Virginia Pearson, Eric Mayne. Survival status: Prints exist in Cinémathèque Royale (Bruxelles), Archives du Film du *Cnc* (Bois d'Arcy) and Lobster Films (Paris).

The Perfect Sap—released 1/16/27. First National Pictures. Six reels. Dir. Howard Higgin. Cast: Ben Lyon, Pauline Starke, Virginia Lee Corbin, Lloyd Whitlock, Diana Kane, Bryon Douglas, Christine Compton, Charles Craig, Sam Hardy, Tammany Young, Helen Rowland. Survival status: Presumed lost.

Play Safe—released 1/30/27. Monty Banks Enterprises. Five reels. Dir. Joseph Henabery. Cast: Monty Banks, Virginia Lee Corbin, Charles Hill Mailes, Charles Gerard, Bud Jamison, Rosa Gore, Syd Crossley, Max Asher, Fatty Alexander. Survival status: Prints exists in Library of Congress.

No Place to Go—released 10/30/27. First National Pictures. Seven reels. Dir. Mervyn LeRoy. Cast: Mary Astor, Lloyd Hughes, Hallam Cooley, Myrtle Stedman, Virginia Lee Corbin, Jed Prouty, Russ Powell. Survival status: Print exists in BFI National Film and Television Archive (London).

Bare Knees—released 2/1/1928. Gotham Productions. Six reels. Dir. Erle C. Kenton. Cast: Virginia Lee Corbin, Donald Keith, Jane Winton, Johnnie Walker, Maude Fulton, Forrest Stanley. Survival status: Prints exist.

The Little Snob—released 2/11/1928. Warner Bros. Six reels. Dir. John G. Adolfi. Cast: May McAvoy, Robert Frazer, Alec B. Francis, Virginia Lee Corbin, Frances Lee, John Miljan. Survival status: Presumed lost.

The Head of the Family—released 12/14/1928. Gotham Productions. Seven reels. Dir. Joseph Boyle. Cast: William Russell, Mickey Bennett, Virginia Lee Corbin, Richard Walling, Alma Bennett, William Welsh, Aggie Herring. Survival status: Presumed lost.

Jazzland—released December 1, 1928. Gotham Productions. Six reels. Dir. Dallas M. Fitzgerald. Cast: Bryant Washburn, Vera Reynolds, Carroll Nye, Forrest Stanley, Virginia Lee Corbin, Violet Bird, Carl Stockdale, Edward Cecil, George Raph, Nicholas Caruso. Survival status: Presumed lost.

Jazz Mammas—released 6/30/1929. Mack Sennett Comedies. Two reels. Dir. Mack Sennett. Cast: Virginia Lee Corbin, Vernon Dent, Jack Cooper, Robert Seiter, John J. Richardson, Dave Morris, Billy Gilbert, June Gittelson, William Davis, Harry Ming, Bud Ross, Thelma Hill, Patsy O'Leary, Kathryn Stanley. Survival status: Presumed lost.

Footlights and Fools—released 11/4/1929. First National Pictures. Eight reels. Dir. William A. Seiter. Cast: Colleen Moore, Raymond Hackett, Fredric March, Virginia Lee Corbin, Mickey Bennett, Edward Martindel, Adrienne D'Ambricourt, Frederick Howard, Sidney Jarvis, Cleve Moore. Survival status: Only the Vitaphone sound discs survive in the UCLA Archive.

Morals for Women (aka ***Big City Interlude***)—released 10/25/1931. Tiffany Productions. 65 minutes. Dir. Mort Blumenstock. Cast: Bessie Love, Conway Tearle, John Holland, Natalie Moorhead, Emma Dunn, June Clyde, Edmund Breese, David Rollins, Lina Basquette, Virginia Lee Corbin, Crauford Kent, Otis Harlan, George Olsen, Ethan Allen, Norman Budd, Wilbur Higby, John Hyams, Walter Perry, Lillian Rich. Survival status: Prints exist.

Shotgun Pass—released 11/1 1931. Columbia Pictures. 58 minutes. Dir. J.P. McGowan. Cast: Tim McCoy, Virginia Lee Corbin, Monte Vandergrift, Frank Rice, Joe Smith Marba, Dick

Stewart, Ben Corbett, Harry Todd, Chris Allen, Tom Bay, Hank Bell, Roy Bucko, Ace Cain, Jim Corey, Rube Dalroy, Frank Ellis, Herman Hack, J.P. McGowan, Bob Reeves, Archie Ricks, Glenn Strange, Blackjack Ward, Slim Whitaker. Survival status: Prints exist.

X Marks the Spot—released 11/29/1931. Tiffany Productions. 72 minutes. Dir. Erle C. Kenton. Cast: Lew Cody, Sally Blane, Wallace Ford, Mary Nolan, Fred Kohler, Charles Middleton, Virginia Lee Corbin, Joyce Coad, Richard Tucker, Clarence Muse, Henry Hall, Lloyd Ingraham, Hank Mann, Bradley Page, Helen Parrish. Survival status: Prints exist.

Forgotten Women—released 12/1/1931. Monogram Pictures. 67 minutes. Dir. Richard Thorpe. Cast: Marion Shilling, Beryl Mercer, Rex Bell, Virginia Lee Corbin, Carmelita Geraghty, Edna Murphy, Edward Earle, Jack Carlyle, Eddie Kane, Gordon De Main, William Beaudine, Thomas A. Curran, Billy Franey, Gordon Griffith, William H. O'Brien, Dorothy Vernon, Charles Williams. Survival status: Prints exist.

Letter of Introduction—released 7/29/1938. Universal Pictures. 104 minutes. Dir. John M. Stahl. Cast: Adolphe Menjou, Andrea Leeds, George Murphy, Edgar Bergen and Charlie McCarthy, Rita Johnson, Ann Sheridan, Ernest Cossart, Frank Jenks, Eve Arden, Jonathan Hale, Virginia Lee Corbin (uncredited). Survival status: Prints exist.

Little Accident—released 10/27/1939. Universal Pictures. 63 minutes. Dir. Charles Lamont. Cast: Hugh Herbert, Florence Rice, Richard Carlson, Ernest Truex, Joy Hodges, Kathleen Howard, Howard Hickman, Edgar Kennedy, Etienne Girardot, Fritz Field, Virginia Lee Corbin (uncredited). Survival status: Prints exist.

The Howardso Virginia—released 9/14/1940. Columbia Pictures. 122 minutes. Dir. Frank Lloyd. Cast: Cary Grant, Martha Scott, Sir Cedric Hardwicke, Alan Marshal, Richard Carlson, Paul Kelly, Irving Bacon, Elizabeth Risdon, Ann Revere, Richard Alden, Virginia Lee Corbin (uncredited). Survival status: Prints exists.

So Ends Our Night—released 2/14/41. United Artists. Dir. John Cromwell. Cast: Fredric March, Margaret Sullavan, Frances Dee, Glenn Ford, Anna Sten, Erich von Stroheim, Allan Brett, Joseph Cawthorn, Leonid Kinskey, Alexander Granach, Virginia Lee Corbin (stand-in for Frances Dee). Survival status: Prints exist.

Chapter Notes

Chapter 2

1. *Yavapai County Directory 1913.* Arizona Directory Company, Phoenix, AZ.
2. Ames, Hector. "Two Baby Stars and How It Happened." *Motion Picture Magazine.* June 1918.
3. *Ibid.*
4. Brownlow, Kevin. "The Franklin Kid Pictures. Ably Directed, Lavishly Mounted, Well Acted, Deserve a Special Place in Film History." *Films in Review.* August-September 1972.
5. *Let Katie Do It* review. *Variety.* December 10, 1915.
6. *Let Katy Do It* review. *Motion Picture News.* December 18, 1915.
7. Virginia Lee Corbin personal scrapbook clipping; publication and date unknown.
8. "'The Birds' Christmas Carol' Ready for States Rights Buyers." *Motion Picture News.* April 14, 1917.
9. Virginia Lee Corbin personal scrapbook clipping; publication and date unknown.
10. "In and Out of West Coast Studios." *Motion Picture News.* September 23, 1916.
11. Virginia Lee Corbin personal scrapbook clipping; publication and date unknown.
12. "Grow Up With Business." *Los Angeles Times.* April 21, 1916.
13. *Pidgin Island* review. *Moving Picture World.* January 13, 1917.
14. "*Pidgin Island* Has Thirty-Five Acting Roles." *Statesman Journal* (Salem, OR). December 30, 1916.
15. Virginia Lee Corbin personal scrapbook clipping; publication and date unknown.
16. *Ibid.*
17. *Ibid.*
18. "A Christmas Performance." *Los Angeles Times.* December 31, 1916.
19. Lane, Rose Wilder. "Twinkle, Twinkle Little Stars." *Sunset Magazine.* January 1918.
20. Virginia Lee Corbin personal scrapbook clipping; publication and date unknown.
21. "19th Century American Theater." University of Washington. https://content.lib.washington.edu/19thcenturyactorsweb/essay.html.

Chapter 3

1. *Heart Strings* review. *Variety.* February 2, 1917.
2. *Heart Strings* review. *Motion Picture News.* January 27, 1917.
3. *The Old Toymaker* review. *Moving Picture World.* January 27, 1917.
4. "R. Henry King in 'Fortune Photoplay.'" *Moving Picture World.* April 21, 1917.
5. Virginia Lee Corbin personal scrapbook clipping; publication and date unknown.
6. *Ibid.*
7. *Ibid.*
8. *Ibid.*
9. *The Light of Love* review. *Motion Picture News.* June 2, 1917.

Chapter 4

1. "Hollywood Hookum." *Motion Picture News.* February 17, 1917.
2. "Virginia La Verne Corbin." *Moving Picture World.* April 14, 1917.
3. Brownlow, Kevin. "The Franklin Kid Pictures. Ably Directed, Lavishly Mounted, Well Acted, Deserve a Special Place in Film History." *Films in Review.* August-September 1972.
4. "Children Will Make Films for Children." *Los Angeles Times.* April 29, 1917.
5. Brownlow.
6. *Ibid.*
7. *Ibid.*
8. *Ibid.*
9. *Ibid.*
10. *Ibid.*
11. *Ibid.*
12. Virginia Lee Corbin personal scrapbook clipping; publication and date unknown.
13. *Jack and the Beanstalk* review. *Motion Picture News.* August 18, 1917.
14. "Teller's Shubert Theater." *Brooklyn Daily Eagle.* September 2, 1917.
15. Brownlow.
16. "Our Films for Action: William Fox Says the World Gives Them First Award." *Los Angeles Times.* July 8, 1917.

Chapter 5

1. Virginia Lee Corbin personal scrapbook clipping; publication and date unknown.
2. *Jack and the Beanstalk* review. *New York Times.* July 31, 1917.
3. *Jack and the Beanstalk* review. *Variety.* August 3, 1917.
4. *Jack and the Beanstalk* review. *New York Tribune.* Undated.
5. *Jack and the Beanstalk* review. *Motion Picture News.* August 18, 1917.
6. Virginia Lee Corbin personal scrapbook clipping; publication and date unknown.
7. *Motion Picture News.*
8. Virginia Lee Corbin personal scrapbook clipping; publication and date unknown.
9. "Francis Carpenter and Virginia Lee Corbin Will Be Presented by Fox in Elaborate Production." *San Francisco Chronicle.* October 21, 1917.
10. "William Fox Production." *Altoona Tribune.* October 22, 1917.
11. Huston, N.W. McGhie Theater Notes. *Columbus (KS) Daily Advocate.* December 29, 1917.
12. Virginia Lee Corbin personal scrapbook clipping; publication and date unknown.
13. "Screen: Miller's." *Los Angeles Times.* September 2, 1917.
14. "*The Spy* Featuring Dustin Farnum Will Reveal Them." *Los Angeles Times.* September 9, 1917.
15. *Los Angeles Times.* September 2, 1917.
16. Virginia Lee Corbin personal scrapbook clipping; publication and date unknown.
17. *Ibid.*
18. *Ibid.*
19. *Ibid.*

Chapter 6

1. Clancy, Carl Stearns. "A Really Truly Princess." *Photo-Play Journal.* August 1917.
2. "Mere Heresay." *Lima News.* February 3, 1917.
3. *Ibid.*
4. *Ibid.*
5. Virginia Lee Corbin personal scrapbook clipping; publication and date unknown.
6. *Ibid.*
7. *Ibid.*
8. *Ibid.*
9. "Society: Manhattan Beach." *Los Angeles Times.* April 14, 1918.
10. "Women's Work and Women's Clubs: Children's Festival." *Los Angeles Times.* April 28, 1918.
11. "Prosperity Note." *Motion Picture News.* October 20, 1917.
12. Virginia Lee Corbin personal scrapbook clipping; publication and date unknown.
13. *Ibid.*
14. *Ibid.*
15. Wood, Corinne. "Four-Year Old Girl the Wonder of the Movies, a Perfect Dresden Doll." *Santa Cruz Evening News.* April 4, 1917.

Chapter 7

1. "William Fox Says the World Gives Them First Award." *Los Angeles Times.* July 8, 1917.

2. "The New Fox Pictures. William Fox Tells How They Were Produced and Who Made Them." *Moving Picture World.* August 4, 1917.
3. "In and Out of West Coast Studios." *Motion Picture News.* July 28, 1917.
4. "In and Out of West Coast Studios." *Motion Picture News.* August 4, 1917.
5. "Fox's *Aladdin* Plays Second Week at Globe. Second of Kiddie Series Surpasses Even *Jack and the Beanstalk* in Popularity—Many Ingenious Effects Produced." *Motion Picture News.* October 13, 1917.
6. "Old Fairy Tale Revived on the Screen, *Aladdin* Capital Fun for All Ages." *Motion Picture News.* October 13, 1917.
7. "Fox Kiddies' Feature at Criterion Theater Has Beauty and Charm." *Atlanta Constitution.* December 21, 1917.
8. Virginia Lee Corbin personal scrapbook clipping; publication and date unknown.
9. *Aladdin and the Wonderful Lamp* review. *Variety.* September 28, 1917.
10. *Ibid.*
11. *Ibid.*
12. "*Aladdin and His* (sic) *Wonderful Lamp* Make Great Hit." *Altoona Times.* November 30, 1917.
13. "McGhie Theatre Notes." *Columbus (KS) Daily Advocate.* December 29, 1917.
14. Virginia Lee Corbin personal scrapbook clipping; publication and date unknown.
15. *Ibid.*
16. *Ibid.*

Chapter 8

1. "Prescott Infant Making Good in Pictures." *Weekly Journal-Miner* (Prescott, AZ). May 2, 1917.
2. *The Babes in the Woods. Moving Picture World.* October 27, 1917.
3. *Ibid.*
4. Virginia Lee Corbin personal scrapbook clipping; publication and date unknown.
5. *Ibid.*
6. "*Babes in the Woods* Again at the Strand, Today Program." *San Bernardino County Sun.* December 22, 1917.
7. *Babes in the Woods* review. *Daily Republication* (Cherryvale, KS). March 5, 1918.
8. Brownlow, Kevin. "The Franklin Kid Pictures. Ably Directed, Lavishly Mounted, Well Acted, Deserve a Special Place in Film History." *Films in Review.* August-September 1972.
9. Semenov, Lillian Wurtzel, and Carla Winter, eds. *William Fox, Sol M. Wurtzel and the Early Fox Film Corporation: Letters, 1917–1923.* McFarland, 2001.
10. "Children Come Here to Film Two Pictures—Thirteen Tiny Actors and Actresses of Fox Film Corporation Here." *Santa Cruz Evening News.* March 26, 1917.
11. Wood, Corinne. "Scores of Santa Cruz Children Play Parts Before Camera." *Santa Cruz Evening News.* April 3, 1917.
12. Virginia Lee Corbin personal scrapbook clipping; publication and date unknown.
13. Wood, Corinne. "Four-Year Old Girl the Wonder of the Movies, a Perfect Dresden Doll." *Santa Cruz Evening News.* April 4, 1917.

14. P.H.E. "Screen Screenings." *Wichita Beacon*. December 29, 1917.

Chapter 9

1. "Choice of Two Standards for Exhibitors." *Moving Picture World*. February 9, 1918.
2. "Gnomes, Sprites Invade Balboa." *Santa Ana Register*. May 31, 1917.
3. *Treasure Island* review. *Variety*. January 25, 1918.
4. "Amusements: Broadway Theatre." *Charlotte News*. March 8, 1918.
5. Virginia Lee Corbin personal scrapbook clipping; publication and date unknown.
6. Semenov, Lillian Wurtzel, and Carla Winter, eds. *William Fox, Sol M. Wurtzel and the Early Fox Film Corporation: Letters, 1917–1923*. McFarland, 2001.
7. Brownlow, Kevin. "The Franklin Kid Pictures. Ably Directed, Lavishly Mounted, Well Acted, Deserve a Special Place in Film History." *Films in Review*. August-September 1972.

Chapter 10

1. Semenov, Lillian Wurtzel, and Carla Winter, eds. *William Fox, Sol M. Wurtzel and the Early Fox Film Corporation: Letters, 1917–1923*. McFarland, 2001.
2. "*Six Shooter Andy* Is Olympic Drama." *Altoona Tribune*. March 18, 1918.
3. "News of Los Angeles and Vicinity." *Moving Picture World*. January 26, 1918.
4. *Six Shooter Andy* review. *Variety*. March 15, 1918.
5. "*Six Shooter Andy*; Gun-Play Picture. It Will Stir You as You Have Not Been Stirred Before." *Wichita Beacon*. March 16, 1918.
6. *Ace High* review. *Variety*. June 28, 1918.
7. *Ace High* review. *Photoplay*. August 1918.
8. *Moving Picture World*. March 30, 1918.
9. "In the Limelight." *Evening News* (Harrisburg, PA). June 5, 1918.
10. Peltret, Elizabeth. "Where Childish Dreams Come True." *Photoplay*. January 1918.
11. "Japanese Fairy Play at Strand. Virginia Lee Corbin and Francis Carpenter in *Fan Fan*." *Hartford Courant*. December 31, 1918.
12. Semenov, Lillian Wurtzel, and Carla Winter, eds. *William Fox, Sol M. Wurtzel and the Early Fox Film Corporation: Letters, 1917–1923*. McFarland, 2001.
13. Krefft, Vanda. *The Man Who Made the Movies: The Meteoric Rise and Tragic Fall of William Fox*. HarperCollins, 2017.
14. Brownlow, Kevin. "The Franklin Kid Pictures. Ably Directed, Lavishly Mounted, Well Acted, Deserve a Special Place in Film History." *Films in Review*. August-September 1972.

Chapter 11

1. Peltret, Elizabeth. "Where Childish Dreams Come True." *Photoplay*. January 1918.
2. "E-x-t-r-y! Great Hollywood Disaster!" *Photoplay*. April 1919.
3. "Tiny Screen Star Finds Way to Save Her Tires." *Los Angeles Times*. June 9, 1918.
4. Corbin, Virginia Lee. "My Last Christmas and This One." *Photo-Play Journal*. December 1918.
5. *The Forbidden Room* review. *Variety*. March 21, 1919.
6. "Smallest Film Queen to Be Express Guest at Newsies' Program." *Evening Express* (Los Angeles). September 1918 (from Virginia's personal scrapbook; exact date unknown).

Chapter 12

1. "Virginia Lee Corbin." *Muncie Evening Press*. September 22, 1919.
2. "Men and Women of the Stage." *Wichita Daily Eagle*. December 14, 1919.
3. *The White Dove* review. *Harrison's Reports*. April 24, 1920.
4. *San Bernardino Sun*. September 10, 1920.
5. "Virginia Lee Corbin, Tiny Fox Film Star, Coming Here in Person." *Ogden Standard-Examiner*. January 4, 1921.
6. "The Screen." *Santa Cruz Evening News*. April 8, 1921.
7. "The Screen." *Santa Cruz Evening News*. April 21, 1921.
8. "Virginia Lee Corbin Wins Hearts of Orph Audience." *Capital Times* (Madison, WI). June 17, 1921.
9. "The Theatres—Pantages." *Minneapolis Star*. December 12, 1921.
10. "Vaudeville." *Oregon Daily Journal* (Portland). January 22, 1922.
11. "Newsy Events of Society's Affairs from Engagements to Receptions and Dances." *Los Angeles Times*. February 26, 1922.

Chapter 13

1. "New Movie Scandal." *Santa Ana Register*. February 11, 1922.
2. "Hollywood Gossip." *Winnepeg Tribune* (Manitoba). March 11, 1922.
3. "Precocious Miss Wins." *Los Angeles Times*. June 18, 1922.
4. "Events Past, Planned and Talked About by Society's Devotees." *Los Angeles Times*. June 25, 1922.
5. Virginia Lee Corbin First of Many Stars to Make Pictures Here." *San Francisco Chronicle*. September 18, 1922.
6. "Child Star, Known Here, Signed by New S.F. Film Company." *Santa Cruz Evening News*. November 3, 1922.
7. "Clever Child to Sing at Granada." *San Francisco Chronicle*. November 14, 1922.
8. "*Enemies of Children* Is First Mammoth." *Moving Picture World*. September 8, 1923.
9. *Enemies of Children* review. Variety. December 20, 1923.
10. Jungmeyer, Jack. "Film Prodigy Weathers Break Period." *Evening Press* (Muncie, IN). June 11, 1923.

Chapter 14

1. Jungmeyer, Jack. "Film Prodigy Weathers Break Period." *Evening Press* (Muncie, IN). June 11, 1923.
2. *Moving Picture World*. Various dates July-August 1924.

3. "Former Child Favorite Now More Mature." *Los Angeles Times*. September 11, 1924.

4. *Sinners in Silk* review. *Harrison's Reports*. August 23, 1924.

5. *Sinners in Silk* review. *New York Times*. September 8, 1924.

6. *Sinners in Silk* review. *Variety*. September 10, 1924.

7. *Wine of Youth* review. *Harrison's Reports*. July 19, 1924.

8. *Wine of Youth* review. *New York Times*. August 1, 1924.

9. *Wine of Youth* review. *Variety*. August 13, 1924.

Chapter 15

1. "Virginia L. Corbin Given Lasky Role." *Los Angeles Times*. June 12, 1924.

2. Nangle, Roberta. "Cruze Gives New Slant on Naughty N.Y." *Chicago Tribune*. September 30, 1924.

3. Jungmeyer, Jack. "Prohibition Is Now a Popular Movie Theme." *Daily Times* (New Philadelphia, OH). October 6, 1924.

4. "Director Thinks Virginia's Tears Are Finest Art." *Los Angeles Times*. September 7, 1924.

5. *The City That Never Sleeps* review. *Moving Picture World*. October 11, 1924.

6. *The City That Never Sleeps* review. *Movie Weekly*. Date unknown.

7. *Broken Laws* review. *New York Times*. January 21, 1925.

8. *Broken Laws* review. *Harrison's Reports*. January 24, 1925

9. *The Chorus Lady* review. *Moving Picture World*. February 21, 1925.

10. *The Chorus Lady* review. *Harrison's Reports*. January 31, 1925.

11. *The Chorus Lady* review. *Variety*. February 4, 1925.

12. "On the Set and Off." *Movie Weekly*. August 9, 1924.

13. Kingsley, Grace. "Strutting Oolong Lane with Lounge Lizzie." *Los Angeles Times*. August 20, 1924.

14. Gardner, Mona. "Blond Infant Plays Adults." *Los Angeles Times*. September 20, 1925.

Chapter 16

1. Jungmeyer, Jack. "Page Peter Pan! Who Will Play the Role?" *Capitol Times* (Madison, WI). January 2, 1924.

2. Klumph, Helen. "Gloria Candidate." *Los Angeles Times*. July 20, 1924.

3. Dean, Daisy. "Virginia Lee Corbin Selected from Long List for Role in *Peter Pan* of J.M. Barrie." *Los Angeles Times*. July 6, 1924.

4. "Daily Squint at Movie Stars." *Star-Gazette* (Elmira, NY). July 29, 1924.

5. Pickard, Margery. "It's Settled, Absolutely, Positively That She'll Be Movie Peter Pan." *Morning Call* (Allentown, PA). September 7, 1924.

6. "Old Theme with New Twist Entertains in Feature." *Los Angeles Times*. December 3, 1924.

7. "Banner Officials Elated as 'Shooting' Ends on *3 Keys*." *Moving Picture World*. November 22, 1924.

8. Advertisement. *Moving Picture World*. March 7, 1925.

9. "Straight from the Shoulder Reports." *Moving Picture World*. March 14, 1925.

10. *The Cloud Rider* review. *Moving Picture World*. February 21, 1925.

11. "Baby Vamp Thrilled." *Los Angeles Times*. April 19, 1925.

12. *Lilies of the Streets* review. *Harrison's Reports*. May 9, 1925.

13. "Treat Seen in *Lilies of the Streets*, Unique." *Santa Cruz Evening News*. June 8, 1925.

14. *Headlines* review. *Harrison's Reports*. July 18, 1925.

15. *Headlines* review. *Moving Picture World*. August 1, 1925.

16. The Bystander. "Over the Teacups." *Picture Play*. September 1925.

17. *The Handsome Brute* review. *Film Daily*. July 18, 1926.

18. "Amusements." *Palladium-Item* (Richmond, IN). December 10, 1926.

19. "Bathing Beauties or Trick Dog—Your Choice Offered." *Chicago Tribune*. February 9, 1926.

20. *North Star* review. *Harrison's Reports*. February 13, 1926.

21. "Ingenue Ambitious to Play New Roles." *Los Angeles Times*. December 27, 1925.

22. "Must Take Rest." *Argus-Leader* (Sioux Falls, SD). December 31, 1925.

Chapter 17

1. Los Angeles (CA) County Court Record. Complaint. Earl A. Maginnis, Inc., a corporation, vs. Virginia Corbin, defendant. 1924–1928.

2. "Driving Ability Basis of Suit." *Los Angeles Times*. October 24, 1925.

3. Los Angeles (CA) County Court Record. Complaint for Slander and Damages. Ralph I. Magee, Plaintiff, vs. Virginia Lee Corbin, Mrs. Jane Doe Corbin, and Howard Estabrook, Strongheart Productions Company, John Doe company (a corporation), Defendants. Undated.

4. Los Angeles (CA) County Court Record. Answer of Defendant's First Strongheart Unit, Inc., a corporation, and Howard Estabrook. Undated.

5. "Kidnapping Victim Believed with Mate." *Los Angeles Times*. August 5, 1925.

6. Liebman, Roy. *The Wampas Baby Stars: A Biographical Dictionary, 1922–1934*. McFarland, 2000.

7. Romeo, Ramon. "Guess Who's in Town." *Moving Picture Stories*. June 16, 1925.

8. "The Charge of the Light Brigade." *Motion Picture Magazine*. July 1925.

9. Gardner, Mona. "Blond Infant Plays Adults." *Los Angeles Times*. September 20, 1925.

10. *Ibid.*

11. *Ibid.*

12. Kerr, Walter. *The Silent Clowns*. Alfred A. Knopf. 1975.

13. Mitchell, Glenn. *A-Z of Silent Film Comedy*. B.T. Batsford, 1998.

14. Kauffmann, Stanley, and Bruce Henstell. *American Film Criticism*. Liveright, 1972.

15. *Hands Up!* review. *Harrison's Reports*. January 23, 1926.

16. *Hands Up!* review. *Variety*. January 20, 1926.

17. "Virginia Lee Corbin Explains Screen Lovers." *Pittsburgh Daily Post*. January 31, 1926.

18. Woolridge, A.L. "Pauline So Excited Over Marrying Lowell Sherman She Wore Mismatched Shoes." *Des Moines Register*. February 21, 1926.

19. *The Whole Town's Talking* review. *Harrison's Reports*. June 26, 1926.

20. "Amusements." *Tampa Tribune*. October 18, 1926.

21. *The Whole Town's Talking* review. *Photoplay*. October 1926.

22. *The Whole Town's Talking* review. *Film Daily*. September 12, 1926.

23. Manners, Dorothy. "The Sketchbook." *Picture Play*. May 1926.

24. "Veterans Relate Seeing Actress in First Picture." *Los Angeles Times*. February 14, 1926.

25. Tinee, Mae. "Title Is Only Thing Wrong in This Picture." *Chicago Tribune*. September 9, 1926.

26. *The Honeymoon Express* review. *Harrison's Reports*. August 21, 1926.

27. *The Honeymoon Express* review. *Variety*. September 8, 1926.

28. *The Honeymoon Express* review. *Photoplay*. October 1926.

29. Pickard, Gilbert. "Behind the Screen." *Star Press* (Muncie, IN). October 10 1926.

30. Hall, Mordaunt. "Ladies at Play" review. *New York Times*. November 16, 1926.

31. *Ladies at Play* review. *Variety*. November 17, 1926.

32. *Ladies at Play* review. *Harrison's Reports*. November 27, 1926.

33. Hall.

34. "*Ladies at Play* Amusing Farce." *Los Angeles Times*. November 21, 1926.

Chapter 18

1. *Not Herbert* contract. Warner Bros. Archives. University of Southern California School of Cinematic Arts. Los Angeles, CA.

2. "Holds up Train for Photograph." *Washington Post*. September 19, 1926.

3. *The Perfect Sap* review. *Moving Picture World*. January 22, 1927.

4. *The Perfect Sap* review. *Variety*. January 12, 1927.

5. *The Perfect Sap* review. *New York Times*. January 24, 1927.

6. "Ben Lyon in *Perfect Sap* Role in Film at Capitol." *Reading Times*. February 21, 1927.

7. "Miss Corbin of Films Returns Heart Whole." *Los Angeles Times*. October 29, 1926.

8. *Driven From Home* review. *Variety*. June 1, 1927.

9. *Driven From Home* review. *Green Bay Press-Gazette*. October 7, 1927.

10. "Who's Who in *Driven from Home*." *Moving Picture World*. January 15, 1927.

11. *Ibid.*

12. *Play Safe* review. *Moving Picture World*. January 29, 1927.

13. *Play Safe* review. *Variety*. April 20, 1927.

14. *Play Safe* review. *Photoplay*. April 1927.

15. *Moving Picture World*.

16. First National contract. Warner Bros. Archives. University of Southern California School of Cinematic Arts. Los Angeles, California.

17. "Gotham Signs Miss Corbin." *Moving Picture World*. January 22, 1927.

18. "Virginia Corbin and Mother Are 'Pals.'" *Moving Picture World*. March 12, 1927.

19. First National memo from Mr. Allison to Mr. Thompson dated July 9, 1927. Warner Bros. Archives. University of Southern California School of Cinematic Arts. Los Angeles, California.

20. First National letter to Duke Worne Productions dated November 21, 1927. Warner Bros. Archives. University of Southern California School of Cinematic Arts. Los Angeles, California.

21. "Los Angeles River Is Used for Film Scene." *News Journal* (Mansfield, OH). September 11, 1927.

22. "*No Place to Go* Is Breezy Comedy." *Los Angeles Times*. October 30, 1927.

Chapter 19

1. Los Angeles Superior Court records February 10, 1926, to December 19, 1927.

2. "Miss Corbin Testifies in Theft Case." *Los Angeles Times*. March 10, 1927.

3. Wooldridge, Jack. "Movieland." *Oakland Tribune*. June 5, 1927.

4. "Gossip of All the Studios." *Photoplay*. January 1928.

5. "Hunting Girl to Play Lorelei in Screen Version." *Detroit Free Press*. May 15, 1927.

6. "'Sorrows' Only Half and Half." *Los Angeles Times*. October 17, 1927.

7. Letter from Welt-Detektiv to First National Studios dated March 25, 1927. Warner Bros. Archives. University of Southern California School of Cinematic Arts. Los Angeles, California.

8. Letter from First National Studios to Welt-Detektiv dated April 15, 1927. Warner Bros. Archives. University of Southern California School of Cinematic Arts. Los Angeles, California.

9. "Gossip of All the Studios." *Photoplay*. October 1927.

10. Nye, Myrna. "Society Cinemaland." *Los Angeles Times*. November 27, 1927.

11. Author's telephone interview with Esther Linn, April 22, 2001.

Chapter 20

1. "Mrs. Corbin Tries Suicide." *Los Angeles Times*. November 7, 1927.

2. *Ibid.*

3. *Ibid.*

4. "Actress Makes Insanity Plea Against Mother." *Chicago Tribune*. November 7, 1927.

5. "Screen Star Has Mother Held On Insanity Charge." *St. Louis Star and Times*. November 7, 1927

6. "Actress Frees Mother." *Los Angeles Times*. November 8, 1927.

7. *Ibid.*

8. *Ibid.*

9. "Star Drops Sanity Charge on Mother." *Reading Times*. November 8, 1927.

10. "Actress to Plead for Guardian." *Los Angeles Times*. November 13, 1927.

11. "Last Bar in Miss Corbin Case Falls." *Los Angeles Times*. November 17, 1927.

Chapter 21

1. "Virginia Corbin Breaks Contract." *Los Angeles Times*. January 24, 1927.
2. First National contract termination letter. Warner Bros. Archives. University of Southern California School of Cinematic Arts. Los Angeles, CA.
3. First National memos dated June 7, 1927, and June 16, 1927. Warner Bros. Archives. University of Southern California School of Cinematic Arts. Los Angeles, California.
4. Loan-out agreement letter dated December 8, 1927. Warner Bros. Archives. University of Southern California School of Cinematic Arts. Los Angeles, CA.
5. *Bare Knees* review. *Film Daily*. January 29, 1928.
6. Tinee, Mae. "Bare Knees" review. *Chicago Tribune*. March 7, 1928.
7. *Bare Knees* review. *Exhibitors' Herald and Moving Picture World*. November 3, 1928.
8. Wolf, Howard. "Strand Patrons Like Virginia Both Ways." *Akron Beacon Journal*. June 5, 1928.
9. "All About The Flapper Told Here." *Washington Post*. April 29, 1928.
10. *The Little Snob* review. *Variety*. May 2, 1928.
11. "*The Little Snob* Opens at the Majestic." *News Journal* (Mansfield, OH). May 3, 1928.
12. "At the Deluxe Theatre." *Times* (Munster, IN). June 23, 1928.
13. *The Head of the Family* review. *Film Daily*. December 16, 1928.
14. *The Head of the Family* review. *Variety*. December 22, 1928.

Chapter 22

1. *Jazzland* review. *Film Daily*. March 10, 1929.
2. "This One? Well, It's Another Film!" *Chicago Tribune*. January 23, 1929.
3. *Jazzland* review. *Variety*. March 20, 1929.
4. "Film Actress and Mother in Quarrel." *New Castle (PA) News*. May 7, 1929.
5. *Footlights and Fools* contract. Warner Bros. Archives. University of Southern California School of Cinematic Arts. Los Angeles, CA.
6. Schallert, Edwin. "Colleen Moore Remarkably Versatile." *Los Angeles Times*. October 27, 1929.
7. Schallert, Edwin. "Colleen Moore in Novel Role." *Los Angeles Times*. November 20, 1929.
8. *Footlights and Fools* review. *Variety*. November 13, 1929.
9. Hall, Mordaunt. *Footlights and Fools* review. *New York Times*. November 9, 1929.

Chapter 23

1. "Whereabouts of Virginia Corbin Are in Dispute." *Chicago Tribune*. July 18, 1929.
2. Nye, Myra. "Society of Cinemaland." *Los Angeles Times*. November 3, 1929.
3. "Virginia Grows Up." *Picturegoer*. April 1930.
4. Goldbeck, Elizabeth. "Little Bread-Winner." *Motion Picture Magazine*. May 1930.

5. "Miss Corbin Home with New Accent." *Los Angeles Times*. November 25, 1930.
6. "A Line O' Type or Two." *Chicago Tribune*. November 26, 1930.
7. Gloss, Edward R. "Player Hopes Accent Will Open Film Gate." *Akron Beacon Journal*. December 2, 1930.

Chapter 24

1. *Morals for Women* review. *Film Daily*. November 22, 1931.
2. *Morals for Women* review. *Harrison's Reports*. November 21, 1931.
3. *Morals for Women* review. *Photoplay*. January 1932.
4. *Shotgun Pass* review. *Film Daily*. March 13, 1932.
5. *Shotgun Pass* review. *Motion Picture Herald*. November 7, 1931.
6. "Hard Riding Thrills in *Shotgun Pass*." *Evening Standard* (Uniontown, PA). December 4, 1931.
7. *X Marks the Spot* review. *New York Times*. December 7, 1931.
8. *X Marks the Spot* review. *Harrison's Reports*. December 12, 1931.
9. *Forgotten Women* review. *Film Daily*. February 28, 1932.
10. *Forgotten Women* review. *Photoplay*. March 1932.

Chapter 25

1. "Virginia Lee Corbin, Baby, Feared Stranded in Europe." *Akron Beacon Journal*. June 19, 1934.
2. "Virginia Corbin Sues Mate in Cross-Bill." *Chicago Tribune*. August 21, 1936.
3. "Ex-Movie Star Blames Broken Home on Bridge." *Chicago Tribune*. August 28, 1936.
4. "Divorce Battle." *Chicago Tribune*. August 29, 1936.
5. Divorce File: 37S-13223. Theodore Krol, Plaintiff, versus Virginia L. Krol, Defendant. December 8, 1937.
6. Phil Krol email to Bob (Robert) Krol. October 4, 1998.
7. *Ibid.*

Chapter 26

1. *San Francisco Examiner* file photo. September 26, 1939.
2. "Virginia Lee Corbin Appears with Sandy." *Times* (Munster, IN). October 8, 1939.
3. McLaughlin, Will. "Twixt Stage and Screen." *Ottawa Journal* (Ontario). March 16, 1940.
4. *Ibid.*
5. "Ex-Stars, Still Young, Are Extras at $10 a Day Now." *Pittsburgh Post-Gazette*. June 4, 1940.
6. *Ibid.*
7. Hoagland, Vernon. "Hollywood Sights and Sounds." *St. Cloud Times*. June 26, 1940.

Bibliography

Books

Astor, Mary. *Mary Astor: A Life on Film*. Delacorte Press. New York. 1967.

Baer, D. Richard, ed. *Harrison's Reports and Film Reviews 1919–1928, Vols. 1–3*. Hollywood Film Archive. Hollywood, 1994.

Braff, Richard E. *The Braff Silent Short Film Working Papers*. McFarland. Jefferson, NC. 2002.

Codori, Jeff. *Colleen Moore: A Biography of the Silent Film Star*. McFarland. Jefferson, NC. 2012.

D'Agostino, Annette M. *Filmmakers in the Moving Picture World: An Index of Articles, 1907–1927*. McFarland. Jefferson, NC. 1997.

Jensen, Richard D. *The Amazing Tom Mix: The Most Famous Cowboy of the Movies*. iUniverse. Bloomington, IN. 2005.

Kauffmann, Stanley, and Bruce Henstell. *American Film Criticism*. Liveright. New York. 1972.

Kerr, Walter. *The Silent Clowns*. Alfred A. Knopf. New York. 1975,

Krefft, Vanda, *The Man Who Made the Movies: The Meteoric Rise and Tragic Fall of William Fox*. HarperCollins. New York. 2017.

Laurie, Joe, Jr. *Vaudeville from the Honky Tonks to the Palace*. Henry Holt. New York. 1953

Liebman, Roy. *Silent Film Performers: An Annotated Bibliography of Published, Unpublished and Archival Sources for Over 350 Actors and Actresses*. McFarland. Jefferson, NC. 1996.

Liebman, Roy. *The Wampas Baby Stars. A Biographical Dictionary, 1922–1934*. McFarland. Jefferson, NC. 2000.

Mitchell, Glenn. *A-Z of Silent Film Comedy*. B.T. Batsford. London. 1998.

Moore, Colleen. *Silent Star Colleen Moore Talks About Hollywood*. Doubleday. New York. 1968.

Munden, Kenneth W., ed. *The American Film Institute Catalog of Motion Pictures Produced in the United States 1911–1930, Vols. 1–2*. R.R. Bowker. New York. 1971.

Quirk, Lawrence J. *The Films of Fredric March*. The Citadel Press. Secaucus. 1971.

Semenov, Lillian Wurtzel, and Carla Winter, eds. *William Fox, Sol M. Wurtzel and the Early Fox Film Corporation: Letters, 1917–1923*. McFarland Jefferson, NC. 2001.

Sherk, Warren, ed. *The Films of Mack Sennett*. The Scarecrow Press. Lanham, MD. 1998.

Slide, Anthony. *The New Historical Dictionary of the American Film Industry*. The Scarecrow Press. Lanham, MD. 2001.

Slide, Anthony. *Selected Film Criticism 1912–1920*. The Scarecrow Press. Metuchen, NJ. 1982.

Slide, Anthony. *Selected Film Criticism 1921–1930*. The Scarecrow Press. Metuchen, NJ. 1982.

Solomon, Aubrey. *The Fox Film Corporation, 1915–1935: A History and Filmography*. McFarland. Jefferson, NC. 2011.

Variety's Film Reviews 1907–1929, Vols. 1–3. R.R. Bowker. New York. 1983.

White, Wendy Warwick. *Ford Sterling: The Life and Films*. McFarland. Jefferson, NC. 2007.

Periodicals

Akron Beacon Journal. 1928–1934.
Altoona Tribune. 1917.
Argus-Leader, Sioux Fall, SD. 1925.
Atlanta Constitution. 1917.
Brooklyn Daily Eagle. 1917.
Capital Times, Madison, WI. 1921–1924.
Charlotte News. 1918.
Chicago Tribune. 1924–1939.
Columbus Daily Advocate, Columbus, KS. 1917.
Daily Republican, Cherryvale, KS. 1918.
Daily Times, New Philadelphia, OH. 1924.
Des Moines Register. 1926.
Detroit Free Press. 1927.
Evening Express, Los Angeles. 1918.
Evening News, Harrisburg, PA. 1918.

Evening Press, Muncie. 1919–1923.
Evening Standard, Uniontown, PA. 1931.
Exhibitors' Herald and Moving Picture World, New York. 1928.
Film Daily, New York. 1926–1932.
Films in Review. August-September 1972.
Green Bay Press-Gazette. 1927.
Harrison's Reports, New York. 1920–1931.
Hartford Courant. 1918.
Lima News. 1917.
Los Angeles Times. 1916–1929.
Minneapolis Star. 1921.
Morning Call, Allentown, PA. 1924.
Motion Picture Herald, New York. 1931.
Motion Picture Magazine, Chicago. 1918–1930.
Motion Picture News, New York. 1915–1917.
Movie Weekly, New York, 1924.
Moving Picture Stories, New York. 1925.
Moving Picture World, New York. 1917–1927.
New Castle News, New Castle, PA. 1929.
New York Times. 1917–1931.
New York Tribune. 1917.
News Journal, Mansfield, OH. 1927–1928.
Oakland Tribune. 1927.
Ogden Standard. 1921.
Oregon Daily Journal, Portland. 1922.
Ottawa Journal, Ontario. 1940.
Palladium-Item, Richmond, IN. 1926.
Photoplay, Chicago. 1918–1932.
Photo-Play Journal, Philadelphia. 1917–1918.
Picture Play, New York. 1925.
Picturegoer, UK. 1930.
Pittsburgh Daily Post. 1926.
Pittsburgh Post-Gazette. 1940.
Reading Times. 1927.
St. Louis Star and Times. 1927.
San Bernardino County Sun. 1917–1920.
San Francisco Chronicle. 1922.
San Francisco Examiner. 1939.
San Francisco Times. 1917.

Santa Ana Register. 1917–1922.
Santa Cruz Evening News. 1917–1925.
Star-Gazette. Elmira, NY. 1924.
Star Press, Muncie, IN. 1926.
Statesman Journal, Salem, OR. 1916.
Sunset Magazine, San Francisco. 1918.
Tampa Tribune. 1926.
Times, Munster, IN. 1928–1939.
Times, St. Cloud. 1940.
Variety, New York. 1915–1929.
Washington Post. 1926–1928.
Weekly Journal-Miner, Prescott, AZ 1917.
Wichita Beacon. 1917.
Wichita Daily Eagle. 1919.
Winnepeg Tribune, Manitoba,. 1922.
Yavapai County Directory 1913, Phoenix, AZ.

Miscellaneous

Divorce File: 37S-13223, Cook County Courthouse, Chicago, IL, 1937.
Internet Archive Digital Library. https://archive.org/index.php
Krol, Bob (Robert), various emails, telephone conversations, personal interviews, 1998–2002.
Krol, Phil, various emails and telephone conversations 1998–2017.
Los Angeles Superior Court records 1926–27.
Newspapers.com
Telephone interview with Esther Linn, April 22, 2001.
Telephone interview with Patsy Karp, 1999.
Virginia Lee Corbin archival records held in Warner Bros. Archive, University of Southern California School of Cinematic Arts, Los Angeles, California. 1927–28.
Virginia Lee Corbin's personal scrapbook
Washington University, University Libraries. St. Louis, MO. https://wustl.edu/

Index

Numbers in **bold italics** indicate pages with illustrations